W9-CHB-693

Mandate Days

British Lives in Palestine
1918–1948

A.J. Sherman

Mandate Days

British Lives in Palestine
1918–1948

With 61 illustrations

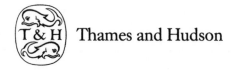

Thames and Hudson

IN MEMORY OF ORI

© 1997 A.J. Sherman

First published in the United States of America in 1998 by Thames
and Hudson Inc., 500 Fifth Avenue, New York, New York 10110

Library of Congress Catalog Card Number 97-60324
ISBN 0-500-25116-9

Printed and bound in Slovenia

Contents

Preface

In the nearly half-century since the British left Palestine, there has been a virtually ceaseless outpouring of analysis and polemic about the Mandate and its policies, yet curiously little assessment of the experience and self-understanding of British individuals, officials and others, who actually lived and worked in that unquiet country. As if their presence in the Holy Land, their reactions to it, had somehow been irrelevant, the British men and women of the Mandate have with rare exceptions been omitted from histories of Palestine, their daily lives, relations among themselves and with Arabs and Jews unexamined or taken for granted. This book aims to remedy that omission, largely by permitting the participants in the Mandate to tell their own stories. Although a posting to Palestine was never conceived of as a colonial service plum, and the Mandate represented to most British at best a burden and in the end a supreme mortification, those who served there ultimately came to feel their own version of imperial nostalgia. If few of the British community stationed in Palestine ever fully understood the growth of Arab nationalism, or the dynamics of the Jewish state within a state that was to become Israel, virtually all were affected by their stay. Mysterious as it was, frustrating and often infuriating, the Holy Land worked a subtle alchemy on its British rulers, and few of them remained untouched by their experience of its peoples, landscape and history.

My own life began in Jerusalem under the Mandate, and I retain a few but vivid memories of earliest childhood there: sunlight on the local stone walls, the scent of eucalyptus trees, snatches of song, certain words in Hebrew and Arabic. Growing up in the United States, I heard countless stories of a life in Jerusalem that even then had an almost mythic quality: a moment in time before the great bitterness of the Second World War, when it seemed not hopelessly quixotic for idealists such as my parents and their small circle to dream of a commonwealth in Palestine in which Arabs and Jews might dwell together in peace. Later, amid the violence of the Jewish revolt against the Mandate, my parents deplored the facile demonizing of Palestine's rulers, and recalled individual British neighbours from Jerusalem with respect and sympathy. The lives of those British sojourners in Palestine have always exerted a great fascination for me: perhaps a residue of the child's curiosity about the doings of grownups in authority. Their voices, quite unmistakably of their time and that place, continue to resonate from the texts to which that last generation of assiduous letter-writers and diarists confided feelings as well as facts about where they were and what they were doing.

The British of the Palestine Mandate left a vast trove of private papers, and I am most grateful to the custodians of those collections to which I had access. I am in the first place indebted to the Warden and Fellows of St Antony's College, Oxford, for welcoming me on several lengthy visits to their most agreeable society. It is a particular pleasure to thank Dr Derek Hopwood, Director of the Middle East Centre, St Antony's College, Oxford, who generously assisted me in consulting the rich archive of Private Papers deposited there, largely through the initiative of the late Miss Elizabeth Monroe. I wish also to acknowledge the efficient helpfulness of Mrs Diane Ring, Librarian of the Middle East Centre, St Antony's College, and of Mrs Clare Brown, Archivist of the Private Papers Collection. My thanks are due as well to the librarians and staff of Rhodes House, Oxford; the Imperial War Museum, London; the Research and Jewish Divisions of the New York Public Library; and the library of Middlebury College, Vermont. The staff at the Central Zionist Archives, Jerusalem, in particular Mr Reuven Koffler, curator of the Photographic Archive, were most helpful in locating materials I would not otherwise have seen. I am grateful to Mr Stephen Bank for his contributions to the Biographical Index. I am much obliged to Thames Television for permission to quote from transcripts of interviews broadcast in 1978 in their series on the British Mandate in Palestine; to Mr Leslie Perowne, for his consent to my quoting from his late brother's papers; to Miss Mary K. Burgess for allowing me to quote from her letters; and to Mr R.D. Chancellor, for leave to quote from his late father's papers.

I have also been fortunate in the kind assistance and encouragement of the following, to whom I offer collective and individual thanks: Dr David Arnow; Mrs Anna Biegun; Mr and Mrs R.D.N. Bird; Sir Isaiah Berlin; Maj. General H. Bredin; Professor William Brinner; Dr Jules Cashford; Professor E. Mason Cooley; Lord and Lady Dahrendorf; Faith Evans; Mr James Hatch; Mr Edward Horne; the late Mr Albert Hourani; Mr J.D.F. Jones; the late Mrs Philippa Keith-Roach; Professor Christoph Kimmich; Professor A.H.M. Kirk-Greene; Mrs Mary MacKenzie; Professor Margaret Macmillan; Mr Theo Mainz; Mr R. David Mann; Dr Jorge Martín; Professor Joseph Nevo; Professor Joaquín Martinez Pizarro; Mr Steven M. Riskin; the late Mrs Sarah Stein; Mr Anthony Verrier; Mr George Warburg; Professor David Wasserstein; Professor Michael Wood. To several others, who prefer anonymity, profound thanks for insights and information.

Although I have greatly benefitted from the views of several friends and critics, I remain solely responsible for the entire contents of this book. It is, finally, salutary to be reminded, in the words of Benny Morris, that "the possibility that his findings and conclusions might subsequently be used by propagandists and politicians of this or that ilk is surely no concern of the historian....The historian must be judged acording to the degree of accuracy and understanding he has achieved regarding the past -- nothing else."[1]

A. J. S.

Jerusalem security pass used
by British residents

chapter 1 ~ **In the Beginning**

The British Mandate in Palestine, surely one of the least glorious episodes in the long history of the Empire, was nonetheless one of the great dramas in that history, productive of more emotion and certainly more criticism than any other part of the vast enterprise. The Mandate, in form a trusteeship under the authority of the League of Nations over a territory "inhabited by peoples not yet able to stand by themselves under the conditions of the modern world", was in fact consistently administered as a Crown Colony, to the abiding frustration of all its inhabitants. As to Palestine, Eretz Israel, Filastin: the very names of the country have always aroused passion, an immense freight of history, the clash of ideologies, communities and individuals. The phrase "Britain in Palestine" also carries an emotional charge, evoking the British Empire at its zenith and in decline, and the whole complex of feelings arising from the domination of non-Europeans by European powers. The nearly fifty years since the Mandate ended have not diminished the strong passions associated with it, either in the Middle East or elsewhere: British policies, promises, her mere presence in Palestine are all still argued, deplored, or less frequently admired.

Yet it was all so brief. When the last British High Commissioner slipped away from Jerusalem on a May morning in 1948 through a cordon of heavily armed troops and a few feebly clapping spectators, his exit ended an imperium that had lasted a mere thirty years, the product of expedient but incompatible undertakings made to Arabs and Jews amid the dire exigencies of the first World War. The High Commissioner and his colleagues departed with the consciousness of failure, the knowledge that they had left the Holy Land torn by strife, its inhabitants united only in their detestation of

British policies and their sour conviction of betrayal by His Majesty's Government. All the machinery of a large and intricate administration now lay in ruins; its officers in every part of the country, numerous departments of state, several police forces and nearly 100,000 troops had failed in their fundamental task: to maintain the authority of the Mandate and keep Arabs and Jews from mutual slaughter. As the High Commissioner was piped aboard a British warship in Haifa Bay, few who witnessed the ceremony could have felt emotions other than embarrassment, sadness and relief.

A quarter of a century before, in the very earliest, relatively peaceful days of the Mandate, C.R. Ashbee, a town planner and architect, had remarked that "chance, some idea we are not yet able to comprehend, has set us to our work, and will turn us out of Palestine as it has the other conquerors before us."[2] Dark though Ashbee's personal vision was, he could not have conceived that British authority in the land would collapse so utterly, nor that the Mandate would end with scuttle, the abandonment of Palestine to savage warfare between its Arab and Jewish inhabitants. After a brief moment in history, the intolerable burden of Palestine was not so much laid down as flung aside, freeing Britain at last from the long unhappy shadow of its promise to the Jews, the Balfour Declaration, but without thereby cementing friendship with the Arabs in the Middle East, and at the cost of grievous loss in world standing. The abject end of British rule in Palestine, a revelation of impotence not lost on independence-minded nationalists in the remaining Empire, both engendered and reflected a mood of exhaustion and disgust that accorded with the dismal icy winter of 1947 in which British morale sank further than in the darkest days of the war. "Palestine", wrote one official, "was indeed a tragedy. It moved to its fated conclusion like the Oresteia of Aeschylus. We who worked there could do no more than attempt to mitigate the operation of fate."[3]

It was military victory over the Turkish Empire and its German ally that brought Britain to Palestine in the first place, but the history of the British in

Palestine was played out against a larger background of defeat. The with-drawal from Empire was a slow ineluctable recessional, punctuated by episodes of conflict and occasional gallantry that halted but never staunched the steady seepage of will and resources, resulting at last in abandonment of all but a trivial few imperial possessions. At a more self-confident moment, a critical stage in the First World War, the British Government had enuncia-ted in the Balfour Declaration of 2 November 1917 a policy favouring the "establishment in Palestine of a National Home for the Jewish people... it being clearly understood that nothing shall be done which may prejudice the civil and religious rights of existing non-Jewish communities in Palestine".[4] The "National Home" thus promised to the Jews was never clearly defined and had no precedent in international law. The very vague-ness of the National Home concept implied that its meaning was somehow to evolve over time; but the disparate understandings, fears and desires of Zionists, Arabs and the British implied anything but a peaceful evolution. At once hailed as a declaration of unprecedented imaginative generosity, or condemned as monstrous hypocrisy and a dreadful blunder, the Balfour Declaration was destined to put Great Britain on a collision course with the Arabs and ultimately the Jews of Palestine as well. The resulting tragic dilemma of the British Mandate in Palestine was stated in elegiac language by the Royal Commission reporting in 1937, after investigating the causes of the Arab Rebellion that had begun the preceding year:

Under the stress of the World War the British Government made promises to Arabs and Jews in order to obtain their support. On the strength of those promises both parties formed certain expectations....An irrepressible conflict has arisen between two national communities within the narrow bounds of one small country....There is no common ground between them....This conflict was inherent in the situation from the out-set....we cannot -- in Palestine as it now is -- both concede the Arab claim of self-government and secure the establishment of the Jewish National Home... this conflict between the two obligations is the more unfortunate because each of them, taken separately, accords with British sentiment and British interest....[5]

British sentiment and British interest were indeed in the consciousness of those men and women who came out to Palestine on assignment, whether they were soldiers, civil servants, policemen, teachers, missionaries, medical officers or wives. British sentiment: the comfortable conviction that the success of its arms entitled Britain to a pivotal role as arbiter of the Middle East, and the concomitant notion that as the paramount power in the region, Britain had obligations to all its peoples. Underpinning that ground of sentiment was the confident reliance on "a long tradition of executive responsibility towards the colored races,"[6] that enabled individual British men and women to live out an imperial role according to a code inculcated and reinforced from early childhood by family, school, church and the wider society. As to British interest, Palestine was felt to be a vital component of the British imperial presence in the Middle East, a region of utmost significance, not least because of its vast oil resources. Despite all its intentional and irreconcilable ambiguities, the "Jewish National Home" in Palestine, with its fanciful vision of a possible Jewish state in the far-off remote future, secure and prosperous under British auspices, was conceived as a potential bulwark of stability, a helpful counterweight to anti-British feeling in Egypt and elsewhere in the region. In Palestine, it was optimistically hoped, an industrious, educated Jewish population grateful for British protection would, with the financial assistance of Jews throughout the world, develop the country to a point of sufficient economic well-being to reconcile its Muslim and Christian communities to Zionist aspirations. The creation under British suzerainty of a flourishing and stable Palestine, preferably with minimal cost to the British taxpayer, was thus an integral part of a larger strategic vision, in which the solidity of the British position in the Middle East guaranteed the safety of maritime routes to India and other imperial possessions, as well as access to critically important oil. Despite rationalizations and much talk of imperial priorities, it was almost invariably emotion rather than cool calculation of strategic advantage that predominated in the evolution of British policies in Palestine.

British occupation of Palestine was undertaken in full awareness of geopolitical realities, but also with largely unconscious and unexamined assumptions of natural authority that pervaded the entire imperial enterprise: the self-evident superiority of British institutions, the incorruptibility of her colonial civil and military servants, the selflessness of the British ambition to extend to ill-governed, neglected peoples the benefits of an impartial and just administration that would enable them, under appropriate guidance, to develop and flourish. That the British alone knew what would be suitable and beneficial for their imperial wards was unquestioned. As Lord Cromer put it in 1908, each issue arising in colonial governance was to be "decided mainly with reference to what, by the light of Western knowledge and experience tempered by local considerations, we conscientiously think is best for the subject race, without reference to any real or supposed advantage which may accrue to England as a nation..."[7] It was dimly appreciated that Palestine might present something of a problem, since it contained not merely a native Arab population firmly attached to their lands and traditions, but also a European-educated, sophisticated class of Zionist Jewish immigrants and settlers; but the Mandate was undertaken with that mixture of sang-froid and wishful thinking that had reliably served for muddling through, despite occasional unfortunate episodes, in most of the Empire. Palestine would somehow fit into the large-scale Pax Britannica that was to be established throughout the Middle East and on into India.

As was pointed out even at the time, after the First World War Britain no longer had the resources to realize such a vision; "and its intended beneficiaries might have wondered why a country which had just lost a million men in a war nobody knew the meaning of should be offering to bestow Peace on the tranquil East."[8] The presence in Palestine of communities so different as the Arabs and the Jews, despite their common Semitic origin, constituted that division of the indigenous population into "good" and "bad" tribes that the British had repeatedly encountered elsewhere in their colonial experience. Splitting the original inhabitants, the unknown "other", into two groups was a sturdy cliché of imperial governance, notably in Africa and India. In Palestine, as for example in Kenya, the self-appointed role of British officials was to protect the indigenous inhabitants against European settlers with expansionist ambitions. Moreover, the notion of "good" and "bad" peoples, often associated with differences in culture, skin pigmentation and occupation, had a lineage going back to the Bible. Few British individuals who came to Palestine were unaware of the contradictions in their mission, or had not already encountered in literature or in personal experience the opposing archetypes of Jacob and Esau, Isaac and Ishmael. The Zionists were fated to remain the "bad" and tiresome tribe whether or not they spoke European languages, were law-abiding and nominally cooperative; the Arabs, even when in outright rebellion, somehow were "good" and even attractive in the perception of their British rulers.

Strategic and military considerations brought the British to Palestine to begin with, but these were not the sole preoccupations of the individuals who arrived to undertake the multiple tasks of governance in what had been a relatively neglected province of the Ottoman Empire. Many of them came as well with other intellectual and emotional baggage: a pre-formed vision of the Holy Land almost invariably shaped by reading and listening to the King James Bible and the Book of Common Prayer, and influenced by a tradition of scriptural illustration and Orientalist art seen from earliest childhood, often vividly recalled. "At school", wrote one, "I probably knew far more about the geography of Palestine than of my own country".[9]

British official photograph of General Allenby
entering Jerusalem, 9 December 1917. Allenby
entered on foot, in deliberate contrast to the pompous
entry of Wilhelm II on a white horse when he visited
Jerusalem in 1898

Jewish soldiers with the British army celebrating
Passover in Jerusalem, 1918

Lord Allenby, Lord Balfour and Sir Herbert
Samuel at the opening of the Hebrew University,
Jerusalem, 1925

Lord Plumer, staff and members of the British
community at a race meeting at the Jaffa Race
Club, 1925

Official reception in Jaffa for Lord and Lady Plumer
on their landing in Palestine, 1925

Interior of J.H.H. Pollock's house
in Jaffa, 1937

18

British family group on the beach at the Jaffa
Club, 1934

Colonel and Mrs Saunders
at prize-giving at the Police
Sports, Jerusalem, 1935

Wedding of Araminta MacMichael, St. George's
Cathedral, Jerusalem, June 1943

Colonel and Mrs Saunders, M. and Mme de Courcelle,
Katie Antonius and Mr and Mrs Whitcomb at King's
Birthday garden party, Government House, Jerusalem,
June 1938

Poster advertising Spinney's Soda
Water, 1935

Spinney's shop in Mamillah Road, Jerusalem,
sand-bagged against bombs, 1948

The Jerusalem Dramatic Society presents
The Mikado, 1933

Sir Harold MacMichael, aide and guests at King's
Birthday garden party, Government House, Jerusalem,
June 1938

Highlanders dancing in the
gardens of Government House,
Jerusalem, King's Birthday,
June 1938

New Year's Eve celebration at the King
David Hotel, Jerusalem, 1937–38

Guests at King's Birthday
garden party, Government
House, Jerusalem, 1938

British children and Father
Christmas at the British Police
Christmas party, Jerusalem,
December 1941

Members of the Royal Commission headed by
Lord Peel arrive in Jerusalem, 1936

Derailed train at Kilometer 107 after an attack by Arab
saboteurs, 1936

Expecting Palestine to look "Biblical", they were often thrilled to see their imaginations confirmed: actual shepherds tending their flocks of sheep, camel caravans, olive groves, the rock-strewn slopes of the Judaean hills, all somehow familiar, often evoking specific passages from Scripture. The names of towns, hills, rivers were for the most part known, each with its web of associations, sometimes tied to a specific Biblical episode or parable, or a well-remembered phrase. Palestine was always a vividly real country of the spirit and the imagination, as well as a concrete geographical place. The British came also with ideas and emotions about Arabs, Jews, and "the East".

Upon the Arabs of Palestine, improbably including both town-dwellers and the impoverished *fellahin* of the countryside, the British tended to project expectations and feelings absorbed largely from a romantic literary tradition of Orientalism, itself based on an attribution to the desert Beduin of chivalric virtues prized in the English public school, that testing place of physical hardship, tribal loyalties and intense male camaraderie. The Palestine Arabs, like their brethren elsewhere in the Middle East, were felt to be attractive by virtue of their physical courage, pride in their traditions, and above all the exquisite courtesy and generous hospitality that enabled most British individually to enjoy social and official encounters with them. Loyalty, a well-developed sense of personal honour and of humour were also imputed to Arabs, a set of character traits much appreciated and indeed claimed personally by many among the British, who moreover felt they uniquely understood and had an affinity for Arabs, and could therefore guide them by gentle persuasion, reference to shared values, and only as a last resort physical coercion. Even repeated rebuffs and disappointments such as the costly and demoralizing Arab Rebellion in the late 1930s, or the tepid and sometimes hostile Arab response to Britain's needs in the Second World War, could not materially alter the cherished British fantasy that the Palestine Arabs and their colonial masters shared both profound understanding and uncomplicated mutual affection.[10] To be sure, relationships with Arabs, perhaps especially of the higher social strata, were not entirely free of ambiguity, as reflected in the report of an official's wife on arrival at her husband's post in Nazareth:

> we went to the office first, which is a <u>very</u> grand & spacious building & Ken <u>will</u> have a lovely big office. There we met the District Officer who is an Arab but a sort of top drawer one & one treats him as an equal <u>almost</u> but apparently not <u>quite</u> -- all these things seem to be very important & he took us to look at the only three available houses....[11]

Among the British in Palestine, even devoted admirers of the Arabs could on occasion display a casual contempt and feelings of superiority: "the people here are not Arabs," wrote one, "nor do they have anything in common with the 'mystic East', with the sole exception of their great dislike to any kind of work. They are simply Arabic-speaking Levantines, a type which may speak Greek or Turkish or Arabic, but is much more in sympathy with the West than with the East."[12] Another voice: "It is difficult not to sympathize with the majority, and the Jews do not tend to make themselves popular; but one feels too that the Arabs are a lazy and unenterprising people, and if they do lose ground they will do so largely owing to their own lack of effort."[13]

Jews, whether of Oriental or European origin, known personally or not, were uneasily felt to be less malleable altogether, certainly less amenable to British charm or moral leadership than Arabs. Whether perceived in ancient archetypal guise as deniers of Christ, clannish and rootless wanderers, or exotic wielders of vast international power as financiers, revolutionaries or both, the Jews seemed to most British observers more threatening and altogether less appealing than their Semitic cousins; in the last days of the Mandate they were often feared and hated by their British rulers, but seldom if ever patronized. If the British rulers of Palestine had encountered individual Jews at all before their arrival in the country, it was either in school or military service, or as part of the colourful background elsewhere in the Middle East, where Jews were often impoverished, but sometimes could be found also among the very highest social class, as in Egypt. "What does the average English boy know of Jews?" asked Sir Ronald Storrs rhetorically, years after his tenure as first Military Governor of Jerusalem.[14] Proclaiming nonetheless "that there was in the world no aspiration more nobly idealistic than the return of the Jews to the land immortalized by the spirit of Israel", Storrs added that England was uniquely qualified to understand and help foster this return, since England "was more steeped in the Book of Books" than any other nation.[15] Storrs could not be held to speak for England or indeed for most of his colleagues: the majority of British officials posted there had no great sympathy for the establishment of a Jewish National Home in Palestine, even if they could have explained what was meant by the phrase. They considered the notion quixotic, onerous, of doubtful benefit to Great Britain -- and resented the fact that it compelled them to deal with a group of thrusting, self-confident Zionist functionaries whose mostly Russian backgrounds made them in turn deeply suspicious of officialdom and government regulation in any form. If most British officials had little knowledge of Jews in general, they had even less of the teeming Jewish populations of Eastern Europe from which most of the Zionists came. The complex history, traditions and ideology of these Zionist settlers from Eastern Europe tended to be lumped together by the British in broad categories such as "religious Orthodox", "secular socialist", or simply "Bolshevik". Since few British officials knew Hebrew, the complex political and ideological controversies that agitated the Jewish community, reflected in lively press and public debate, were unknown to all but a few, whose job it was to monitor these developments.

The majority of the British official community in Palestine were, as one observer wrote towards the end of the Mandate, "either pro-Arab or strictly impartial in detesting both sides....Off the record, most of the officials here will tell you that the Jews are above themselves and want taking down a peg."[16] Even for a Jewish British officer, the Arabs, "whether they whined, or threatened, or cajoled, or protested", were always "picturesque, ingratiating, sympathetic", while the Jews, right or wrong, were "clumsy, fussy, and aggressive".[17] On a social level, the British found the urban Arab upper classes attractive for their "French culture, amusing, civilized, tragic and gay",[18] and admired the Arab *fellahin* for their stubbornly traditional ways, including their natural courteous deference to social and official superiors. Eastern or Central European Jews, on the other hand, were perceived as "tense, bourgeois",[19] bereft of humour, seldom open and straightforward, lacking the small talk and ease of manner that lubricated social encounters. "Somehow we like the Arabs even though they fight us, and we dislike the Jews even if our interests run together." [20] Put another way, "we find it difficult to sympathize with the Jews because they do not seem to want to get on with us, while the Arabs are our friends, not because we do not recognize their weaknesses, but because we believe we understand them." [21] There were those among the British for whom visceral dislike of Jews went deeper. One described with distaste their "fat aquiline features" and wide-hipped women wheeling prams; another claimed to see a "Soho, Strand, flashy, overdressed look" about Jews who, even in the early days of Zionist settlement, were notorious for the negligence bordering on extreme minimalism of their dress.[22] Not a few officials, especially as the troubles multiplied, would express a wish that the Jews could somehow be cleared away, leaving Palestine to the Arabs -- and the British.

There were also among the British, notably from evangelical Low Church backgrounds, a few exceptional individuals for whom Zionism and Jews were interesting or appealing for religious or sentimental reasons. But for most British in Palestine, Zionism was associated dimly with Bolshevism, international conspiracy theories and notions of widespread

Jewish influence, and tainted, paradoxically, by both its German and East European intellectual origins. On the level of ordinary official dealings, anti-Jewish feeling arose from the contrasting impressions garnered from daily contact with both Arabs and Jews: "the Englishman", one officer recalled, "'gets on' with the Arab. He finds him a cheerful, courteous and companionable sort of chap, often a bit slippery in his business methods but rather as one playing a game than making any deliberate effort to cheat. The Jew in Palestine is inclined to be surly, morose and un-cooperative: the Arab at least looks as though he is glad to see you."[23] The native-born Zionist settlers of Palestine represented a quite different breed from Diaspora Jews of whatever provenance: their tough self-confidence verging on brashness, and supreme lack of European Jewish doubts, fears, or arts of ingratiation made a deep impression on all observers, and often evoked ungrudging respect from even those British with overt pro-Arab sympathies. Speaking for these unabashed, hearty new-model Palestinian Jews, David Ben Gurion admonished Richard Crossman, a member of the Anglo-American Committee of Inquiry in 1945, not to "make the mistake of thinking of us as Jews like the Jews you have in London. Imagine that we're Englishmen fighting for our national existence, and calculate that we shall behave as you would behave if you were in our situation."[24] Although individuals among them were occasionally perceived as attractive, courageous, even heroic, the Zionist settlers of Palestine on the whole made their British colonial masters feel uncomfortable; and for those who were well-informed, even irrelevant.

Under the authority of the Jewish Agency, the Jewish community in Palestine had created its own virtual state within the superstructure of British administration under the Mandate, with autonomous Jewish community taxation, government departments, highly efficient military and intelligence forces and clear long-term goals. The mutual dislike of official representatives of Palestine Government and the Jewish Agency was reinforced by the notorious fact that the Jewish Agency was consistently informed by its agents, sometimes well in advance, of British plans and intentions. The Agency's representatives, moreover, neither deferential in manner nor deliberately charming, were sometimes better educated than the British officials they encountered, and refused ostentatiously to be intimidated or much impressed, even when these officials wielded virtually dictatorial powers under emergency regulations. At the very top, the British respected and some felt personal affection for the exceptional and impressive figure of Dr Chaim Weizmann, the Zionist leader who exerted a moral authority based on his well-known Anglophilia, crucial scientific contributions to the British cause in the First World War, and his universally acknowledged eloquence and charisma. One former Palestine Government official summed it all up: "There was a saying that everyone who came to Palestine came there to a certain degree pro-Jew, but after a time became essentially pro-Arab, and generally ended pro-British." [25]

The East, the Middle East in particular, was a palpably imagined region in the minds of many English men and women, an attractive half-known world of "minaret and muezzin... camel and veil and palm". [26] A place of romantic adventures, long and complex history, colourful landscapes made familiar by artists yet fascinatingly alien, the Middle East was geographically near Europe but unimaginably foreign: "the place of Europe's greatest and richest and oldest colonies, the source of its civilizations and languages, its cultural contestant, and one of its deepest and most recurring images of the Other." [27] Vivid from travellers' tales, the Arabian Nights, histories of the Crusades and of European-Ottoman conflicts, the memoirs of colonial administrators and explorers, the East was a region whose natives had once ruled themselves, who had in historic times achieved greatness, but who were now to be ruled for their own good by Europeans. Indubitably fascinating, even romantic, the peoples of the East were assumed to be incapable in their irrationality and technological backwardness of deciding their own best interests, and were therefore to be guided by Britain, gently if possible, firmly if necessary, towards a better future. The East was intellectually conceived of but also felt as passive, lethargic, immeasurably ancient, incurably corrupt and despotic. Europe, by contrast, with its overwhelming technological and military superiority, its comparatively youthful masculine energy, its entrepreneurial and missionary zeal, its largely democratic institutions, was to take the once-great peoples of the East into tutelage, and direct their slow but sure progress under stable and just governments to an improved life for all.

In addition to all these notions, the new rulers of Palestine had absorbed and consciously aimed to emulate a set of imperial role models based on widely admired examples from the colonial services in India and Africa. Many in the Palestine administration had lived in African and other colonies, not a few had seen service elsewhere in the Middle East: virtually all accepted without question the assumption of European superiority and its corresponding privileges and responsibilities, a belief in the imperial enterprise based on the "traditional aristocratic claim to 'leadership'... where those to be governed seemed also eminently qualified by their primitiveness to be led."[28] This claim and its attendant self-image clashed almost immediately with the reality of Palestine, where much of the population, both Arab and Jewish, refused to play the same role as subject races elsewhere in the Empire, setting up tensions that remained unresolved throughout the Mandate years. The colonial ideal, refined in the Indian Civil Service tradition, contemplated a well-administered, calmly prosperous country in which an official could recall "so many little worlds lived side by side, understanding each other very imperfectly, disliking each other often very heartily, and yet all dwelling peaceably on the whole under the strong hand of British law and order."[29]

The model of the peaceful colonial kingdom never applied in Palestine. Administered by the Colonial Office, but held in trust under the loosely worded League of Nations Mandate, Palestine was emphatically not a

British possession like any other. Perennially the focus of Parliamentary questions, journalistic scrutiny, often partisan international attention from press and politicians, the Mandate was never a quiet backwater, much to the chagrin of local officials, who often felt themselves second-guessed by London, and forced to acknowledge and occasionally bend to international protests skilfully orchestrated by the Zionists, and later by the Arab states on behalf of their Palestinian brethren. Consistently undermined by noises-off in London, then in Geneva and later in New York, the British officials in Jerusalem never enjoyed the wholehearted support of their own people and Government, and were forced to steer a zigzag course between Arabs and Zionists, incurring the wrath of both. Moreover, in the prophetic words of Lord Balfour, "directly the native populations have that instinctive feeling that those with whom they have got to deal have not behind them the might, the authority, the sympathy, the full and ungrudging support of the country which sent them there, those populations lose all that sense of order which is the very basis of their civilisation, just as our officers lose all that sense of power and authority, which is the very basis of everything they can do for the benefit of those among whom they have been sent."[30] So it was to be in Palestine: as support from home eroded, so too did the Palestine administration's crucial sense of its mission and authority. Moreover, at no time in the history of the Mandate could parades, trumpets and flourishes conceal from the inhabitants of Palestine the true state of British morale.

A considerable number of the British, men and women, came voluntarily to Palestine, many with enthusiasm; but most arrived under orders, a number cordially loathing, from the very beginning, their assignment to the country. Very few, however, can have been unmoved by the sheer drama of their situation, in the footsteps of Romans, Crusaders, Ottomans, ruling the Holy Land that for most had been vividly imagined since childhood. Palestine evoked strong feelings even among the career colonial administrators, and few were proof against the transforming moments offered by experiences of personal danger, the peculiar intensity of the local climate and landscape, and the encounter with a colourfully varied, occasionally disturbing population. For the British who came out to Palestine, only a few of whom would have claimed to be remarkable, the ordeal of living and working amid physical risks and constant challenges was made bearable by a still coherent imperial ethos that enjoined attitudes of superiority and prescribed rigid, socially approved behaviours for virtually all contingencies. Dealing at least with the Arab population, many of the career officials "had a sense of mission and an implicit faith in the psychological ascendancy they derived from knowledge, a knowledge which seemed all the more powerful because it was believed to be unilateral."[31] By the end of the Mandate, both sense of mission and psychological ascendancy had largely evaporated, but while they lasted, they served as powerful stiffeners of resolve, vital ingredients in sustaining morale. British officials and their wives of the Mandate years lived within a culture that emphasized decorum, deference and the avoidance of shame; feeling themselves almost always on parade, even within their own small community, they were concerned above all not to let the side down. Few of them felt they had much autonomy of action, and virtually all assumed without question that rule over non-Europeans, throughout large areas of the globe, was simply part of the natural order.

These individuals were a disparate group, some formed by the public school and Oxbridge imperial tradition, others by churches and missionary culture, still others of humbler social origins having found in the military or police the steady employment otherwise scarce in the diminished peacetime economy of Britain and Ireland. Some of the expatriate officials were highly self-conscious, striving to advance within the career service, whether Colonial Office, Foreign Office or military: they and their wives moved in a carefully choreographed round of official and unofficial entertaining, always with a keen eye to prize postings and advancement up the administrative ladder. In the struggle for preferment, no social or administrative detail was too minor to overlook. Placement at dinners, mention in Honours Lists and invitations to Government House, seat of the High Commissioner and the administrative and social centre of the Palestine Mandate, were minutely scrutinized; the game of relative advantage was played in offices, clubs, dining rooms and on occasion bedrooms. Military and civil officers were graded in terms of rank and seniority, listed in the Palestine Gazette and the other official lists: salaries of all ranks were published, and everyone in the small official community knew precisely which officers had private means to supplement official emoluments.

The churches and their emissaries to Palestine moved in their own world of intense relationships and often competitive enterprise, mingling with government and military representatives on social and diplomatic occasions, or in the context of official church-going. There were British businessmen as well in Palestine: Barclays Bank and Shell Oil were but two major British enterprises with a solid position in the country, and representatives of engineering, insurance, and a host of other firms were also in residence, some for long tours of duty.

Most of the British community of lesser rank, constrained by deficits in education, experience or social connection, were in Palestine under orders. With exiguous incomes, often confined socially, they lived in barracks or other institutional housing, met mostly one another, and tended to spend even less time exploring the country than their officers. Although the soldiers and police for the most part regarded both Arabs and Jews as alien "wogs", they were the likeliest to mingle with the ordinary inhabitants wherever they were posted, and to seek opportunities for intimate relationships with locals, overwhelmingly among the Jewish rather than the closely guarded Moslem Arab women. Despite all odds, a number of these relationships, and a few among Englishmen and Christian Arab women, resulted in marriage, especially in the ranks of the Palestine Police, and towards the end of the Mandate.

Arriving either by train, usually from Egypt or, most often, off steamers docking at Jaffa or Haifa, bombarded with unfamiliar sights, sounds and smells, then plunged into sometimes arduous assignments, the British often had strong reactions to the country in which they found themselves, and above all to its people, whether Arabs or Jews. In all but the most phlegmatic, Palestine evoked a host of emotions, ranging from hostility and repulsion to an almost messianic fervour and a yearning to know and care for the land and its people. The impulse to record, to describe and communicate, somehow to make sense of all this rich experience was nearly universal. At the end of each day or week, time was set aside to write, sometimes voluminously, whether letters home, private diaries, sketches or stories. Much of this writing was spontaneous, informal, addressed to an individual or the family circle, some carefully polished and deliberately aimed at a wider readership. Whatever their rank or tasks, their limitations of perception or experience, whether idealistic or cynical, most of the British in Palestine were conscious of participating in an extraordinary adventure.

The official start of British rule in Palestine was 11 December 1917, when General Sir Edmund Allenby, having routed the Turkish army in a mobile cavalry campaign that contrasted vividly with the muddy immobility of the Western Front, entered the city of Jerusalem on foot, followed by a parade of troops, to receive the plaudits of the assembled notables of the city, and savour his triumph as liberator of an impoverished and war-devastated Turkish province. To a young subaltern who witnessed the occasion, romantic associations and optimistic hopes were uppermost:

It was a perfectly glorious day, cold, bright sun and not a cloud....At 12 o'clock the C. in C. entered the Jaffa Gate accompanied and followed by the various people according to arrangement... with a crowd of local dignitaries, Syriac, Arab, Abyssinian, Coptic, Roman Catholic, Greek, Armenian, Austrian and other church dignitaries all beautifully got up with all their jewels....The moment when we walked in under the Jaffa Gate the C. in C. as Chief of a victorious army after 600 years was one not to be forgotten.[32]

The euphoria of victory and being genuinely welcomed as liberators made a lasting impression on the first British to arrive in Palestine. Lord Milner wrote, "You cannot imagine anything more interesting and Biblical! We are quite popular in Palestine, because we are still a novelty, and people there have not, like the Egyptians, had time to forget all the atrocities to which our coming has put an end." [33]

In the beginning and always there was the land itself, and the British soldiers and administrators observed it with an eye to the exotic new flora and landscapes, but with perennially nostalgic, sometimes improbable comparisons to the country they left behind, an England evoked in home-sick letters and diaries.

On the hill tops, clumps of olive trees, also blue gums here and there, and patches of very green corn just coming up. Over the whole the bluest of blue skies and away in the distance the blue hills of Judaea, the immediate surroundings remind me rather of parts of Hampshire with its undulating country and little hill tops growing larch, and here moreover the Jewish Colonies, all consist of neat little houses with red roofs which make them look very English indeed.[34]

Much later, in the last days of the Mandate, English diarists could still rhapsodize over the landscape, even the air of Palestine:

But to-day has been our first glorious Spring day; the air itself almost coruscating in the brilliant sunlight in which every stone and tree becomes a jewel -- urbs Sion aurea, Jerusalem the golden....Palestine light is of incredible clarity. It is brittle rather than glaring; translucent like cold spring water. In March and April among the hills of Samaria, Galilee and Transjordan, the wild flowers sprinkle the rocky and pale green landscape with red, yellow and blue. Sometimes the red anemones cover a whole hillside, and the blue lupins shine for miles like great splashes of ultramarine paint spilt among the young grass.[35]

Jerusalem and the Holy Places always occupied a special place in the English imagination, and had a correspondingly strong impact.

We had surmounted Scopus, had had a view of the Dead Sea to the east and were approaching Olivet when, westwards, the Noble Sanctuary, the ancient Temple area, came into sight. I stopped the carriage and looked down. There the Holy City lay, without compare, without parallel. I determined that I would serve her.[36]

C.R. Ashbee, who was to have a key role in town-planning in Palestine, wrote of Jerusalem: "And how the poetry of the place gets hold of you." [37] "The atmosphere of the whole place is what makes the fascination", wrote another officer, "apart from sentiment, it is attractive as quite the most untouched mediaeval town I have ever seen". He went on:

The walls are good, the Haram esh Sharif is a marvel and the streets are picturesque. You clatter up and down weird alleys paved with stone, passing perpetually under ancient arches and at times wandering through vaulted bazaars. There is no open space anywhere and big buildings old and new are swallowed up by dingy houses on all sides. Every now and then from a higher point you catch a vista of roofs over a ruined wall covered with flowering plants. There are picturesque corners without number, but the "ensemble" gives a feeling of compression which does nothing to take away the bad taste of grimy people and dirty streets....Few towns can be fuller of history and certainly none can have such associations. The Church of the Holy Sepulchre is a fraud and as tinsely as any church you can find anywhere. It is a pity because you have to see it all anyway. At first it is rather disgusting to watch the jealousy of the sects and to think that nearly all the holy sites are fakes, but it doesn't really matter. After a bit you come to look on them symbolically just as they might be put up in any other Church only here you are at any rate sure the actual spots are quite close and a little imagination does the rest.[38]

The same observer found that Jerusalem despite its squalors was fascinating, and castigated his fellows for "saying it is a dirty town with filthy inhabitants. I can't understand them. What they say is quite true but how could it be otherwise? The people are really one of the principal attractions. The variety and colouring are marvellous, while as for the town itself, any corner of it would bring people miles in any European town." [39]

Despite doubts as to the authenticity of this or that site, history was uppermost in many minds: to those soldiers and civil servants who knew the Bible, Josephus, the course of the Crusades, Palestine was rich in associations, enthralling altogether.

When you think that Thothmes III, Rameses II, Sennacherib, Cambyses, Alexander, Pompey, Titus, and Vespasian, Saladin, the Crusaders, Beybars, the Sultan of Egypt, Napoleon, and Mohamed Ali, all passed quite close to our camp, that Joshua and all the Judges fought the Philistines here or hereabouts, and that the Kings of Israel and Judah fought each other and the Maccabees fought the Romans all in the neighbourhood, it is rather wonderful.[40]

The very moment of arrival was always vividly recalled:

I woke at 5 a.m. and got up to see the Holy Land which is just exactly as one has always imagined. Donkeys, camels and people working in the fields dressed exactly the same as the pictures of Biblical incidents....You can picture us in a lovely country -- with a lovely climate -- we have been lucky.[41]

Recalling many years later his first experience of Palestine, Stewart Perowne said to an interviewer:

Well it was overwhelming, I'd never seen anything like it before... brilliant crystalline light... the moment I arrived, I went out as secretary to the Anglican Bishop and ... it was the 6th January 1926 and he drove me straight up to the top of the Mount of Olives, and there we looked down on Jerusalem, lying before us like a beautiful jewelled model... unforgettable to this day... you felt you were very much part of the original Palestine, that you might find Rebecca at the well, or the woman of Samaria coming out... literally, I mean one had that feeling, a tremendous sort of feeling... that the Holy Land was still Holy.[42]

Not all, of course, were comparably enthusiastic. Some thought the country unappealing: "The country we went through was very striking but not a patch on Portugal.... Some of the views are wonderful, but it's all spoilt by the barrenness."[43] Others commented on the bickering, squalor and commercialization encountered in the Holy Places:

In Jerusalem and Bethlehem one sees greater disregard for all the great principles common to all faiths than anywhere I've ever been. It is absurd to talk of the brotherhood of man here....Everyone has to make money out of religion here, either by fair means or foul and one is thoroughly disgusted by the tricks that are resorted to.[44]

But even when they found that Palestine lacked charm, or were repelled by aspects of its appearance or its population, virtually all who first saw it felt that the place stirred memory, evoked texts remembered since childhood, suggested meanings.

> The whole country is littered with rocks & stones in between which there is a few patches of stony ground for the growing of crops. "And some of the seed fell upon stony ground". I often wondered when reading the bible where they got the material from to stone people to death, I can see now. There are many passages in the bible the true meaning of which is not clear unless you have been out here...[45]

Arriving in a country laid waste by military operations, extensive deforestation for fuel, plagues of locusts and widespread crop failures, the British and Empire troops occupying Palestine found a local agricultural economy that had virtually collapsed, leaving almost universal poverty, malnourishment and disease among both Arabs and Jews. Although military operations against the Turks were still going on, the occupying army found itself obliged initially to undertake widespread relief measures on behalf of a starving population. Within a very short time, they also found themselves caught between growing, vocal Arab hostility to the Zionist enterprise, and the often impatient behaviour of the Zionist settlers and their official representatives, who had in their initial euphoria over the Balfour Declaration expected outward and visible signs of the new dispensation, such as the use of Hebrew as one of the official languages, the right to fly the Zionist flag, and other concessions with both symbolic and practical impact. Although "framed unmistakably in the Zionist interest",[46] the Palestine Mandate was shot through with ambiguities, not least concerning the meaning of "National Home" and the geographic boundaries within which the Mandate was intended to apply. Each of these ambiguities was to be fruitful of discord, in which both Arabs and Jews freely imputed to each other treacherous aims and underhand methods.

At the beginning, some officers were intrigued by their new responsibilities, and fascinated by Palestine. "Life here is really amazingly interesting and picturesque," wrote C.R. Ashbee to his family. "You've no idea of all the wonderful things that are going on. In the morning yesterday I was picking flowers in the Garden of Gethsemane, after rereading St. Luke. In the afternoon, it being the Fourth of July, I was the guest of the American Colony, among generals, bishops, and the 'Best Society' of Jerusalem -- 'all the World and his Wife.' In the evening there was an official banquet, another section of the 'Best Society', oriental, the Governor in the chair, all the Arab chiefs, and Imams, and Greek Archimandrites in black flower-pot hats, and a Moslem aristocracy that goes back to the Prophet -- 'all the World without his Wife.' We were recruiting for the new army that is being raised, with the aid of colour, music, oratory, and poetry." [47] But for most of the officers attached to the army of occupation, political tensions and disillusionment with the pro-Zionist British policy quickly soured initial enthusiasm, and made it virtually impossible to maintain the requisite stance of impartiality and proconsular hauteur.

The provisional military government established by General Allenby shortly after the conquest of Jerusalem was meant to last only as long as military operations continued in Palestine, but in the event operations ended in October 1918 and the military government went on until the summer of 1920. The administration was initially headed by a dual executive consisting of a Chief Administrator, Major-General Sir Arthur Money, and a Chief Political Officer, Brigadier-General G.F. Clayton, who had headed the Arab Bureau in Cairo, the war intelligence organization for the Middle East. These officials worked in reasonable personal harmony, but after their departure in mid-1919 their successors could not; and Occupied Enemy Territory Administration, or OETA as it was known, became notorious for dissension at the top and a good deal of muddle throughout. The officers of OETA, a variegated collection of men who in civilian life had been engaged in virtually every occupation but colonial administration, were thrust into their multiple tasks with little guidance except the general principle to maintain as far as possible the status quo that had obtained in Palestine before the war. The very vagueness of their instructions meant that individual officers wielded virtually unfettered local authority, an experience of autocracy that was exhilarating for some, intimidating and confusing for many others.

It rapidly became evident that even the smallest local administrative decision could be fraught with political significance, and that British military officers, unprepared and unwilling, were drawn from the very outset into the cockpit of Arab-Zionist conflict. In that conflict, the British of OETA were almost unanimous in their dislike of the pro-Zionist policy they were required to uphold, and correspondingly frustrated and angry when their representations to London expressing reservations about that policy were firmly rejected. The officers on the spot in Palestine tended always to view Arab opposition to the Zionists as a grave threat; Arab unrest was, at least in the earliest years, consistently downplayed in Whitehall. The visit in March 1918 of the Zionist Commission, an official body sent to Palestine with a view to coordinating policies for establishment of the Jewish National Home, was viewed with deep forebodings by the officers of OETA, who felt that unappeasable Arab hostility to Zionism might endanger the entire British position with Muslims in the Middle East and India. They were concerned above all not to be pushed by Zionist influence in London into having to "undertake the unpalatable task of imposing Zionism on Palestine at the point of a British bayonet,"[48] and made efforts to deflect Arab opposition to British policies by banning most Jewish immigration and land purchases in the Holy Land.

Often frustrated in their civil tasks, British officers were able to mobilize their energies in the non-political work of relief and rehabilitation: units of the Royal Engineers built roads, dug drainage systems and wells, worked to restore the shattered railways, and brought in medical supplies and food-stuffs, largely from Egypt, for the population. Officers restored the Palestine economy by establishing a Palestine currency pegged to the Egyptian sys-tem, and helping local farmers to cultivate their neglected fields.

The trusteeship of the Great Powers enshrined in the League of Nations Mandate system was designed to look after those dependent and backward populations whose well-being and development should be fostered as "a sacred trust of civilisation".[49] The League distinguished among territories of varying stages of development, conceding that "certain communities for-merly belonging to the Turkish Empire have reached a stage of develop-ment where their existence as independent nations can be provisionally recognised", subject however "to the rendering of administrative advice and assistance by a mandatory until such time as they are able to stand alone." [50] Although Palestine Arab society was in 1920 still composed overwhelming-ly of impoverished peasants, either smallholders or tenants, dominated by a small, often absentee land-owning aristocracy, the nascent Arab nationalist movement asserted that Palestinians had in fact reached political maturity, and should have been granted independence instead of the vague assurances contained in the Balfour Declaration and subsequent British interpretations of the Mandate. Despite these claims, and the undoubted political sophisti-cation and educational level of the Zionist settlers for their part, the govern-ment ultimately established by the British in Palestine was of the pure Crown Colony variety, under the authority of the Colonial Office, with a High Commissioner instead of a Governor as in the African Mandates. There was a small Executive Council of high-ranking officials, a mixed Advisory Council with no executive authority, and a country-wide adminis-tration in which the senior ranks were occupied by British men, mostly ex-Army officers, and junior positions distributed among carefully selected Palestinian Arabs and Jews. British judges presided over all courts higher than Magistrates' Courts. The police were Palestinian with British officers, supplemented for a time after 1922 with an all-British gendarmerie recruited largely from men who had served in Ireland.

In practice, the task of promoting the "well-being and development" of the people of Palestine meant in large part turning a blind eye to Jewish development, and protecting the Arabs by attempting to improve living conditions for the impoverished Arab peasants, the *fellahin*. British officers in each district kept the peace, administered justice, surveyed and mapped the country, established schools and clinics, advised on agriculture, foresta- tion, and public health. The Jews, aided by an international outpouring of funds mobilized by the Zionist movement, largely looked after their own community's needs, forging acomprehensive network of labour enterprises, an educational system from kindergarten to university, and land investments on a large scale. Jewish settlement and immigration were coordinated by the Jewish Agency, a central administrative body representing the Zionist movement and established in conformity with the Mandate. Arriving Jewish immigrants found homes either in agricultural settlements ranging from the collectivist kibbutz to villages of individual farmers, or in burgeoning small towns and such cities as Tel Aviv, Haifa and Jerusalem. Industrial and commercial enterprises of all kinds were also established; and despite their varied backgrounds and political commitments, the Jewish Palestinians rapidly organized themselves into a community on a level of political and social development so advanced that it compelled the uneasy admiration of the British and evoked fear among the Arabs.[51]

Despite the imperturbability on public display, the new rulers of Palestine had their doubts from the very beginning about the entire Mandate undertaking. A British Jewish officer wrote home:

The after-war politics of Palestine are very obscure and there are many problems that will require very delicate handling....I believe the British

Government is aware of this, but they have to hold the balance very evenly so as not to offend Muslim opinion which would endanger the whole Empire, or Jewish opinion either which would raise difficulties throughout the World....[52]

Sir Ronald Storrs, first British Military Governor of Jerusalem, later recalled that from the outset he and his staff felt surrounded "by an atmosphere always critical, frequently hostile, sometimes bitterly vindictive and even menacing",[53] and that "what with the feasts, the fasts, and the anniversaries, the impassioned conferences and congresses... the protests, the boycottings, the shuttings of shops, the stupid provocations and the disgusting retaliations"[54] there were those of them sufficiently alienated to condemn both communities out of hand.

Virtually all the British longed at some stage for the appointment in Palestine of a traditional colonial governor who would ruthlessly impose the order obtaining in African colonies, silencing the clamorous agitations of Arabs and Jews alike.

Even within the microcosm of a small, mixed student body in the Jerusalem Girls' High School, an Anglican-sponsored establishment, difficulties loomed. The Headmistress confided to her diary,

the Jews are much the most pushing, and if there were very many of them they would lower the tone of the school. It is queer, -- one hears people at home talk of the return of the Jews to Palestine, but it wouldn't be any good, one sees, for they are hated by both Christians and Moslems....Nothing but a thorough-going despotism for a hundred years will pull this country together, for there is no section of the community which you could trust to rule at all, and the country has lived for so long under the Turks, that it will take ages to instill into the people any idea of public service, or truthfulness, or cleanliness.[55]

Perhaps the least enviable of the new rulers of Palestine were the few British Jews among them, for whom the experience was "little better than one long embarrassment",[56] trying in good conscience to fulfil obligations to the Government and its policies, while under constant attack from both Arabs and Jews for presumed partiality, disloyalty or double dealings. The tensions inherent in their position came to a head over the issue of the so-called Jewish Legion, the Jewish battalions attached to the Royal Fusiliers. This all-volunteer force, numbering some 5,000 men, was recruited from Jews in England, Palestine and the United States, officered mostly by English Jews, and was the object of much suspicion and rancour on the part of all ranks in the British military. Anxious to appease Arab misgivings about the Jewish battalions, the senior military authorities in Palestine issued orders concerning the deployment of the battalions and their ability to display the Zionist flag that were considered by the Jewish troops insulting and demeaning. Moreover, Zionist attempts to have those orders modified or reversed in London predictably enraged senior military officers in Palestine. The battalions were ultimately considered a source of more difficulty than utility, and were demobilized after armistice lines had been established. One of their British Jewish officers commented:

> Time is not yet ripe for the garrison of Palestine to be specifically Jewish or Arab or even partially so. For some years Non-Jewish and Non-Arab administration and troops are necessary and then it will be possible to say what the destiny of the country should be. We have now no role and so the sooner we are demobilised the better. I don't think hot-headed Zionists realise this, but though I am only a sympathiser with their aspirations and not an active Zionist, I am sure that my views are sound.[57]

When Arab anti-Zionist activities in Haifa caused Jewish troops to be ordered outside the city, the Palestinian Jews demanded for the first time the right to bear arms in their own defence; and when the British authorities insisted that Jews instead be disarmed to avoid provoking the Arabs, this was deemed conclusive proof of British anti-Semitism, justifying attempts to smuggle arms into Palestine and engage in clandestine military training. Dr Weizmann retained to the end of the Mandate the belief that English Jews in the Palestine administration would serve as a link between the Zionists and the British. Instead, all too frequently the more prominent among them, notably the chief law officer of the Palestine Government, Norman Bentwich, found themselves in an impossibly controversial position, their loyalties strained and their every action and utterance subject to criticism from one or another side. Bentwich, despite an unblemished reputation for personal integrity and fidelity to his oath of office, was ultimately compelled to step down because as a Jew he was deemed impossibly controversial in the office of Attorney-General of Palestine.

The divided loyalties of even quite junior Arab and Jewish employees of the British government were also reflected in the notorious security leaks that plagued the administration throughout the Mandate. "To seal a document or label it 'Secret and Confidential' only provoked curiosity,"[58] according to a former functionary of the Palestine police. Routine monitoring and indeed interception of telephone, telegraph and postal communications meant that the Zionists and sometimes the Arabs frequently were in possession of important information before it reached the hapless official who was the nominal addressee. Jewish or Arab officials were moreover expected to turn a blind eye to or actually cooperate in pilferage of arms for their respective underground armies, and Jewish or Arab police and judicial officers were under constant pressure to intervene in favour of their fellows in litigation or investigations that came before them.

The new rulers of Palestine, "a collection of unqualified amateurs haphazardly thrown together by the war and told to run a country",[59] devoted much of their efforts to reconstruction in the country, while keeping a wary

eye on developments in Syria, where the French had replaced British gar-
risons but Arab nationalists were demanding the establishment of an independent united commonwealth including both Palestine and Syria. The
OETA officials introduced several innovations in Palestine life, for one a
daily work timetable that eliminated the customary two or three hour siesta
each afternoon. Henceforth in British Palestine, office work hours started at
7.00 a.m. and continued until 1.00 p.m., when offices closed for the day.
European social life too became the norm. The moderate climate of Palestine made it possible, once civilian government was established, to bring out
wives and children, who normally stayed with their parents until old enough
to be sent back to England to school. Houses were rented or built, gardens
planted, clubs founded, social relations established and maintained. The
British brought with them the ritual round of formal calls, luncheons, dinners and other events familiar from home, a full social calendar that went on
despite recurrent crises practically to the end of the Mandate. Most British
expatriates socialized exclusively within their community: it was at the higher levels of political administration, especially in Jerusalem, that foreign consuls and notables from the Arab or Jewish communities were added to the
guest list, and then mostly on large public occasions such as the King's
Birthday. Despite the efforts of some, British society in Jerusalem at least
tended to "degenerate into a cross between a Garrison Town and a Cathedral City, and to be overwhelmed by the official element,"[60] sub-divided in
its turn among civil and military, and the inevitable cliques based on various
affinities.

To a non-British observer outside these circles, British social goings-on,
irrelevant to her daily life in Haifa, nonetheless made a splendid show:

At the foot of Mount Carmel, just below the beautiful Bahai gardens, the
British officers banquets were held outdoors, under the silvery leafed olive
trees. The tall, Egyptian servant, in his snowy white galabia, red sash and

red tarboush, standing at attention behind each officer, looked more like the master than a servant. Accompaniment for the banquet, the music of the band of the Seaforth Highlanders reverberated through our Colony and provided a beautiful concert for us.[61]

From the very beginning, and even while military operations were still continuing, the British in Palestine engaged in a wide range of social activities, both within individual homes and on a more official level at headquarters and later Government House. In the early Mandate years, Miss Annie Landau, Headmistress of the Evelina de Rothschild School for Girls, an English Jewish woman of impeccable Orthodoxy and great personal charm, glided without challenge into the position of doyenne of Jerusalem society, and invitations to her dances and receptions were much prized. Described as "more British than the English" and "more Jewish than the Zionists",[62] Miss Landau nevertheless managed to be friendly with all communities, whose selected representatives mingled at her celebrated parties. Traditional hostesses received at fixed days and times, and at least at the beginning of the Mandate with a certain formality, not unleavened in some cases with a sense of mischief:

> I was invited to an "At Home" by Colonel Storrs, the Governor of Jerusalem....we were offered baklaweh, (a very sweet sticky Arab pastry made with nuts and honey) but no plates or spoons, and most of the ladies were wearing long white kid gloves![63]

Especially in the early years, the King's Birthday, Armistice Day, and anniversary of the deliverance of Jerusalem by Allenby were observed with considerable ceremony, including a special service in the Anglican Cathedral, prayers in all the official languages, and a formal reception to follow. In addition, from the beginning, arrivals and departures of high-ranking

ETON DINNER

JERUSALEM, 4TH JUNE 1918.

HORS D'OEUVRES

CONSOMMÉ

MAYONNAISE DE POISSON

BOEUF A LA PAYSANNE

ASPERGES

GATEAUX

OEUFS AUX ANCHOIES

FLOREAT ETONA.

Menu for Eton dinner party; Jerusalem, 4 June, 1918

officers, Christmas, Easter and other holidays, were all celebrated with what pomp could be mustered in Palestine. Attendance at these events was obligatory for all British officials and many others in the community, and there were ample opportunities for social rivalry and display, for wounded amour-propre and subtle social warfare. Old Etonians held a commemorative dinner in Jerusalem so early in the military occupation that their names could not be printed on the menu for security reasons. Oxford and Cambridge men had their own reunion dinners, and the whole web of British university and school affinities was reproduced in Palestine as elsewhere in the Empire. But there were also many less formal occasions: dinners and lunches, tea parties, tennis matches, picnics, amateur theatricals, recitals and simple "at homes" of both official and unofficial character. Life for senior officials was a constant round, occasionally including local guests, and attendance throughout the year at the many services celebrated by all the religious communities. For non-officials, such as the staff of mission schools, pleasures were perforce simpler: during the early years there was no library, no cinema and no radio in Jerusalem, so the principal pleasure was organizing picnics, if possible at some spot of historical or Biblical interest. After wives arrived, there was an English Dramatic Society in Jerusalem that staged amateur productions of Shakespeare, Gilbert & Sullivan and other plays. For those interested in music, opportunities to play and listen abounded, especially when the sizeable influx of German Jews in the 1930s brought enough first-class instrumentalists into the country to establish the Palestine Philharmonic Orchestra and a number of chamber ensembles.

Sporting occasions were not lacking either in Palestine. Within the all-male, military society of the earliest days of the Mandate, race meetings were organized, athletic competitions among Army and Police units, bathing in the Mediterranean, and hunting for small game. Before the Huleh swamps were drained, they contained ample game, and British officers organized hunting parties at weekends. For the more adventurous, there were excursions to Trans-Jordan, Syria and Lebanon, where in the winter season skiing was possible. Later in the Mandate, a mounted hunt was established by an Inspector of Police nostalgic for fox-hunting, dubbed by its members the Ramle Vale. With a Master resplendent in the traditional pink coat, the Ramle Vale pursued jackals across cactus-strewn fields as if the Jordan valley were the Cotswolds.

In the OETA days, other needs of the troops were also catered for: one or two streets in Jerusalem and other main centres were set aside for prostitutes, under medical supervision; compliance with the hygienic regime was encouraged by making the transmission of venereal disease to a British soldier a criminal offence. When the military occupation ended, it was considered that prostitution was incompatible with the sanctity of the Holy Land, and first medical supervision and then official permission for prostitution were withheld. It was also noted that in Palestine, as elsewhere after 1918, prostitution naturally declined with the increasingly available alternatives of "complaisant girlfriends, protected by contraception" and "same-sex solutions if opportunity presented itself."[64] Ultimately, keeping a brothel became a criminal offence, a prohibition that was maintained until the massive influx of troops to Palestine in the Second World War made enforcement impracticable.

Visitors to the Holy Land, numerous at all times, provided a source of entertainment and an official reason for celebration. There were constant arrivals and departures of military units and their officers, officials of the Administration, newly appointed ecclesiastics and teachers. Farewell and welcome parties and receptions filled the social calendar, and most officials were wearily familiar with the little Jerusalem railway station and its few amenities. If despite multiple recreations Palestine social life was recalled by many as relatively tame, that was because the same small circle of resident personalities recurred in entirely predictable combinations, moving according to a well-known script at fixed and moveable feasts. Throughout the Mandate years, the excitements of Palestine were amply evident outside the British community, and largely beyond its control. The ominous awareness of clashing nationalisms, anxiety over personal or family security, the sheer uncertainty of policy all overshadowed the ordinary concerns of individuals, and lent to life in Palestine more than the usual ration of imperial drama. Moreover, local officials knew that they were being swept along by a current generated far from Jerusalem.

From the earliest stage in the troubled history of the Mandate, local officials chafed against their inability to shape the essential course of Palestine policy. In July 1919, frustrated by their vain attempts to carry out a pro-Zionist policy with which they were in profound, irreconcilable disagreement, Generals Money and Clayton resigned the service and left Palestine, to the relief of the Zionists who exerted considerable pressure in London for the appointment as successors of British officials more in sympathy with the Jewish National Home. British officers in Jerusalem were uncomfortably aware that the Zionists in London had access to the home government at the most senior levels, and were not slow to mobilize pressure against any measures taken in Palestine that did not accord with Zionist policies. Yet with the resignation of several pro-Zionist officials in London, the Zionist-British entente had already begun to erode, and the Zionists were increasingly thrust upon their own resources.

The first Palestine Arab Congress met in Haifa in November of 1919, and evidence in the early months of 1920 of increasing Arab nationalist activity heightened already existing tensions between Jews and Arabs. Senior officers of OETA openly sympathized with the increasingly anti-Zionist atmosphere in Palestine, and storms and food shortages added to the unrest of the Arab population. In April 1920, the religious pilgrimage of *Nebi Musa* brought Arabs from all Palestine to Jerusalem, where there was a serious outbreak of anti-Jewish rioting, accompanied by loss of life and significant property damage. The civil police proved useless when its Arab members joined the rioters, and the British troops that were called out remained unhelpfully deployed outside the Old City walls while arson and other violence went on unchecked within. The Zionists bitterly accused the military authorities of negligence and pro-Arab partiality resulting in a "pogrom". The Arabs on their side first submitted a petition to the Chief Administrator asking for the removal of the Military Governor of Jerusalem, Ronald Storrs, and then retracted their demand. The military government did not, however, escape censure: although the official investigation blamed the disorders primarily on Arab fears of Jewish immigration and settlement, the military's handling of the riots was criticized, both in Palestine and in England. At the San Remo conference in May 1920 it was agreed that Great Britain should be awarded the Mandate for Palestine, on the basis of the Balfour Declaration, and France reluctantly signified its assent, giving up long-cherished pretensions to overlordship of a unified Levant. The first High Commissioner, Sir Herbert Samuel, a distinguished Liberal statesman and former Cabinet member, was appointed and came out promptly to Palestine, taking over from the military at the end of June 1920.

In a pessimistic private comment, Humphrey Bowman, Director of Education in the Palestine Government, wrote in his diary:

It is indeed difficult to see how we can keep our promises to the Jews by making the country a "National Home", without inflicting injury on 9/10ths of the population. It is the old story of the unfit going to the wall, for undoubtedly the Jews are cleverer and more industrious than the Moslems & their Zionist education is decidedly good... The mistake seems to be that we supported Zionism officially in the so-called "Balfour Declaration"... if we had merely let things take their course we shd. not have made ourselves responsible for this "interesting political experiment"....But we have now got the onus of it on our shoulders, & have incurred odium from the Moslems & Christians, who are not appeased by vague promises that their interests will not be affected...[65]

Sir Herbert Samuel's landing at Jaffa on 30 June 1920 was staged with all the viceregal pomp that could be mustered by the local garrison: caparisoned in tropical whites, with plumes and cocked hat, Samuel was greeted by a guard of honour, ceremonial artillery salutes, even a Royal Air Force fly-past. The occasion was only slightly marred by the persistent assassination threats that persuaded his staff to have Samuel driven by armoured car to the special train that bore him to Jerusalem. Upon his arrival as the first High Commissioner of mandatory Palestine, Samuel embarked on a carefully measured policy committing the British government as "trustee under the Mandate for the happiness of the people of Palestine"[66] not to impose measures which "that people" considered contrary to their interests, but fulfilling with fidelity the positive obligation of the Mandate to promote the establishment of the Jewish National Home. Samuel, who had first visited Palestine in the winter of 1919-20, came away then with a deep impression of the strength of Arab opposition to the Zionist enterprise, and prior to his appointment had expressed private doubts, subsequently overcome, that a Jew should be put in the position of governing Palestine. His concerns can only have been increased by the riots of April 1920 with their toll of dead and wounded, overwhelmingly among the Jewish population.

The appointment of Samuel, a prominent and practising Jew, was greeted with enthusiasm and unrealistic, almost messianic expectations by the Jews, and corresponding dismay by the Arabs of Palestine. Samuel's personal integrity was never impugned, but it was generally observed, at least among Jews, that his very high-mindedness and sensitive awareness of being a Jew made him unfit to take the really tough decisions required in Palestine, and that "when a question arose between the Jewish and the Arab demands...the High Commissioner would, time after time, give the Arabs all, or at any rate most, of what they wanted."[67] Nearly four years after Samuel's arrival in Palestine, his Director of Education expressed in his diary doubts that Samuel, as a Jew, could, despite all his efforts at impartiality,

> view affairs from the view of an Englishman. When he receives an Arab deputation, he does not -- cannot -- weigh the arguments for or against what is right, but what is expedient. "If I answer them so & so, will it be taken as favouring or not favouring the other side? I know I must not be thought to be favouring the Jews, so perhaps I had better give way."... I believe he is perfectly honest, as far as he can be in his position: but he is not English, and therefore he is the wrong man for the job....I do not see how any good can come to this country, until the Administration is British at the top, and until the preferential clauses in the Mandate are changed....[68]

Shortly after the arrival of Sir Herbert and Lady Samuel, and the transition to civilian rule in Palestine, the country came under the jurisdiction of the Colonial Office, and by the end of 1920 life began to take on the pace and even some of the atmosphere of other British colonial possessions. Wives and young children were sent for, houses purchased, gardens planted. Social life and its concomitant round of entertaining implied staff, and even quite junior officials could afford and were expected to engage household servants. British officials and their wives most often engaged chief servants from Egypt or the Sudan, usually considered more reliable and authoritative than Palestinians, to administer their households, but depended on local people, almost always Christian or Muslim Arabs, for the lesser domestic staff. Those British wives who came from posts in India or Egypt were often disappointed with Palestinian servants, complaining of incompetence, laziness and excessive wage demands as well as the generally low level of cooking and other domestic skills. Others recalled their household staff with affection, respect and gratitude.

> We had Moslem staff instead of Christian women. This meant not Palestinians but Sudanese, the recognised household staff of the Middle East... alluded to as Suffragis, meaning waiters, although they were cooks and everything else. Our Suffragi, named Abdu, stayed with us the two years we were there....They had a tradition of honesty doing the household shopping, although this may have contained a traditional percentage from the shops in the market, and they had to uphold their dignity by employing a local boy to carry their basket when marketing....If you gave a party, you would not be surprised to find helping the suffragis of your guests and perhaps your guests' dishes as well. I fancy they came for the fun of it as much as anything for you did not pay them. A suffragi always took off his shoes and put on his tarbush before coming into the sitting room to require the mistress's orders, as a necessary sign of respect. He did not stay in the house....[69]

When Edward Keith-Roach was District Commissioner of Jerusalem, his household was smoothly run by a small staff presided over by a Palestinian Arab from Bethlehem who did the shopping and kept the other servants in order: these included a Christian Arab cook from Bethlehem, a batman-valet who accompanied Keith-Roach on his daily round, a gardener and outside man, and a number of boys engaged to help inside or out wherever needed, especially at the regular Tuesday receptions, where up to 100 guests would gather for tea and sandwiches in the house and garden. Mrs Keith-Roach recalled that the servants took immense pride in these occasions: "it was to their honour to make the parties a success."[70] Others referred less fondly to their Palestinian servants. Writing to her mother, one district

57

officer's wife reported, "such a busy morning, spent mostly abusing people! We had bad eggs for breakfast -- so there was a scene with Abdul, followed by scene with small girl who had brought them yesterday, followed by scene with her mother!!"[71]

Another memsahib described trying to settle in to a Jerusalem house with virtually no useful help

in a world where half the population won't work and the other half are too frightened to show themselves to be working.... I am maid of all work, plumber, electrician, porter, painter, hostess, sanitary inspector, shrew, shopper. I had almost added bitch!.... At the moment we have... a Greek cook, who knows everything except a language, a possible but problematical Soudanese bearer, an Arab char, and a Russian laundress. The only answer to that is Esperanto....[72]

To attain a smooth-running household by European standards required a regime of eternal vigilance and a willingness to engage in virtually nonstop household combat:

Housekeeping in Palestine is more difficult and far more expensive than anywhere else in the world - bar the jungle. Servants are unutterably bad and foully overpaid, and each day is one long exhausting battle against the wickedness, the imbecility and the clumsiness of the "rest".... Everything is as expensive as at home, and many things just a little more so. I pay out every day on my ordinary shopping over a pound. How people on small salaries exist here I just don't know. My servants think I'm a demon on legs because I've got it all taped down to the last penny.... This sounds as if we were in the last stages of starvation -- far from it. We live very well and entertain a lot. No it merely means I have to be a lynx-eyed, fox-nosed, vinegar tongued Argus.... It is the first time I've had to do it in ten years of housekeeping in the East - and I don't enjoy it. I have a hate about something every day....[73]

With the arrival of wives and families and the creation in Palestine of a familiar microcosm of British society, there came also the Club. Centres for sports and social gatherings, the principal British clubs were in Jaffa and Jerusalem, offering tennis courts, a club house, writing and dining rooms. The point of the Club, exclusion as well as inclusion, was adhered to as rigidly in Palestine as elsewhere in the Empire: the Club was not in general open to "natives" except as they might be guests of members. An exception was made in the Jerusalem sports club for one outstanding tennis player who was an Arab.[74] Although towards the end of the Mandate, British social clubs might include a token handful of Jews or Arabs, these seldom came, somewhat to the relief of the regular members, one of whom remarked that

Programme for Race Meeting, Lydda, 1925

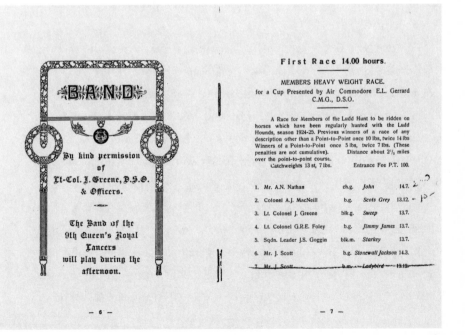

non-British members would simply "have sat together at the bar drinking coffee and playing tric-trac."[75] Nor, of course, were the clubs open to all ranks among the British. Troops or police had their own canteens and favourite local pubs and cafés, where indeed there might be some mingling with the indigenous Palestinians of several communities. Sports competitions, especially boxing and football, were organized within and among units, and other occasions sought for relieving the tedium of weekends, and slightly lessening the consumption of alcohol for which British other ranks were notorious. For a young woman just out from England, sister of a junior civilian official, whether or not she came on the local version of the "fishing expedition" famed in Anglo-Indian lore, the Club was an indispensable institution, offering opportunities to meet eligible men, extend her social circle, and above all escape from all too alien local colour into comfortably English predictability:

"There were lots of people up at the Club to-day watching as well as playing & some of them are decidedly unmannerly & catty. One thing about joining the Club is that you can see the latest papers & magazines & entertain friends to tea."[76]

With relatively few exceptions, in Palestine as elsewhere in the Empire, the British stayed close to their own kind. Ralph Poston, who served as an aide to the High Commissioner from 1931 to 1938, recalled that "there was virtually no mixing between the British and Arabs and very little with the Jews at all."[77] One factor certainly was language: almost none of the British knew Hebrew, while those who knew Arabic were seldom truly fluent; and knowledge of English was relatively rare among Jews and even the educated class of Arabs, who mostly preferred to speak French. Summing up British life in Palestine, Poston pronounced it "on the whole plain boring I think", adding that his colleagues were generally incurious about the past and indeed the present of the country: they "didn't really go out and see what was happening. I mean most of the ordinary British officials had never been to a Jewish kibbutz or seen what they were doing...."[78] By comparison with India or Egypt, in Palestine British officials kept relatively little state: the social tone was set by Government House, and there almost all the High Commissioners tended to follow the precedent set by the Samuels, entertaining with a certain sobriety, scrupulously following the protocol reflected in rules of precedence, and ending their evenings early after allocating their time with some precision according to the rank of their British and native guests. The very smallness of the British community in Palestine enforced social conformity: opportunities for breaking the rules were few when virtually every British man and woman was known to many others, and surveillance on and off the job was inescapable. There were of course lapses from decorum or legality: episodes of notorious adultery or drunkenness, two officials dismissed the service and deported from Palestine for issuing bad cheques, a Major cashiered for turning a blind eye to arms smuggling into Haifa port, one young aide to a High Commissioner who quite abruptly decided imperialism was wicked, embraced Communism, and after resigning his post was politely but firmly asked to leave Palestine.[79] And throughout, especially towards the end of the Mandate, there were numerous cases in which weapons, ammunition and other materiel were "lost" from military stores, and courts martial convicted only a fraction of those involved in the lucrative arms traffic with both Arabs and Jews.

In the relatively peaceful beginning of Samuel's High Commissionership, life in Palestine for most British officials was placid. The eastern and northern boundaries of the country were eventually established, the French seen off in their attempted encroachment from Syria on Trans-Jordan, and the work of post-war reconstruction continued. Sir Herbert Samuel himself radiated public confidence that all communities could be reconciled to living together under a benevolent and just Pax Britannica. Indeed, the relative peace of Jerusalem early in the Samuel administration led a senior British official to muse that "this may be the beginning of a new era, in which Jew and Moslem, Catholic and Protestant, Greek Orthodox and Samaritan, Druse and Armenian, Copt and Abyssinian, may not only live together in harmony, but may even come together and unite in one harmonious whole."[80] Samuel's private doubts were, however, reflected in his reluctance to accede to pressures from London for further reduction of the Palestine garrison below its then strength of 7,200 men.

The High Commissioner's optimistic hopes, grounded on the notion that the Arabs might somehow peacefully acquiesce in a growing Jewish population, were destroyed quite abruptly when on the Orthodox Easter Sunday of 1921, which fell on May Day, a minor clash in Tel Aviv between rival parades of Jewish Communists and Socialists led to outbreaks of serious rioting and looting that began in Jaffa, with random attacks by Arabs on Jewish residents, and spread to other parts of the country. The disturbances, which lasted one week and ultimately required the intervention of the Royal Air Force, resulted in significant loss of life and property in several places. Samuel immediately responded with a provisional ban on further Jewish immigration, a gesture which did not significantly alter Arab opinion but predictably infuriated the Jewish community, and won Samuel no plaudits in London for what was seen as a less than firm response to the challenge of disorder. The official inquiry into the 1921 riots concluded that they were caused by Arab hostility to the Jews, rooted in fear of the steady increase of Jewish immigration which the Arabs saw would result ultimately in a Jewish majority in Palestine, a prospect openly pursued by Zionists of all political views. Despite subsequent British efforts to placate the Arabs, ranging from new services and reduced taxes to a reinterpretation of the Mandate in a 1922 White Paper that moderated the Jewish National Home concept, the Arabs continued to regard "the benefits accruing to their countrymen from Zionist investments as unwelcome gifts from foreign intruders."[81] The Arab leaders consistently rejected British offers of a larger role in the working of the Mandate, making clear their fundamental objections to the Mandate itself and the Balfour Declaration at its core. In dismissing the offer of an Arab Agency designed to represent the Arab community and parallel the Jewish Agency, the President of the Executive of the Arab Congress wrote to Sir Herbert Samuel: "The Arab owners of the country cannot see their way to accept a proposal which tends to place them on an equal footing with the alien Jews,"[82] a refusal that put an end to all British efforts to co-opt Arab representatives in any advisory or legislative capacity into the mandatory regime. Undeterred by the constitutional deadlock, the Palestine Government continued to function as a benevolent dictatorship, its officials attempting doggedly to undertake the impossible task of continuing to favour, or at least permit, burgeoning Zionist development while somehow simultaneously accommodating Arab opposition.

In the small world within a church-sponsored school, it was possible to create by fiat relationships between British and the locals that could be cordial:

The Government had asked us not to fly the Union Jack, but to "merge our nationalities". Previously the British staff had always been addressed by their surnames, and collectively referred to as "The Ladies", and the ladies had done few, if any, playground duties. The Palestinian staff, on the other hand, had been addressed as "Miss Kareemeh" or "Miss Rosie" without a surname, and had been referred to as "the teachers", and they had done all the playground duties. Miss Warburton swept all this away, at a memorable staff meeting. From now on, all members of staff would be addressed in the same way, with surnames, not Christian names, and all would take their due part in school duties. It was a real step forward, and was much appreciated by everybody on our staff....[83]

Within the larger society, the creation of an inclusive Palestinian identity was recognized as an increasingly unrealistic goal. British officials nonetheless pursued a social policy that aimed to integrate, or at least not to offend, the disparate religious and political groups in Palestine which frequently were not on speaking terms with one another: official representatives of the various communities continued to meet under British auspices on ritual occasions, and the social calendar included regular calls by senior British officials on religious notables of all creeds. The social diary of H.V. Luke, then Assistant Governor of Jerusalem, is replete with social and official occasions ranging from a large-scale service at the Anglican Cathedral to commemorate the anniversary of Allenby's victory, to dances or other parties at Miss Landau's and in other private houses, including that of the High Commissioner; picnics, receptions, parades, luncheons and teas. "Hard at work all day on preparations for the dance. Latter a success, cloister lit up & looking charming, helped by full moon. About 250-300 guests, including Admiral & the Iron Dukes & Ajaxes [officers from Royal Navy ships sent from Malta to suppress riots], H.E. & Lady Samuel, & the Emir Abdullah."[84]   In one month, February 1922, Luke recorded a virtually nonstop round of dinner and luncheon parties, participation in a Shakespeare play, guests to stay, calls on Arab or Jewish notables. Attendance at religious services was also *de rigueur* for the higher British officials: in the Spring, there were the Orthodox and Armenian washing of feet ceremonies, the Holy Fire of the Greeks, Abyssinian, Orthodox and Catholic Easter as well as the Anglican holidays and Jewish Passover. On the official King's Birthday, there was invariably a parade, followed by a reception at Government House, and all the notables would pay ritual calls on senior British officials. Even in country districts the local British officer would receive indigenous representatives with whatever ceremony seemed fitting in rural social terms. Luke records that on one King's Birthday in Jerusalem, the two Chief Rabbis omitted their visit since the celebration fell on the Jewish Sabbath, but called later with apologies, saying they had held special services that day for King George "*und haben sehr gut gebeten*".[85]

For British District Officers in the Palestine countryside, showing the flag was an important part of the job, and of daily life. A great deal of work was done on horseback, often with the local doctor and one or two junior Arab officers in attendance. Villages would be visited, and after ritual greetings and hospitality there would be a discussion of local needs and problems: a road, help from the doctor, water supply, education, a dispute requiring conciliation. Many officers felt great satisfaction in such work: "it was a tremendous lovely life to lead in the open air... doing what we were there for... and lift the country up."[86] Edwin Samuel, son of the High Commissioner, was an officer in his early twenties when he became a District Officer in an Arab area of about 30,000 hill folk. He recalled it as a heady experience:

I was a townsman and here I was in one of the most primitive parts, more or less God Almighty and it went to my head. The place was exceedingly poor, they'd had four centuries of Turkish misrule... these were very barren hill lands and the villages were rather like the Italian villages, all built on the hill tops for defence. There was no sanitation, there was no electricity, there were no roads, they were peasants, poor peasants walked, so the middle class peasants went on donkeys and the very rich people had a horse and camels were used for transport... they were using wooden nail ploughs that only ploughed a few inches, they'd counted then on the rains, they were only active twice a year when they were ploughing and when they were reaping and threshing the corn. It was very Biblical and very beautiful to watch the winnowing of the corn, throwing it up with shovels and let the wind blow away the chaff and the grain would fall down. Most of the people were heavily in debt, you couldn't get bank loans because the title deeds were defective.... The Government began issuing agricultural loans and one of my jobs was to dish out the money and try and recover them later. Taxes were very difficult to collect, I had to go around with police to support the tax collectors.

Samuel went on to recall that he found the local Arabs fascinating, and appreciated the opportunity as a magistrate to learn all aspects of peasant life. He had no doubts about his role at the time, explaining to an interviewer that any questioning of Britain's right to rule Palestine "never entered one's head because... there'd been a war, the Turks had been defeated, the Middle East was divided up between France and England and it was the white man's burden." He further remarked, "I felt that I'd be doing some good, at least these people needed a lot of help, so one did what little one could, but chiefly I was learning."[87]

One District Officer, trying as part of his mission to reconcile the Arabs and Jews under his jurisdiction, proposed a meeting between them, only to receive the following reply from the headman of the Jewish colony:

> With great joy we received your invitation to come to Ber-toviya to-morrow, and we are thanking you infinitely for your Kindness. But, dear Sir, although there is a complete peace and a full mutual understanding between us and our neighbours **north** of Gaza, the road is not as secure yet as to venture travelling on it. If you could come over to us, dear Sir, we believe that the success of your undertaking to favour peace, would have been sure.[88]

The Jewish settlements were largely autonomous, wary of the British administration, and only in relatively formal relations with local British officers, very few of whom knew Hebrew or had much sympathy for the Zionist collectives, widely considered nests of Bolshevik ideology in the Palestine countryside. In contrast, British officers looking after Arab districts frequently became attached to the local villagers:

> We have come to bid you good-bye after you had spent among us two years of good service and strong exertion. Your connections with the

natives in general and with the Municipality in special, had been personal more than official. No problem had risen between you and the Beladiya, either from the natives or from the Government, but was solved with mutual understanding which was due to your wisdom and excellent management. So it is not strange to see us gathered to-day to explain our utmost regret for your departure. Gaza will never forget your efforts and hard struggles to uplift the district in every way. You had worked and toiled day and night for the welfare and happiness of the town.

Good-bye, our good Governor, good-bye, supplied with our best wishes for you and your honourable wife, and we wish you would always be the source of goodness and virtue to all.... So it is a comfort for us all to see that our beloved Governor has left us a good successor; and we hope that his days would be the same as yours, days of work and energy. In conclusion, I again bid you farewell and ask the Almighty to protect you day and night and guard you wherever you go or live.[89]

Other British officers in Palestine, especially in the north, took advantage of the open countryside to explore the pleasures of hunting and riding which they might have enjoyed elsewhere in the Empire or indeed at home:

Boxing Day meet -- at 14th Sqdn. R.A.F. Ramleh. Fine day, rather hot, but a rare scent. 43 people riding.... Had a very good day - 3 good hunts - - the last two very fast.... Ran our second one to ground in a cactus hedge. The first time I have seen this happen out here with a jackal. Took a proper toss on the flat.[90]

And, a few days later:

Up at 0400. Cup of tea & a bit of bacon then afloat in 2 boats & up the W. Coast [of Lake Huleh] towards Melahah. No luck & no chance of a shot at any duck, though many passed over us in the murky darkness. Glorious dawn & sunrise. Our next move was along the edge of the reeds on the North end, at the mouth of the Jordan, but could not conceal the boats here enough. Many duck on the wing. Finally posted in through small channel on N.E. corner & emerged into typical broadland, exactly like Hickling broad, except that this is framed in the most gorgeous scenery, with Hermon snowcapped towering above it all -- wonderful. We took up positions in the papyrus & waited for duck. A strong breeze sprang up about midday for about an hour & duck began to move. I got 11 but only picked 8... & so home across the Lake. Our quarters were in the house of a little Jew farmer, & quite comfortable, but the sanitary arrangements in most of these Jewish colonies are NIL! Hearty meal, a couple of pipes & ditto a couple of "drams", & so to bed, & here endeth the year 1923. I wonder what 1924 will bring forth?[91]

On into the next year, Major McNeil's diary is filled with descriptions of other sporting occasions: the Ludd Hunt Point to Point, other races, inter-unit games and other "good shows" including celebrations featuring Circassian dancers, march-pasts and bonfires. His was not a boring existence.

Other expatriate officers were, however, condescending about the pace and variety of British life in Palestine, comparing it unfavourably with society in other parts of the Empire, and ascribing its relative dullness to low official salaries and high local prices. One observed that the key to Mandate social life was "the magnification given to individuals by the smallness of the place" and complained that fine distinctions of social standing were "worked out to several places of decimals" wherever the officials gathered.[92] Noting that the romantic possibilities of the Indian hill station were also remarkably absent in Jerusalem, the same officer speculated that the "comparative moderation of the climate adequately restrained the more tropical human manifestations", but concluded the real deterrent to adventure was the closed smallness of a town "where it was impossible for any man to take any woman to dine in any restaurant, without the whole population of the restaurant, not merely knowing their identity, but speculating acutely then and there as to their actual or prospective relations, and the episode becoming common property throughout the length and breadth of the city the very next minute."[93] Towards the end of the Mandate, one civilian recalled, a saying current in Jerusalem described the city as "half the size of a cemetery in New York, and twice as dead."[94]

The club world was of course even smaller, and afforded meetings with the same officials and their wives who were encountered on innumerable other occasions, though perhaps in the context of tennis seen with greater clarity: "She was playing with her husband who is a disagreeable looking old thing & pitches into his wife for missing balls, etc. She plays far better than he does."[95] But in the glow of much later recollection, one British officer recalled Jerusalem society as on the whole harmonious, except when the Flower Show brought out latent animosities within the British community, with "Mrs. X defying Mrs. Y to grow a bigger and better gloxinia".[96]

Palestine did afford many opportunities for British indignation and moral superiority, especially in that reliable area of cultural misunderstanding, the treatment of animals:

A camel was kneeling down outside one house... tarred all over his back to prevent rubbing. Some of them have hardly any fur left on their poor old bodies but look like dried leather. The camels appear to be far better treated than the donkies whose skins must be as hard as iron they are always being whacked & having things jabbed into them. I am wondering when the English attitude towards animals will begin to have effect in Jerusalem -- it probably will in time. Even now they realise that the English have a bee in the bonnet on this subject. I brushed some flies off a donkey's sore the other day & the small boy with it immediately covered the place over with a sack. No doubt he was expecting baksheesh. Another beastly custom they have in the east is the carrying of fowls upside down. They tie the legs together & then carry three or four of the poor wretches through the streets with their heads hanging down. It makes you feel sick.[97]

Many British observers expressed varying degrees of shock at the unrestrained fervours of the Holy Fire and other religious ceremonies, in which only a line of stolid British policemen prevented beatings and other mayhem among the congregation. More recent arrivals tended to find almost all non-Anglican worship distressingly alien and mysterious:

At 8 o'clock this evening we went to the Abyssinian service on the roof of the Church.... There was a great crush -- but thanks to being English & a woman the gendarmes passed me forward & I even got inside the tent.... The service was most weird.... A tom-tom was beating all this time.... The Procession now moved slowly out of the tent & to my amusement McInnes - the English Bishop - marched after the Black Bishop with his gorgeous green & gold umbrella being held over him. McInnnes is low church, I imagine, & a Scot & there was something incongruous about this clean shaven Scotch looking man in his University robes walking after this weird procession with the tom-tom beating excitedly. McInnes has been asked to take part in several of the Easter celebrations & must sometimes feel rather at sea I think.[98]

The same observer, at a Greek Orthodox celebration:

I trade abominably on being English & find that generally speaking the officials leave me alone & do not "move me on" if they can avoid it. If a gendarme has to clear a path he is apologetic & says "please". The Greek priests too are kindly & careful not to shove more than they can help.... It is extraordinary how little idea the Greeks have of organizing & the fitness of things. Fancy allowing one of the choir to walk round among his gorgeously clad brethren in a striped shirt, braces & no coat. I saw that yesterday.[99]

But for the familiar little exchanges of English social warfare, it was reassuring to be among one's own: "dined with the Rowlands & went to the amateur production of 'Dear Brutus'.... There were one or two weak characters but no one down right bad.... I saw the notorious Sir Ronald Storrs Governor of Jerusalem to-night. He was making himself conspicuous in the front row -- gazing at the wild animals around him at intervals. The Rowlands hate him though they have to be polite."[100]

Palestine always had more than its share of misfits, enthusiasts and remittance men. Something in the thin clear air of Jerusalem and Galilee was conducive to religious or other obsessions that occasionally inspired otherwise ordinary visitors to flights of irrationality, or in a few cases descent into emotional or spiritual chaos. Among the places that always attracted the eccentric was Lake Tiberias, where a little society gathered in a local Catholic hospice, to be observed by an English visitor:

This is a lovely little place... The garden is full of trees & shrubs & two lemon trees laden with fruit throw their shadow over the garden seat where we spend a great part of our time. We pick them at meal times & make fresh drink with them. Little land crabs scuttle about & at night the jackals come howling quite close to the house. We all meet for meals & sit at a long table with Father Jäpper at the head. He is a jolly individual with cropped head, rosy cheeks & bushy beard & his laugh does one a world of good. He roars with delight. He wears a long white gown with girdle & a sun hat. Next to him on either side sit two young men who have been at the Hospice for some time. One is Turville Pater an antiquity student who affects long hair & shirts ties & socks to match each other.... He is excavating a cave quite close here & is very pleased with the flints he has come across. He is an ardent R.C. The other man is Briant of no particular occupation but 2 years ago he was painting now he is apparently an author. He is a queer individual very fond of arguing & Miss Dixon thinks his relations probably pay him to stay out here. Mrs. Stevenson & Mrs. Barnes complete the party. The former - an elderly lady wanders about painting while her husband wanders about in cargo boats seeing the world. Mrs. Barnes (middle aged) is interested in antiquities & helps Turville Pater with his flints.[101]

British educators in Palestine were unshakeable in the conviction that Shakespeare, Latin, the values of the English public school were appropriate for the natives, even though they never made significant inroads within the autonomous Jewish school system:

The [inter-school] Sports themselves were really quite a success... St. George's naturally won them, because they are of such a completely different type to all the others... It certainly is interesting to see the difference that the application of English methods does make. One naturally has qualms about forcing English ideas and institutions upon these people, but there is no doubt, that if you are going to do it at all, it is best to go the whole hog. You can see that in the case of the scouts: the best troops are the ones that are most English in dress and ways, just as the best Schools are the ones that are run most completely on English lines... it is an absolute fact that the boys in the schools here find their Arabic poets dull and uninteresting, while they lap down Shakespeare with avidity. By giving them an English education, therefore, one is not really de-nationalising them, because for the most part they have not the remotest idea of what their nationality implies; they have no traditions, and they are likely to find, on the whole, more akin to their own aspirations in Nelson and Cromwell than in Salah ed Din and Suleiman the Magnificent. That is a generalisation, but there is truth in it. The difficulty comes, of course, in finding careers for those you educate. There is absolutely no future for them in this little apology of a country. The agricultural basis of Society is hopelessly inadequate, and its only alternative, an industrial one, is impossible. There is, of course, emigration, which is largely resorted to by an increasing number; but what is the good of that for the 'Palestine for the Palestinians'? And there are always the Jews waiting to get hold of anything they can.[102]

If Arab nationalism seemed tiresome though just comprehensible to many officials of the Palestine administration, the Zionist variety was less attractive altogether; even among the few English officers who approved of Zionism, the Zionists themselves were perceived as self-righteous, implacable and egocentric: "the vigour of the Jewish agitation makes me tired.It wearies me so that even my sympathy flags and I find myself becoming antagonistic. Their belief in what they are doing is terrible and selfish in its intensity.... They ask bounty and protection from England, but they never pause to consider how many troubles have been heaped upon us in the past few years."[103] British policemen complained that the Jews were not always quick or "reasonable" in obeying police orders, and that both they and the Arabs were unduly sensitive to the rough language they occasionally provoked. And then, commented one official, "the inability to give a straight answer to a plain question is very characteristic of all races in Palestine except the British, and even they are not entirely immune from the infection."[104]

Those who were in a position to observe the steady growth of Jewish population, from some 55,000 in 1918 to 108,000 by the spring of 1925, were either impressed or alarmed by the increase in Jewish numbers, as well as every measure of economic and social progress. Zionist development was expressed not only in population growth but also in the proliferation of agricultural colonies, industrial and commercial enterprises, and a highly developed educational, social and cultural infrastructure, whose most notable achievement was perhaps the revival in less than a generation of Hebrew as the everyday language for large portions of the Jewish population of Palestine.

Fond Colonial Office hopes that a moderate nationalist Arab party with widespread support would somehow emerge in Palestine were never fulfilled, and the Palestine conflict, with steadily larger international ramifications, continued to elude any attempts at conciliation. Without a constitutional structure that might unify the disparate communities of Palestine, each pursued development quite independently of the other, forging communal institutions that came to resemble quasi-governments in embryo. The British governors of Palestine thus found themselves ruling a country that had *de facto* been partitioned politically, if not yet officially and on the ground. The Zionists, absorbed in the development of their burgeoning community, continued to exist "in a strange twilight zone, seeing the Arabs and at the same time not seeing them",[105] deluding themselves, depending on their ideology, with notions that only the class of feudal *effendi* landlords prevented the Arab masses from realizing the advantages accruing from Jewish settlement, or that the British authorities with characteristic duplicity were subtly undermining the Zionist enterprise, and could if they were sufficiently determined simply impose the Jewish National Home in Palestine. Most seemed unable to understand that neither generally increasing prosperity in Palestine nor gestures such as King Feisal's one-off meeting with Dr Weizmann, or any number of Weizmann's conciliatory speeches, would reconcile the Arabs to large-scale Jewish settlement in the country. Only David Ben Gurion and his supporters saw clearly that an armed conflict with the Arabs was likely. The Arabs on their side steadfastly refused any participation in all-Palestine affairs that might be construed as acquiescence in the Mandate and its hated pro-Zionist policy.

The continuing conflict was epitomized by the angry Arab reaction, a General Strike, to the arrival of Lord Balfour in Palestine in 1925 to participate in the formal opening of the Hebrew University in Jerusalem, an occasion for pride and celebration by the Jewish community. Sir Herbert Samuel felt nonetheless able to report upon relinquishing office at the end of June that his conciliation policy had borne some fruit: "I trust", he wrote, "that work, accomplished under conditions sometimes of difficulty, will be considered in the retrospect not unworthy." A British observer wrote of Samuel's time as High Commissioner: "Sir Herbert ruled with patient justice, but he had small thanks from the people of the land. The Arabs could not imagine that a Jew could possibly treat them justly, and the Jews disliked him because he really was just."[106] Samuel had tried with all the strength of his Liberal convictions scrupulously to fulfil moral and legal obligations to both the Arabs and the Jews of Palestine. He was gratified to observe by the end of his tenure that the more violent Arab opposition to Government had waned. It was left to his successor, Field Marshal Lord Plumer, to reduce military and police forces and still maintain order in Palestine. By 1929 these amounted to one RAF squadron, two companies of armoured cars and a smaller police force. The Permanent Mandates Commission of the League of Nations and other observers expressed disquiet as to the security situation, but Lord Plumer radiated calm reassurance.

Plumer, who landed at Jaffa with Lady Plumer in 1925, was a much-admired military hero of the First World War, a man who commanded authority by sheer presence and proconsular bearing, though he was short in stature. He rapidly acquired local renown by going so far as to request his District Commissioners to cease presenting their routine reports on the political situation. "There is no political situation -- don't create one!" he admonished his officers.[107] Unlike Samuel, Plumer did not have much interest in Zionism, nor did he have any personal reason to curry favour with either Arabs or Jews: a plain-spoken, straightforward military man, he stressed public order, imperial fealty and the strict maintenance of the status quo, preferably at minimal cost to the British and local taxpayers. In one famous incident, Plumer received an Arab delegation objecting to a Jewish parade on the grounds that if it were to take place they could not undertake to be responsible for public order in Jerusalem. Plumer informed them with great firmness that they need not trouble themselves about public order, since maintaining order was his sole responsibility. Plumer was equally clear in consistently resisting any attempts to introduce representative government in Palestine. He and Lady Plumer were much admired and even loved for their unabashed patriotism, personal warmth, and lack of viceregal ceremony. Plumer enjoyed taking unaccompanied walks about Jerusalem, dressed in the officer's mufti of dark suit and furled umbrella that made him even more conspicuous than usual, and was annoyed to discover that his staff had arranged for his protection to have him discreetly followed by a police detective. One officer later recalled that "there he was the great Field Marshal and she was a darling, but they had absolutely no side at all. He always called her old lady, and she would look round and say where's my dear man. Never 'have you seen His Excellency', and at the tea parties... Lady Plumer would say I wonder where so and so is, you know they think I don't notice when they don't come, but I do. And then at the end Lord Plumer told the band to play God Save the King, and then he said now you all will have tea, they weren't going to have anything at all till all the helpers had theirs..."[108]

Despite Lord Plumer's majestically serene denial, there was of course a political situation, not least within the Palestine Administration, where the majority of the senior officers disapproved heartily of the British Government's commitment to the Zionist enterprise in Palestine, though they expressed that opposition only privately. "I agree it [Zionism] ought to go, and I expect it will," the Director of Education confided to his diary, "but why was it ever allowed to come?"[109] It seemed indeed, during the years 1925 to 1929, that the growth of the Jewish National Home had slowed if not stopped: a severe recession caused significant declines in Jewish employment and immigration; in 1927 more Jews left than entered Palestine, and some at least among the Arabs took heart from the prospect of the Zionist settlement perhaps remaining after all a small-scale enterprise. But both Zionist immigration and development soon resumed at an accelerated pace, and the civil calm was deceptive. It was in any event obvious in both Jerusalem and London that abandoning the Mandate and the pro-Zionist promise at its core was not a viable option. British policy-makers were still concerned that leaving Palestine would create a vacuum, of which the French or less friendly powers might be expected to take advantage, thus potentially threatening the British position athwart the Suez Canal. Nor, at that stage in British imperial thinking, would conceding self-government to the Arab majority in Palestine have been a desirable alternative to pressing on with the Mandate and the Jewish National Home. And so, under ever more stringent fiscal constraints imposed from London, the British military presence in Palestine was steadily whittled away: by 1928 the officer commanding in Palestine had at his disposal a handful of aircraft, six armoured cars and only enough personnel to maintain this very small establishment.

Lord Plumer sailed from Palestine in July 1928, retiring early for health reasons, and with his departure the golden age of relative peace in Palestine came to an end. Plumer's successor was Sir John Chancellor, a career Colonial Office administrator with no special knowledge of Palestine or the Middle East, and no sympathy for either. Aloof and suspicious, Chancellor did not mingle with any grace in either British or general Palestine society, and was unable to count on the reservoir of good will that Plumer had effortlessly commanded. Chancellor was, moreover, confronted from the start by renewed Arab demands for a representative assembly which would lead to the self-government that by then had been conceded by the colonial powers in neighbouring Trans-Jordan, as well as in Egypt, Iraq and Syria. He felt that Palestine could not continue to be the colonial exception, and warned that unless some way could be found to associate the populace with government in Palestine there would be serious consequences. In the summer of 1929, Chancellor travelled to London for discussions with the Colonial Office. In his absence, long-simmering Arab resentment burst forth with unprecedented violence.

In retrospect, the signs of trouble had been amply evident. A relatively trivial dispute over Jewish attempts to install a screen to separate men and women praying at the Western Wall, below the Muslim holy places of the Haram esh-Sharif in Jerusalem, an innovation attempted on the eve of the Day of Atonement in September 1928, provoked Muslim outrage and caused the British authorities, anxious as ever to maintain the status quo, to remove the offending screen on the Day of Atonement itself, an act that in its turn aroused passionate resentment among the Jews. The incident was exploited by Arab and Jewish extremists alike, each imputing sinister motives to the other community: the credulous and the cynical on each side were glad to find further fuel to stoke long-smouldering resentments. Arabs and Jews ultimately subsided into sullen silence, but the incident left its residue of bitterness and hostility. The Western Wall dispute was followed by an aggressive nearly year-long campaign by the Mufti of Jerusalem to stir up popular rage over the alleged Jewish threat to Islam's holiest site in the city. The continuing uproar had its predictable effect on both Arabs and Jews. Even aggressively secular Jews were angered by the failure of the mandatory government to take energetic action against the Mufti's campaign. Observant Jews were bitter at attacks on what they claimed as immemorial rights of access to the Western Wall, which in Ottoman times, they alleged, had included bringing religious appurtenances and furnishings to the site, such as the screen that had been forcibly removed on the Day of Atonement by the British authorities. The Arabs for their part, whether Muslim or Christian, were unified and roused to fury by the Western Wall controversy, which represented in microcosm what they perceived as another example of relentless pressure from the Jews to extend their rights and privileges in Palestine.

In the absence abroad of both the High Commissioner, on leave in England, and of the entire Palestine Zionist Executive, who were attending a Zionist congress in Zürich, a large-scale Jewish demonstration and march took place in Tel Aviv on 14 August, followed the next day by a demonstration at the Western Wall itself, in which nationalist Jewish youth groups raised their flag, and with deliberate ostentation shouted Zionist slogans and sang the Jewish national anthem. In response, on Friday, 16 August, thousands of Muslims after morning prayer descended to the Wall, were harangued by incendiary speakers and incited to destroy Jewish prayer books as well as the petitions traditionally left between the stones of the Wall by pious Jews. These acts predictably excited the Jewish community to a fever of outrage, their sense of anger and humiliation heightened by the official British usage of "Wailing Wall" to designate their holiest site in Jerusalem. In the days after this demonstration, emotions among both Jews and Arabs were deftly heightened to boiling point by their extremists. The first Jewish death occurred on 17 August in an affray with Arabs in Jerusalem that resulted also in injuries to other Jews and to Arabs. The following Friday, 23 August, serious Arab rioting broke out in Jerusalem, with widespread looting and random assaults on individuals, and subsequently anti-Jewish violence spread rapidly all over Palestine. In the absence of any effective armed counter-force -- there were only some 292 British policemen in all Palestine, while neither Arab nor Jewish policemen could be relied upon in a situation of communal strife -- mass slaughter ensued, especially brutal in Hebron and Safad, where long-established communities of religious Jews were attacked, suffering many deaths and casualties. The fledgling Haganah, the clandestine Jewish self-defence force, was stretched beyond its limits, and proved unable to counter most of the violence. There were continuing assaults on Jews in Jerusalem, Jaffa and Haifa, and six Jewish agricultural colonies were completely destroyed; the overall death toll among the Jews was 133 killed and 339 wounded, and of the Arabs, 116 were killed and 232 wounded, most by police and British troops who had been hastily mobilized from Egypt to cope with the disorders. Even the swift commissioning of Special Constables from among the male members of the British community could not materially affect the outcome; the disorders subsided only after sufficient numbers of troops were available to patrol troubled areas.

With the High Commissioner out of the country, responsibility for coping with the crisis fell upon the Government Chief Secretary, H.C. Luke, who was subsequently accused of not acting as promptly or decisively as the situation required. When the High Commissioner returned urgently to Palestine, he announced suspension of any talks on constitutional changes, and let the police and courts proceed with their work: some perpetrators were apprehended and convicted, twenty-seven death sentences were confirmed, but after three Arabs were hanged, the remaining death sentences were commuted to prison terms. The show of force by reinforcements of British troops had its effect, and Palestine subsided into a fragile truce that barely masked continuing hatred and clandestine preparation on both sides of the conflict.

The violence of 1929 illustrated beyond any possible doubt the continuing, implacable hostility of the entire Palestine Arab community to the Zionist enterprise, and effectively shattered the delusion that the British could foster a sense of Palestinian citizenship or community that might be shared by Jews and Arabs. The riots also cruelly exposed the inadequacy of police and military in Palestine: the Arab section of the police proved utterly

Official proclamations relating
to the disorders of 1929

PROCLAMATION

I GIVE NOTICE to the public of Palestine that
His Majesty's Forces are operating in the country with
the sole object of quelling the present disturbances
and promptly restoring order.

Exceptional measures of repression will be
avoided so far as possible, but the troops will not
hesitate to use force against disturbers of the peace
without distinction.

H. C. LUKE
Officer Administering the Government.

This twenty-fifth day of August, 1929.

Public   Notice

I order all persons in the Town Planning Area of
Jerusalem to remain in their houses from 11 p.m. to
5 a.m. until further notice.

My Public Notice dated 14th September, 1929,
is hereby cancelled.

23rd October, 1929.

E. KEITH-ROACH
Deputy District Commissioner,
Jerusalem Division.

اعـلان

اني آمر جميع الذين يقطنون ضمن منطقة تنظيم مدينة القدس ان يبقوا في
منازلهم من الساعة الحادية عشرة مساء لغاية الساعة الخامسة صباحاً وذلك لحين
اشعار آخر

ويعتبر اعلاني الصادر في ١٤ ايلول سنة ١٩٢٩ ملغى .

ا . كيت روش
حاكم مقاطعة القدس

في ٢٣ تشرين اول سنة ١٩٢٩

מודעה רשמית.

הריני פוקד על כל האנשים באזור לבנין ערים של ירושלים להשאר
בבתיהם משעה 11 בערב עד 5 בבקר עד הודעה שנית.

המודעה הרשמית שלי מיום 14 סעפטעמבר 1929, בטלה ומבוטלת בזה.

א. קיטרואטש.

81

unreliable and the British forces were hopelessly outnumbered and ineffectual in the crisis. The shock of the riots caused the Arab and Jewish national movements to accelerate their separate internal development, strengthening themselves consciously for the power struggle to come, in the realization that their ultimate destiny would be in their own hands. Those British officials of the Palestine Government who had for years pointed out the perils of the pro-Zionist policy they were reluctantly administering on orders from London could claim only the bleak satisfaction of so many Cassandras whose warnings and advice had consistently been dismissed or ignored. "We have built for 10 years, & it has crumbled to pieces in 10 days", wrote Humphrey Bowman,[110] musing a month later, "people talk terrible lot of rot about Jewish immigration helping Arabs &c. & cousinship of Jacob & Esau. They may be cousins, but relationship forgotten for thousands of years & anyhow, if you own a house, you don't want it taken by somebody else even if he says he is a cousin!"[111]

chapter 3 ~ **Bowl of Scorpions 1929–1939**

Once again, a formal Commission of Enquiry was constituted to examine untoward events in Palestine, and sent out under the chairmanship of an eminent colonial Chief Justice, Sir Walter Shaw. After staying in Palestine from October to December 1929, and completing its thorough investigation, the Shaw Commission exonerated Luke of negligence, concluding that he had in fact done everything possible, considering the inadequate forces at his disposal, to maintain order. The Commission also satisfied itself that the Arab attack had not been directed against the British administration, and was not planned or incited by the Mufti of Jerusalem and the Arab Executive. Unsurprisingly, the Commission found that the outbreak could be ascribed to widespread Arab hostility towards the Jews, based on the fear that continuing Jewish immigration and land purchases in Palestine would block any progress towards national self-determination, and ultimately transform the Arab population of the country into a landless minority. The Shaw Commission had thus, after laborious deliberations, come to almost precisely the same findings as its predecessor after the 1921 disturbances, the Haycraft Commission. The Permanent Mandates Commission of the League of Nations, for its part, refused to exonerate the Palestine Administration of negligence in its handling of the disturbances, criticizing it harshly for lack of foresight and inattention to Arab disaffection, and arguing without much evidence that an economic "fusion of interests" might have helped integrate Arab and Jewish aspirations in Palestine.

In the wake of the League of Nations report, the British garrison in Palestine was substantially reinforced, the Palestine Police Force reorganized, and another eminent colonial servant, Sir John Hope Simpson, formerly of the

Indian Civil Service, appointed to find facts and make recommendations concerning land settlement, immigration and development in general. Hope Simpson's subsequent report, designed to establish an objective measure of Palestine's economic absorptive capacity, failed in its object. The Report, based on an estimate of cultivable land in Palestine that later was shown to be erroneous,[112] concluded that pending further development, especially of water resources, there was not enough room in the country for any further Jewish agricultural colonization without doing irreparable harm to Arab interests. Convinced, moreover, that there was widespread Arab unemployment, Hope Simpson was also discouraging on the prospects for Jewish non-agricultural immigration. This blow to Zionist aspirations for the Jewish National Home was compounded in October 1930 by a new statement of Government policy, a White Paper signed by the Colonial Secretary, Lord Passfield, which set forth more stringent controls on immigration and land transfer, and explicitly restated the principle that "economic absorptive capacity" was to limit future immigration. The Passfield White Paper repeated that the Palestine Mandate involved a double undertaking, to the Arabs as well as the Jews, and stated that the British Government "will not be moved, by any pressure or threats, from the path laid down in the Mandate".[113]

Such comfort as the Arabs on their side might have felt in British assurances was undermined by a reaffirmation in the White Paper that the Arabs could not hope for any kind of constitutional change, any progress towards self-determination that would block the British Government from carrying out its double promise. There thus remained, seemingly eternal and immutable, the fundamental contradiction between Arab nationalist aspirations and the undertakings assumed by the British Government in the Balfour Declaration and the Mandate itself. While "ink flowed from the Government and the League, the Jews and the Arabs all through 1930",[114] the sullen quiet of Palestine was broken by renewed rioting in Nablus in

August, continuing random murders of Jews, and chronic rural unrest as well as sporadic violent efforts by Arab groups to prevent illegal Jewish immigrants from entering the country.

Sir John Chancellor, as High Commissioner the target of harsh criticism from all sides, thoroughly disliked his assignment to Palestine. A former colonial governor elsewhere in the Empire, notably Southern Rhodesia, he had no special knowledge of the Middle East, and no prior experience of the Palestine tangle. Isolated and hyper-sensitive to the abuse he had to endure, not least from the Arab and Jewish press, he expressed in private correspondence both weariness and frustration with his task. Describing to his son a meeting with the Arab Executive at Government House, he wrote:

I sent for them to come & see me... & heard what they had to say for about two hours; but was not able to meet their wishes about the Wailing Wall Regulations & other matters... told them that I had heard that they had passed a resolution to the effect that I was not a fit person to be High Commissioner & that they were going to ask the Sec. of State to recall me. I said that I was not disposed to contradict them as to that; but that I was of opinion that under present conditions I knew of no one who would be a good High Commissioner of Palestine except God.[115]

Even a divinity in Government House might have despaired of the High Commissioner's task: to carry out a policy established in London that wavered according to the gales of protest expertly orchestrated by Zionists or Arabs, each adversary now adept at using a variety of international pressure tactics of increasing stridency and boldness. Sir John Chancellor was in any event convinced that the entire Balfour Declaration policy had been "a colossal blunder", unjust to the Arabs and impossible of fulfillment in its own terms.[116] Despite Chancellor's views, and the brave words of the Passfield White Paper, the Government was ultimately moved, by an outcry from

Zionists and their sympathizers in the Conservative and Liberal parties, to issue in February 1931 a clarification and interpretation of the White Paper that was widely perceived as more favourable towards the Zionist case than the original text had been. In a letter from the Prime Minister to Dr Chaim Weizmann, president of the Zionist Organization and the Jewish Agency, the Prime Minister conceded that there would be no obstacle to Jewish land acquisition, particularly in areas that had previously been regarded as uncultivable, and that Jewish labour maintained by Jewish capital would continue to be admitted to Palestine. The interpretation predictably unleashed a storm of protest from the Arabs, for whom substitution of the "Black Letter", as they called it, for the White Paper was incontrovertible evidence of the powerful influence wielded in London by Zionism and world Jewry, adept at swaying Parliamentary opinion despite the advice of the Colonial Office or the Palestine Government. Pressure campaigns from Jews or Arabs, White Papers, Black Letters were all, however, epiphenomena: the basic contentious issue was the Palestine Arabs' desire for self-determination, and their consistent refusal to subscribe to the optimistic notion on which the Mandate was based, namely that somehow, at some future time, both Jews and Arabs would coexist in a spirit of mutual good will and cooperation, engendered presumably by the material benefits conferred on all the inhabitants of Palestine by Zionist investment and general development.

While statesmen argued, lobbyists did their backstage work, and papers flew back and forth, British officials, soldiers and police on the ground tried to maintain the Mandatory's authority in Palestine, fighting loneliness, boredom, and irritation with government policies that seemed to waver even at the level of local law enforcement. From Rosh Pinah in Galilee, where he was newly stationed in the Trans-Jordan Frontier Force, a young officer wrote: "I had a bad introduction to this place as I was ill & very sick when I arrived and I'm feeling very weak after it; and not at all in a fit state of mind to grapple with the problems which hourly present themselves. I have only one man here who can speak any English and he's a bloody fool. The worst part about it is that it's very lonely and I have no form of conveyance of any sort.... I shan't have a very happy birthday here," adding two weeks later, "I am at present without a book, which is the equivalent in this place to being without soap and water."[117] After weeks of desultory patrolling, experiencing both Arab and Jewish realities in Palestine, the same officer exploded: "Transjordan I like, but Palestine is the most frightful country I've ever seen. I'd as soon live in the 'Black Country'. There is no scenery, no climate and no comfort. The people are exceptionally unpleasant, both to look at and in every other way. I wish the Arabs would come and wipe the whole lot out...."[118] And by year end, "I wish I'd known this country was like it is before I came. I would have gone to West Africa, which I'm told is entirely different. All this muddling & changing of policy has an effect upon everyone & nobody knows from one day to another which way they are facing...."[119]

Other British officials were more fortunate in their assignments and some more sanguine or phlegmatic in temperament. But even those who experienced occasional enjoyments and had a general interest in Palestine frequently entertained doubts about the Mandate itself. Still others expressed distaste on aesthetic or political grounds for the Jewish National Home, its bustling enthusiastic Zionist settlers, and its proudest achievement, the burgeoning city of Tel Aviv, always contrasted with the picturesque and suitably "Oriental" ambiance of Jaffa. "It's all very efficient", pronounced one young English visitor about Tel Aviv, "but gruesomely go-ahead... everything bubbling over with expansion... these trodden people from the ghettos have a right to be proud, but it's rather nauseous in a way, this bristling prosperity -- and absolutely unscrupulous."[120] An English journalist found Tel Aviv "a perfect freak in Palestine", "without any flavour of the East" and filled with unattractive Jewish crowds speaking not a word of English, and beat a hasty retreat from his hotel, "pursued by a horrid little Yid waiter."[121]

C.G. Eastwood, a young Private Secretary to General Sir Arthur Wauchope, the much-decorated officer who relieved Sir John Chancellor as
High Commissioner at the beginning of 1931, recorded that at some of
the Government House functions he attended there were interesting personalities and conversation, though Arabs often declined invitations to
events at which Zionists were also invited, and the diplomatic round could
be wearing.

H.E. opens Egyptian Medical Congress & we give tea party for them in
afternoon. Hardly any of the Palestinian Arabs invited turn up. Weizmann & Arlosoroff to dinner in the evening: I sit next to Mrs. W. & have a
long talk to W. himself after. Most interesting. He is v. charming, a mag-
netic personality, tho' I don't feel it as much as some: intensely clever,
seemingly very reasonable. But it is his charm, & his reasonableness that
make him so dangerous, for at heart he is as uncompromising as any of
them. He says that as Arabs must realize that they can't drive the Jews
into the sea, so the Jews must realize they can't drive the Arabs into the
desert. The onus is on the Jews to prove that they do not want to do this.
That is what he says & it sounds very well. But does he mean it? I am sure
not.[122]

Hearing a few months later that the Jewish labour leader Haim Arlozorov
had been murdered in Tel Aviv, most likely by extremist Zionists, Eastwood
expressed personal regret at the loss of a "real friend" and moderate politician, and commented on Palestine, "what a country -- more hatred to the
square mile than in any other country in the world."[123] The assassination,
Eastwood confided to his diary, diluted his feelings of regret at the prospect
of leaving Palestine at the end of his tour of duty. In any event, he described
himself as becoming "more & more - not anti-Jewish but pro-Arab every
day", explaining that he had come to that conclusion because "the Arabs

fear they will be driven into the desert, fear they will be swamped by Jews & their fears seem to me very justifiable. Every year some Arab sells his land to the Jews. No Jew ever sells his land to an Arab. The Jews are prepared to pay fantastic prices to get land so how can you expect the individual Arab, however 'patriotic', to withstand the pressure to sell?" Eastwood's private solution: "I feel sure we should define, define, to try & remove this fear of eventual submergence. Till we have defined we shall never really get co-operation on either side. And definition is what we shall never get, alas -- instead we are to have 'no more White Papers', to 'let things develop', to 'see how things turn out' -- very admirable maxims no doubt in any less artificial a situation than this, but here it simply means letting the Jews have their own way."[124]

Like so many British officials, Eastwood departed at the end of his tour of duty with thoroughly mixed feelings, in which regret predominated. Summing up his entire experience in Palestine, he wrote:

We have repressed disorders, at the price of the last remnants of our popularity, of the confidence of the people in the Police (the Police are now against them) & of much bloodshed. But we have not done & apparently cannot do anything to remove causes of disturbances. H.E [His Excellency] & S. of S. [Secretary of State] repeat that immigration will be regulated by the absorptive capacity of the country - but that is not the point. The Arab grievance is not economic but sentimental. It is the sentimental absorptive capacity that matters. We take steps to chase out illicit immigrants - but only succeed in deporting more Arabs than Jews!... H.E. quite undismayed by the troubles... In a way he is too undismayed. He seems reconciled to the idea that we must go on with the J.N.H. [Jewish National Home] despite Arab feelings & must go on causing Arab distress (sentimental if not economic). He thinks that this is inevitable if we are to carry out our promise to establish the Jewish National Home, & that it is better to carry out this promise at the price of alienating the whole Arab world than to break it or to declare it fulfilled. But he does realize that the time may come, in say 10 years time, when the country will be unable to absorb more & it may then be necessary to declare the J.N.H. established. Then perhaps, with fear of Jewish domination removed, better feelings may come. But as long as the Arabs fear the Jews they will hate them.... Then my own departure. I became most emotional about it. I discovered I was v. fond of Jerusalem & the inhabitants thereof. I was sad to leave both. I was also sad to leave my work & the country at a time when the country is so unhappy. It seemed a little like cowardice, though of course it couldn't be helped.[125]

At the end of January 1933, Adolf Hitler took office in Germany as Chancellor of a National Socialist regime, with the avowed aim of eliminating Jews from the German nation, initially by depriving them of their livelihoods and property, and pressuring them by all means to leave the Reich. With Hitler's ascent to power, one of the fundamental assumptions of the Mandate was revealed as hollow: a vision of the Jewish National Home being realized gradually, over long periods of time, with the orderly immigration of small numbers of well-prepared, mostly young Zionist settlers prepared for industrial labour and hard physical work on the land. It was never conceived by the British Government that Palestine would of necessity become the country of refuge for hundreds of thousands, potentially millions of desperate Jewish refugees, of all ages and conditions, with no place else to go. For the Arabs, fearful of being swamped even by relatively small-scale Zionist infiltration, the advent of Hitler brought into sudden focus their worst nightmare of an overwhelming influx of alien settlers. When Jewish refugees began to stream in increasing numbers from the expanding Reich, they found that in an era of almost universal economic depression countries throughout the world were disinclined to admit any refugee migrants, but especially not those who had been despoiled of their property by the efficient confiscatory regime the Nazis rapidly imposed. Zionist or non-Zionist, thoroughly assimilated or identified as practising Jews, those German citizens now brutally excluded as "non-Aryans" from the new Germany turned as a last resort to Palestine, the one place on the planet where, according to the solemn international undertaking of the British Government, ratified by the League of Nations, they were permitted to enter "as of right and not on sufferance".

And so they came, many initially with some capital and often the large wooden containers, "lifts", in which they occasionally had to shelter after arrival, with much of their furniture, books, professional tools, even the precious pianos that had adorned the comfortable homes they were forced to abandon. Quite unlike the earlier Zionist settlers, most from Poland and quite poor, the German Jewish immigrants to Palestine were often people of means as well as higher education: lawyers, physicians, bankers, and many academics and scientists, not a few of world standing. At least initially, some were able to benefit from special currency regulations designed to foster German exports, that enabled them to expatriate some of their blocked funds to Palestine, thus qualifying for admission to the country as "persons of independent means". In addition to their capital for investment in agriculture, commerce and industry, many of them brought a wealth of managerial and professional expertise hitherto unknown in the country: the German Jews, overwhelmingly of the middle class, had a dramatic impact on the small Palestine economy, especially in such branches as banking, medicine, and publishing. Officially recorded Jewish immigration in 1933 more than tripled from the previous year, to 30,327. Although most of these immigrants still came from Poland, where the economic and political pressure on Jews to emigrate kept mounting, a significant number were refugees from Nazi Germany; their presence and their investments contributed to a boom in housing, the professions, and industrial enterprises of all kinds.

The Arab community observed the landing of every immigrant ship, each trumpeted enthusiastically in the Jewish press, with the most profound disquiet and growing anger. They saw the influx of Jewish immigrants, capital and expertise as not only blocking their dream of self-determination, but lending colour to the notion of a possible Jewish state in which they would be reduced to permanent minority status: all were aware that "economic absorptive capacity", the measure that officially regulated the level of Jewish immigration, was bound to expand the more immigrants were admitted to Palestine. With increasing bitterness, the Arab press and Arab political leaders, represented by the Arab Executive, accused the British Government of deliberately fostering Jewish immigration, with the express aim of displacing Arabs. In August of 1933 the Zionist Congress met at Prague and in response to the rise of Nazism in Germany adopted resolutions demanding that the Jewish National Home be built as a matter of urgency, and on a far larger scale than previously contemplated. By October, the first attempts at a General Strike were organized by the Arab Executive, and there were riots in several parts of Palestine, quelled by the police only with firearms, with significant casualties to both rioters and police in Nablus, Haifa and Jerusalem. A British official in Jerusalem observed with foreboding that the city was "almost too quiet: the absence of traffic & the closure of shops, partly owing to strike, partly no doubt out of fear is unnatural in this town of many people moving, talking shouting.... the attacks have been anti-Govt., not anti-Jew: not that the Arabs love the Jews any more, but they hate the Govt. more."[126] The militant Revisionist Zionists, so called because they demanded a revision of the Mandate to permit Jewish settlement on both banks of the Jordan, also clashed violently in several places with British police.

As conditions for Jews in Germany and Eastern Europe continued to deteriorate, the pressure to enter Palestine grew apace: in 1934, 42,359 official immigrants landed, and 61,854 the next year. It was moreover becoming evident to the British authorities that in addition to the official migrants, unknown and perhaps quite large numbers of illegal immigrants had landed: fictitious marriages, claims of kinship, overstays on tourist visas and other clandestine arrangements reflected the increased urgency with which Jews from Poland, Rumania and Hungary, as well as Germany, were seeking refuge in Palestine. "The Arabs have a genuine fear of hordes of Jews coming in -- as they are coming in now -- & no palliative will quiet those fears except limitation of numbers... a desperate people will not hesitate to take desperate measures", Humphrey Bowman predicted in his diary.[127] Even a first-time visitor to Palestine, a newly-arrived officer previously posted in Nigeria, felt the atmosphere of fear, hatred and increasing tension:

> You see here we were in a more or less temperate climate, lovely stone villas perched in the olive groves, with the religious buildings all round of the various faiths... and over all there was a sort of atmosphere of sanctity and veneration which was extraordinarily satisfying. But the next thing that I found was with all this apparent charm, underneath there was a terrible bitterness.... the Arab that I met bore little relation to what I'd expected to find. He didn't sit on a camel eating dates with flowing robes or anything like that at all. He seemed to be a rather carefully dressed Frenchman living in a prim little villa and with impeccable manners but with absolute feelings of desperation about what the future held for him if more and more Jews were going to come into the country.[128]

As that desperation and Arab hostility to the Mandate mounted, individuals and political groups within the Arab community sank their ideological and social differences and sought a common policy, increasingly radicalized by nationalist youth societies and the political committees that were established in major towns. Selective boycotts, shooting incidents, assassination and sabotage, especially of telephone and railways, gradually increased to the point where ordinary public security seemed threatened throughout large parts of Palestine. By November 1935 the Arab parties formally made three demands on the British administration: an immediate end to Jewish immigration, a prohibition on land transfers to Jews and substantive steps towards democratic self-rule. The first two demands were rejected as incompatible with the terms of the Mandate. To the last, the High Commissioner replied with a proposal for a cautiously crafted Legislative Council in which all communities would be proportionally represented but the British Government would maintain control. Even that watered-down step toward possible self-government by the Arab majority was enough to alarm the Jews, who rejected the proposal out of hand, and in February 1936 so effectively deployed their lobbying skills in London as to kill the scheme outright after it had been debated in Parliament. Arab chagrin over this Jewish victory was compounded by knowledge that in neighbouring Egypt Great Britain had been compelled by a wave of popular unrest to grant Egyptian sovereignty and to evacuate its troops to the Suez Canal Zone. Spurred by this example, Arab nationalists in Syria successfully pressed the French Government into conceding them full national status and formally resigning France's mandate over that country. As if these noises off were insufficient, Palestine Arabs were subjected to a barrage of Italian Government radio propaganda designed to damage British prestige, attack the anomalies of the Mandate, and deflect attention from Mussolini's own brutal campaign of conquest against Abyssinia. By the Spring of 1936, Palestinian Arabs were angrily aware that they were the sole Arab people in the Middle East who had not attained or were not on course to attain national self-determination.

On 15 April, what became euphemistically known as the "riots" or "the disturbances" began with the murder of two Jews on the Tulkarm-Nablus road, followed one night later by the retaliatory murder of two Arabs near Petah Tiqva. Riots and anti-Jewish attacks broke out a few days later in Jaffa, and curfews were imposed there and in Tel Aviv. But the effervescence went on: a General Strike was declared on 21 April, which effectively spread to all Arab labourers and shopkeepers. At the end of April the newly formed Arab Higher Committee vowed to continue the strike until the British Government met their demands for an outright ban on Jewish immigration and land acquisition, and for establishment of a national, representative government. Bound by his instructions, the High Commissioner was compelled to reject all these demands.

Within the British community in Palestine, the first emotion was irritation, then unease. For a young District Officer representing the Administration in Galilee, whose principal challenges thus far had been boredom and the Arabic language examinations required for promotion, Arab unrest initially seemed merely a tiresome interruption of routine. For his wife, preoccupied with social obligations and furnishing their house in Nazareth, the General Strike represented another illustration of Oriental irrationality, a minor interruption in an otherwise placid life. Writing to her mother-in-law in England, Bridget Blackburne reported:

There was a General Strike here yesterday but the only effect it seemed to have was that the roads were delightfully free of traffic!! It was a protest by the Arabs against the "so-called inactivity of the Government after it has been found that the Jews were smuggling in arms" -- they are awful fools -- I think the house is going to look very nice, but none of the curtains are finished of course ...[129]

To Miss Dorothy Norman, teaching in a Church of England school in Jerusalem, the General Strike and its accompanying disturbances meant an unscheduled and certainly not unwelcome holiday. She wrote to her family:

I wonder if you have seen anything about our riots in the papers at home? It occurred to me that you might be getting agitated so I'm sending this by air to calm your anxious spirits!...This morning the buses wouldn't run at all, so altho' about 30 valiant souls walked to school they were all sent home again. We are having a holiday tomorrow as well. Great fun for us isn't it?.... I am writing this at a time when I should normally be teaching Algebra to College V so I feel most awfully bucked with life. Some of the others are playing tennis....[130]

As the low-level violence dragged on, exasperation succeeded Bridget Blackburne's initial insouciance, and she complained in letters home of the High Commissioner's policy of appeasing the Arabs, which she blamed for the continuing unrest. She and every other resident of Palestine was aware that the Turks in their day had upheld iron dominion over the entire country with a relative handful of mounted gendarmerie.

The riots still go on, which is most annoying as we thought they were over on Friday -- its so extremely tiresome as till there is a really good fight somewhere it seems to me it will drag on & on.... H.E. is (we think) being much too lenient & inclined to talk to all these blackguards instead of shooting them!![131]

Mrs Heather Teague, wife of an Intelligence officer newly posted to Jerusalem, wrote of her sense of unease, and attempted to assure her family that the growing disturbances were not directed against the British themselves, but solely against Jews:

I am restless and cannot seem to settle.... This strike (of Arab shopkeepers etc.) is going on much longer than anyone imagined, and things are so hard to arrange. Jew porters won't go into Arab quarters and Arab porters (when willing to work) won't go into Jew quarters, and altogether I feel like banging every silly head in Jerusalem on the ubiquitous stones....

Whatever the papers say - or the marvellous B.B.C. - it is not anti-British.... Any Britishers who have been stoned or attacked have merely been so because they were mistaken for Jews, or have got mixed up in some crowd who no longer knew whether they were attacking Europeans or Jews or themselves. You see, to the untutored eye there is no difference - a hat - a skirt, trousers, bare arms - Jew!.... So to put your mind at rest John is nearly always in uniform, I always wear long sleeves, hat, gloves and stockings -- nothing could more easily prove me non-Jew, and the children never go near the town...[132]

Miss Norman and her charges muddled through, despite steady deterioration in public order:

None of our buses ran yesterday so we have rather few girls again though many struggled to school in the face of great difficulties in order to do their examinations. This morning I walked down our bus-route to collect such girls as were waiting and bring them to school on foot. I found to my horror an enormous bloodstain on the pavement where a man was shot yesterday: but curiously enough it is so common here to see messes in the road that I was not perhaps as horrified as I ought to have been! Anyhow I carefully brought the girls along the other pavement.... Somehow or other, in spite of curfew, telephone wires get cut every night. I can't think how they manage it...[133]

Bridget Blackburne's regular letters home began to reflect increasing insecurity and the need to allay the anxieties of her family:

Things are getting pretty bad I think, & everyone says its only a question of days till Martial Law... really its getting more & more like Ireland ... however don't worry...[134]

As the troubles gradually escalated from isolated acts of brigandage to guerilla warfare and a breakdown in public security in the countryside, another Church of England schoolmistress expressed privately what the authorities themselves were reluctant to confront:

It is nice to think of a peaceful countryside in England these days. We are in a desperate condition of things here.... Until the spirit of fear is eradicated, I see no hope for either Arab or Jew in this country. You cannot have two peoples living in a perpetual spirit of fear and suspicion... what is worrying us all is how long this state of things is to continue.... There is no doubt that Great Britain has greatly lost in prestige, but I believe even the most malcontent would in their heart of hearts rather have British rule than that of any other Western power. One can't help wishing sometimes that we were out of it all, and someone else had the Mandate, but I suppose that is cowardly.[135]

For officials and their wives, however, keeping up appearances was paramount, and public sang-froid very much the rule, with daily life ostentatiously going on as usual, though curfews inevitably curtailed some evening social activities. Military confrontations and other incidents were consistently referred to as "shows"; random, sometimes murderous violence was played down as "riots" or "brigandage"; and long, seldom successful searches for guerilla bands in the countryside were described in terms of rough public-school games of hide and seek, with the police tracker dogs lending the proceedings an improbable sporting atmosphere that reminded some participants of hunting in the English countryside. The British moreover frequently characterized their Arab guerilla adversaries as "brave", "gallant" and sometimes even "chivalrous", crediting them with a sense of humour and of decency increasingly at variance with the random nature of bombs and bullets, as well as the growing campaign within the Arab community of targeted assassination, extortion and intimidation. The Arab rebels were still not considered an entirely credible military or political threat, and the growing disorder they engendered was not in any event allowed to interfere with the ceremonial aspects of British life in Mandate Palestine.

It is one long story of snipings and pottings and ineffective bombs.... The place, as you may imagine, is simply alive with troops, and there are constant shows up and down the roads outside Jerusalem. I go about my ordinary business in the ordinary way.... Yesterday was the King's Birthday, and we stopped the war for an hour to have a birthday parade for Edward VIII.... It was quite a good parade in spite of the fact that all troops are far too busy to practise high stepping! H.E. (General Wauchope) wore his General's uniform and looked a very gallant, brave, dauntless little figure. We were all dressed in our best bib and tucker and sat under marquees. All very fine and debonair like.[136]

Writing to his mother, Kenneth Blackburne confessed to weariness: "this really has been an exhausting time. However at last things seem to be a little quieter -- last night was the first night for six weeks that nothing happened in my area." In an obvious attempt at heartening his family, he added, "even though I secretly have the utmost contempt for both Arabs and Jews, they are both quite pleasant to me personally. Bridget is the one who is having a poor time -- though I took her to Haifa and Tiberias last week."[137]

Despite the tedium, frustration and occasional sudden terror of anti-guerilla operations, some British officers could still be moved by the beauty and the Scriptural associations evoked by Palestine. Years later, recalling his duties in Jerusalem during this period, one wrote,

One routine job that fell to the night duty car patrol, was to go to Tor Village on the Mount of Olives just before dawn, to collect the High

Commissioner's milkman.... I would wait for the eastern sky to light up with the rising sun. All would be quiet as steadily the sky became brighter and then the first rim of the sun appeared and daybreak was upon us as the sun rocketed into the sky. And then at once the cocks began to crow and the donkeys and mules brayed, the dogs barked, doors opened and men and women emerged.... The whole world seemed to spring to life and I thought of the words in The Bible, 'God saw it and it was good'....[138]

Expressing privately the views of many in the British community, Humphrey Bowman complained that "affairs here have got worse instead of better: assassination, bombs, shootings, sabotage continue." More troops from Egypt were transferred to strengthen the Palestine garrison, including artillery, engineers, and armoured cars, but it was widely recognized, as Bowman remarked, that "tho' force can quell riots & sabotage in time, it cannot kill feeling: & that will continue until the cause is settled... immigration: and it is obvious to all of us that unless immigration is reduced to a trickle from the present flood, troubles in one way or another will continue."[139] From her vantage point in a Church of England mission school, Miss Emery wrote that "the people have lost faith in the good-will of the Government, and are feeling desperate, and everybody is miserable.... They are not anti-British, but anti-British policy. To civilians there has been no discourteous behaviour."[140] Despite growing casualties among the ranks of military and police, and the entirely unpredictable hazards of bombs and sabotage, British residents of Palestine continued to cling, at least in their letters to worried relatives, to a roseate version of the disturbances in which the increasing violence was directed only against Jews, not the British themselves. "It is not, I am told, anti-British so unless one looks like a Jew one is fairly safe. So my darlings, please don't clutch your chairs any more," wrote Heather Teague, but then revealing the strain of living in Palestine always on the alert for danger, "they call this the Holy Land; but to me the memory of Christ seems almost submerged under a bitter dust of strife and envy and hatred. Everywhere one turns, even the holiest places, are people struggling to get the better of each other -- the different religious orders -- the Arab-- the Jew. One can quite imagine that it was here they crucified Him."[141]

The mood among British troops and police also was sombre: "Every officer I have spoken to believes the Arabs have a case, & admits the bravery of the armed bands in the hills. The soldiers hate the whole thing and wd. prefer martial law," wrote Humphrey Bowman.[142] For a new recruit to the Palestine Police, the very instant of arrival brought sobering evidence that hazards abounded in Palestine: "At last we reached Jerusalem Station and there to meet us were two police tenders, one for us and one for our luggage. Ours was covered with a wire mesh, and I was told that this was a protection against bombs which might be thrown at us. It was then that I and several of my companions fully appreciated just what we had let ourselves in for, and the type of dangers we might expect to face in the future."[143] The High Commissioner himself was not immune from the general dejection among the British; from Government House, his splendid and well-protected residence atop the Hill of Evil Counsel, Sir Arthur Wauchope wrote: "I was up early this morning, and could have wept as I saw the walls of Jerusalem turn golden under the cloudless sky and thought of -- what you and I think of every sorrowful day."[144]

By the summer of 1936 it was apparent that the Arab rebellion had settled into the pattern of a prolonged irregular little war, characterized by fitful outbreaks of violence in which Arabs fought against the British, the Jews and among themselves, in a campaign of sudden attacks and sabotage: trains were blown up, tracks and roads mined, crops and trees burnt. Hidden snipers made road travel hazardous, and telephone and telegraph wires were repeatedly cut over wide areas. More damaging, targeted assassination and threats almost completely silenced pro-Government informers, destroying the British intelligence network and leaving large areas of the country under virtual control of the guerillas. In efforts not to inflame the situation further, the High Commissioner initially ordered a restrained response: troops were given the essentially defensive role of attempting to keep the railways running and main roads open, an assignment they found uncongenial, and in which they were only occasionally successful. Terror was succeeded by tedium: "and so we go on -- a fire here, a rumour there -- and the Police are getting very tired, as they have to keep on rushing out when these reports come in, and very often they are quite false."[145]

But as in Ireland previously, initial British bafflement and vacillation gave way ultimately to a clumsy brutality that further alienated the local population. Even such minor operations as clearing roads could lead to scenes that both British and Arabs found humiliating and repressive: "broken glass and nails were strewn on many roads in the towns and under The Emergency Regulations, an order was made compelling persons so ordered by the police, to stop and pick up the nails and glass. Many police were needed of course for the implementation of the law. The local notables felt great blows to their dignity when ordered in the street to pick up the glass or nails and some asked if they might be allowed to hire boys to complete the degrading task for them."[146] By early autumn, troop reinforcements brought the Palestine garrison to some 20,000 men, and emergency regulations were enacted that permitted searches without warrant, collective punishment and harsh penalties for possession of arms or firing on British personnel. These still basically defensive measures always stopped short of the imposition of martial law, and the beleaguered High Commissioner was further undermined by chronic civil-military discord, with the soldiers pressing for a stronger response to the rebellion, and the Colonial Office, with one eye on the general Middle East situation, urging restraint and attempted conciliation of the Arabs. Despite all the consequent setbacks to the Mandatory's authority, it was clear that the guerillas could not hope to prevail against overwhelming British arms, and that the long-term effects of the uprising were devastating the Palestine economy for both Arabs and Jews, in the countryside as well as the towns.

The government in London had meanwhile appointed the members of a Royal Commission that was charged to investigate the disorders in Palestine, but it was made clear that the Commission would not be sent out before order had been restored. The continuing strike and military operations had, however, decisively weakened the Palestine Arabs, and by autumn 1936 the influential Arab citrus growers feared they might be unable to market their crop, and urged an end to the revolt. On 11 October, at the express request of several Arab rulers outside Palestine, the Higher Committee officially called off the General Strike and asked the Arab community to abjure violence and suspend further protests pending the investigation and report of the Royal Commission. Towards the end of the year, despite sporadic violent episodes, organized rebellion had died down, and the disorders were officially considered over, thus permitting the Royal Commission to depart for Palestine.

In the midst of these events, the British community in Palestine was caught up in the drama of the Abdication crisis of December 1936, which deflected attention briefly from all but the most urgent local events and problems. The Abdication was a subject of intense concern, and its link with British prestige in Palestine and the Empire a subject of anxious speculation: the King himself letting down the side was to many quite literally unthinkable: "Its all perfectly frightful about HM & Mrs. S... Do you think the Country would really stand for it -- has he gone quite mad -- surely one of the reasons that we still have a monarchy is because they were so quiet & respectable.... everyone out here is terribly agitated about it all," wrote Mrs. Blackburne to her mother-in-law.[147] "Of course we can think & talk of nothing else except about the King & Mrs. Simpson -- somehow one never really believed he was going to do it -- how can he?", she wrote later,[148] adding to another correspondent, "it seems to us that it is the beginning of the end of

OPENING MEETING
OF THE
ROYAL COMMISSION

GOVERNMENT HOUSE
JERUSALEM

NOVEMBER 12th. 1935.

ישיבת הפתיחה
של
הוועדה המלכותית

בית הממשלה
ירושלים.

12 בנובמבר. 1935.

الجلسة الافتتاحية
للجنة الملكية

دار الحكومة
القدس

١٢ تشرين الثاني سنة ١٩٣٥

Programme in English, Hebrew
and Arabic for official opening
of the Peel Commission's
investigation, November 1935

the British Empire, don't you?"[149] As a political officer in the Palestine Government, Kenneth Blackburne was especially distressed by the local implications of the crisis, writing to his father that "this trouble about the King is utterly deplorable. I feel that it is so dreadful that Arabs and Jews and other natives should see that we have such troubles in England.... We thought that Edward's broadcast was very pathetic and it made us think much better of him -- even though he has let us down worse than anyone could ever do."[150] British concern lest the domestic drama of their Royals have a negative impact on the inhabitants of Palestine reflects a quite remarkable ethnocentricity, as if the entire moral authority of the Mandate depended on a perception of impeccable family rectitude among the Windsors. There is no evidence that either the Arabs or Jews of Palestine were much exercised, if indeed more than casually aware that their far-off sovereign was abandoning his throne for the sake of a twice-divorced American commoner.

The Royal Commission headed by Lord Peel, a former Secretary of State for India, arrived in Palestine in November, armed with broad terms of reference to ascertain the causes of the disturbances, and make recommendations to meet and resolve any legitimate grievances of either Jews or Arabs. Some at least of the local British community did not have great expectations for what the Commission might accomplish: "the country is in an awful mess and will continue to be until the Royal Commission has sat -- and they, poor wretches, cannot satisfy both Arabs and Jews, so we don't know what sort of riots we will have to suppress next year!"[151] And a more sombre view, in a private letter from the Palestine Government's Commissioner of Migration to the former High Commissioner:

It is, indeed, intolerable here in many respects and very often incredibly boring. Nearly nineteen years have passed since I first entered the country and I look back and see little that can give satisfaction for hard honest work in the best years of my life. It is true of States as it is of individuals that, if they once embark on a course of moral obliquity, they must for long years take devious courses over uncharted seas. I confess that I do not see how a Royal Commission with the terms of reference now decided can help very much. The Jews will come into Palestine legally or illegally.[152]

The Arab Higher Committee ordered a boycott of the Commission's hearings when it was announced that a small Jewish immigration quota would be permitted during the Commission's investigation, prompting Kenneth Blackburne to explode: "it is impossible for the wretched Royal Commission to please both Jews and Arabs. They are both so utterly unreasonable!"[153] Later, after having met several members of the Commission, Blackburne veered toward cautious optimism: "they are all so quick in the úptake that I am really hopeful that they will do something -- and their main idea is English -- not Arab or Jew -- which is very refreshing."[154]

The Commission, which ultimately did hear official testimony from the Palestine Arabs, concluded its hearings in late January 1937, and presented its Report some six months later. That Report, a model of sober eloquence, concluded that the Mandate could not work: "the difficulty has always been, and, if the Mandate continues, will continue with it, that the existence of the National Home, whatever its size, bars the way to the attainment by the Arabs of Palestine of the same national status as that attained, or soon to be attained, by all the other Arabs of Asia."[155] Since the Palestine Arabs would never acquiesce in the establishment of the Jewish National Home, and neither Arabs nor Jews could plausibly coexist in a community where one or the other would be permanently in the minority, the Commission concluded by recommending the only arrangement it found compatible with equity and the realities on the ground: partition of Palestine into two sovereign states, Arab and Jewish, reserving a British mandatory zone that included such strategic strong points as the ports of Haifa and Aqaba. "Partition", the

Commission concluded, "seems to offer at least a chance of ultimate peace. We can see none in any other plan."[156] Despite much internal struggle, the Jews for their part reluctantly accepted partition, but the Arabs rejected any notion of carving up Palestine, restating through the Higher Committee their demands for independence, an end to Jewish immigration and land purchases, and the replacement of the British Mandate by a treaty between Great Britain and a sovereign Arab state of Palestine.

Responding to several recommendations of the Peel Commission, the Palestine Government then moved to restrict Jewish immigration and land purchases, but also began to impose harsher measures on both Arabs and Jews in an attempt to restore public security. By the summer of 1937 the Arab rebellion resumed with renewed virulence, reaching its climax with the assassination in September of the acting District Commissioner of Galilee, L.Y. Andrews, and his bodyguard. That double murder, accomplished in daylight, which killed a popular officer much admired for his services to the Peel Commission, profoundly shocked the British community and provoked the Palestine Government for the first time to embark on a determined offensive. Summary military courts were established, mandatory death sentences for firearms offences imposed, and energetic measures taken to prevent the importing of arms into Palestine, including the construction of patrol roads and a barbed wire wall with defensive emplacements along part of the frontier. By the end of 1937 more than 800 Arabs had been arrested, the members of the Arab Higher Committee either exiled to the Seychelles or barred from entry into Palestine, and a number of death sentences imposed. Moreover, heavy collective fines and the punishment of house demolition were imposed on villages in the countryside that reportedly had sheltered guerillas. The British writ, however, did not run within the Arab community, where an effective terror continued to reign: individuals of wealth and prominence, those who had displayed undue friendliness to British or Jews, or who had resisted the Mufti's faction openly or by lack of enthusiasm, were cowed into silence, collaboration with the guerilla bands, or brutally removed through intimidation, abduction or assassination. Under cover of the political rebellion, many private scores were also settled, notably within the context of the long-standing and bitter feud of the two preeminent Arab families in Palestine, the Husseinis and the Nashashibis; motives for murder were in some cases only marginally related to the larger political struggle for Palestine.

An Englishwoman teaching in Jerusalem observed,

conditions here are definitely growing worse, & are even now in some ways more difficult than in times of actual rioting, for with the present campaign of murders... no one feels safe. Except indeed women; women - girls are considered to be safe... lately there have been more Arabs than Jews murdered.... all the best people, both Jews & Arabs, hate this constant retaliation....[157]

Goaded by the frustrations of guerilla warfare against an elusive target, some British troops and police committed acts of gratuitous violence, assaulting Arabs at random, looting and wantonly destroying property during searches. One English policeman wrote home with bravado about acts of casual brutality:

The military courts started off well but as we expected are being to lenient and want to much evidence to convict on, so any Johnny Arab who is caught by us now in suspicious circumstances is shot out of hand. There is an average of a bomb a day thrown in Haifa now but few of them do much damage. One was thrown in a Jewish bus last night & the culprit caught. We took him to his house but there was no evidence their, so we let him try to escape in the garden, fortunately I will not have to attend the inquest....[158]

After describing a Christmas celebration interrupted by an attempted Arab bombing of a café frequented by British police, the same policeman wrote:

We then decended into the sook & thrashed every Arab we saw, smashed all shops & cafés, & created havoc & bloodshed... The last thing I remember is hitching a cart horse & racing some one on a donkey down the main street.... I myself drive quite a lot in light Ford pick ups which can do over 80 m.p.h., most accidents out here are caused by police as running over an Arab is the same as a dog in England except we do not report it.[159]

The impulse to punish the Arabs for flouting the government's authority, to hit back as hard as possible, affected civilians as well as military and police. As British forces in Galilee went on the offensive, Bridget Blackburne wrote to her mother:

A terrific battle is in progress all round the Safed hills, the aeroplanes have been passing backwards & forwards all day from Samakh -- do hope they'll get another good haul -- one can't help feeling that the more A's that are killed the better![160]

For ordinary British troops and police, as well as members of the civilian community, the effectiveness of all these measures, including air strikes by the RAF, was dubious. Palestine by 1938 was awash in illicit firearms that had been smuggled over the frontier from Syria and Trans-jordan, or in some cases had been acquired from British troops or police, whose "lost" weapons were saleable to Arabs or Jews at high prices that were tempting to comparatively ill-paid other ranks. "One bright spark... offered me a good price for my 45," reported a policeman in a letter to his family, confessing

"I would have let him have it if I had had a spare one but they are keeping a check on arms since they discovered one of the chief gun runners in the town was a B.P. [British policeman]".[161] A soldier stationed in Haifa in 1938 recalled

> We were all very hard up, while I was in debt... we conceived all sorts of schemes. On pay day "Friday" all the boys in our Hut would toss their wages onto one bed and pool the lot, a trustworthy treasurer being appointed to supply cigarettes, beer etc., rationing them for the week. Everything that could be taken out of the camp was sold to some Jewish dealer in Jaffa Rd. Haifa -- fire extinguishers, picks & shovels and even some spare wheels. The convoys on the road coasted down every hill with their engines switched off to save petrol, most of the big lorries did an average of ten miles to a gallon, so quite a lot of petrol was saved and sold for ten piasters per gallon (2 bob). On one occasion a couple of donkeys disappeared, sold I believe, to an Arab in the village of Samak. The Quartermaster's stores lost hundreds of blankets and other equipment, in fact Jaffa Rd. was like Paddy's Market Liverpool on a Saturday afternoon, we could "flog" anything....[162]

For at least one ordinary soldier, British policies in Palestine were another source of discomfort:

> Our British attitudes towards both Arabs and Jews were confused. Officially, our role was to keep the peace between the two conflicting sides, punishing terrorists of both races. Yet in practice the British showed marked favouritism towards the Jews. I resented this fact, believing that the Arabs always seemed to get a raw deal. A curfew operated from five in the evening till five in the morning and if Arabs broke the curfew they could be shot. Arabs carrying knives over four inches long were shot, but

not the Jews doing the same. Once two Jews were captured after having fired at a bus full of Arabs. The resulting trial lasted two weeks, during which there were mass Jewish demonstrations, the Jews were released. Many of our blokes used to say, "If you run over an Arab make sure you kill him, even if you have to reverse over him. If you injure him you've got to pay his hospital bills."[163]

While common criminals joined politically motivated guerillas to make wide areas of the countryside dangerous for all but armoured convoys, Arab policemen and officials were demoralized by assassinations and threats against them and their families, and were correspondingly unavailable for most public security work. The appointment in February 1938 of a new High Commissioner, Sir Harold MacMichael, was greeted with relief among most of the British community in Palestine: Sir Arthur Wauchope, deemed far too conciliatory to both Arabs and Jews, had been widely unpopular despite the almost viceregal state he maintained throughout his years at Government House, and his undoubted generosity to many individuals and causes within the British community. The MacMichael appointment, fore-shadowing yet another shift in Whitehall, was expected to result in prompt restoration of order in Palestine. It was now accepted that the Mandate as originally conceived was unworkable, but no coherent policy had yet been elaborated to replace it, and growing Italian and German propaganda on behalf of Arab aspirations greatly complicated the task of Government officials struggling to restore public security.

Writing personally to the new High Commissioner on the eve of his appointment, Lord Lloyd, a former High Commissioner of Egypt and the Sudan, predicted

I am afraid you have an angular and thorny task before you. If its solution lay in your hands I should have the greatest confidence, but with no policy charted out from home, your difficulties will be greatly enhanced.... Fortunately for us all, Providence never allows us to see very far down the dark road, but law and order -- and consequently respect, even if only grudging respect -- will show up in clear outline the final solution.[164]

Establishing law and order was then to be the prime task of the new High Commissioner. But the security situation had so deteriorated in Palestine that the restoration of Government authority seemed more wishful thinking than reality.

Brian Gibbs, a young officer writing to his fiancée, counting the days till his leave time and their marriage, described in vivid detail the frustrations of his task in Galilee:

Since Wednesday life has been completely hectic. Earlier in the week... we decided we had about enough and would start a little frightfulness against the villagers, so we arranged with the army to blow up four hous-es in two villages along the road on Thursday morning.... It took us until 2 o'clock to get the four houses blown up, but everything went off alright. It's a depressing business though, as one has to be frightfully careful to get everyone out of range, and there's an awful feeling of suspense after the time fuse has been lit, in case some half-witted villager may go wandering right up to the house....[165]

Somewhat later, he recalled with regret "all the things one used to be able to do here before things went bad -- picnics and riding and moonlight bathing parties at the Dead Sea and at Jaffa", adding "it's very irksome not to be able to go anywhere after dusk now and having an escort even in the day-time."[166]

Aside from their weariness at chasing down fragmentary, sometimes con-tradictory reports of murder, assault and destruction, often arriving too late to apprehend or trace the perpetrators, British officers and men compelled to carry out repressive policies were often convinced of their futility. Both Arabs and Jews were aware that British morale, the essential ingredient in upholding the Mandate's authority, was eroding under the strain of prolonged warfare with shadowy opponents, on behalf of a policy that commanded little respect and less enthusiasm.

The point in blowing up houses, if there is any point, is as punishment on villages that we know have either been harbouring gangs or have been involved in shooting at police posts etc. If we know any names of gangsters from a village we choose their houses but if not we just select two suitable ones and tell the village that's just a warning, and if they cause any more trouble we come back and blow up a lot more! I don't think it does much good, but we haven't found any measures yet that do, short of complete frightfulness, and we're not likely ever to resort to that, and the villagers realise it as much as we do, so it's all a bit of a farce![167]

After a seemingly endless series of barren searches, confused and contradictory orders, and a felt lack of support and guidance from higher authority, even the relentlessly cheerful Brian Gibbs felt his spirits drooping, and he was ultimately capable of writing:

life has really been quite impossible lately... chaos is indescribable, nobody seems to know where anyone else is or what they're supposed to be doing!... I suppose I really ought to be out with both the troops & the Police dogs, as well as being here, but I can't be in three places at once so there's nothing to be done about it! I'm sorry this is such a very depressing letter, darling, but we're all feeling rather browned off with things at present, and all the indications are that they are getting steadily worse, but there's no use getting in a flat spin about it![168]

Individual policemen too felt a sense of impotence and incipient chaos, as the initiative swung unmistakably towards the rebels. Conjuring up a comforting image of cosy English security, Sydney Burr wrote to his family from Haifa: "sitting at home by the fire in England you can not visualise a country only the size of Wales, under British rule, where there is absolutely no law or order. Police & troops are powerless & our only object out here seems to be clearing up the mess after the crime has been committed, we are on the defensive all the time."

He explained that the police were operating largely in the dark, lacking any reliable intelligence information: "all of our regular informers have now kicked the bucket, they have obviously been shopped by someone at headquarters", and then added with feeling, "what I dislike about this war is that more often than not it is the innocent who suffer. Our hospitals here are filled with women & children maimed & blinded for life.... Life for the police is now all work & no play, even at the best of times Palestine is as dull as ditch water but what with curfews & people walking about with the fear of death on them its like living in a cemetery..."[169]

Adding to the sense of futility was the knowledge that increasingly harsh measures, including the death penalty, seemed to have little effect on a deteriorating security situation:

> This afternoon I'm going to Nazareth to see Kirkbride and from there I shall probably go to Haifa for the night as there is an execution in Acre tomorrow morning. It's a pretty grim state of affairs isn't it when our principal relaxation is a night in Haifa before a hanging! I think there's pretty certain to be another one in about a week's time too.[170]

Some servants of the Crown reacted with shame and disgust as rumours of British brutality were confirmed in the wake of engagements that seldom netted more than a handful of suspected guerillas. In a confidential letter to the local District Commissioner, A.T.O. Lees, a junior officer acting as a Settlement Officer, wrote in cold anger:

The raiding, robbing and wounding carried out in the Manshia quarter by three unknown, but traceable, British Policemen in plain clothes at about 2 a.m. during the night Oct. 23-24, 1938, followed by the killing, apparently premeditated and in cold blood, of an unknown hand cuffed Arab by four British Policemen in uniform at about 9.15 a.m. on the 24th Oct. are matters which I feel should be brought in detail to your notice.... It is because I am jealous of the good name of England and Englishmen that I cannot condone murder, looting and wounding, and that is why I now address you when it would be very much less trouble to me, and conceivably safer, if I remained silent....[171]

Equally outraged, Dr E.D. Forster, a physician working at a Church of Scotland mission hospital in Hebron, reported his experience of clumsy British efforts to deal with the Arab insurrection:

from the small hours of Sunday morning, I received at this hospital a series of casualties inflicted by the British, presumably on curfew breakers.... I have the greatest sympathy with individual members of the Forces and the Police, subjected to great strain and provocation for months on end. But I bitterly deplore as much the folly as the immorality of such indiscriminate retaliation.[172]

He later added:

People say that Oriental administration is corrupt. I believe it. I have heard that British Rule is just and merciful. It must surely be true. But here in Palestine we see the opposite established. I do not defend all the rebels' actions in other parts of the country, but I speak of my personal experience in this district. And I fear wherever one tries to balance the cowardly and cruel dealings of the two sides, there is no doubt which party comes with least credit from the comparison. The rebels fight fairly and chivalrously, and rule with kindness. The British kill the innocent, when no other enemy is near, and loot and rob the poor and destitute.... Today the British Empire holds one hill in Hebron, where the troops and police are billeted, and nothing more.... None of the Government Departments is functioning except the P.H.D. [Public Health Department] under quarter-steam and the Post Office, where you can't even buy stamps... The Law Courts are closed, Forests, P.W.D. and Lands have all been withdrawn, and the Police reduced to a cipher.[173]

Looking back on the Palestine experience, a former Army officer admitted there had on occasion been excesses by British troops, but said they had always been minimal, reflecting inexperience, and only following extreme provocation:

Our period in Palestine was the closest we had been to active service since World War I.... At times, tempers flared, soldiers would see Arab atrocities, and there were some of their mates killed and on occasions, they, the troops became bloody angry. In the heat of an action, when a prisoner is brought in, you see your friend near you -- you think "Shoot the B.....d" and I know of one or two occasions where this happened. But it is a source of great pride to all, as a British soldier, that you can count such incidents on the fingers of one hand and that after such an incident, the unit itself, however much they had been provoked, felt ashamed of what had happened in some Regiments. As I have said, these incidents were minimal and no other army would have done so well. Eight years later, it was the Jews who were shooting us.[174]

Allegations of brutality were also made against the police, sometimes by their Army counterparts:

We have had the Army with us on some of these raids & imagine our surprise when we found out that they had written to the High Commissioner protesting against the brutality of the police. What makes it more ridiculous is that 3 of their fellows have been killed in the last week. It was the Ulster Rifles that I think made the complaint, which goes to show what a double-crossing lot of Irish hounds they are. I only hope we play them one day at rugby then they will have cause to complain of the rough policeman. At the moment we are having much more work to do, & their is never a day with less than 5 turnouts... we are being worked night & day. The hills are swarming with bandits & the police are hopelessly inadequate to cope.... All our time is spent in the hills with the troops but we are worse than useless as the fellows we are after can make rings round us when it comes to walking. The only time we came up with any of them we got ambushed just before dark down in a valley & had to run for it... by luck we were not wiped out. After being in the hills all day we are called out continuously at night to colonies which are being shot up. This week I have been under fire 6 times & only seen my opponents once.... I am absolutely fed up with the life here now as we have no time for recreation at all... If things go on like this much longer I am going to resign as I am not at all interested in the cause we are fighting for.[175]

After describing a futile sweep following a guerilla raid on an Arab village, Ivan Lloyd Phillips wrote of his feelings of helplessness and rage:

The infuriating & humiliating part of the whole business is that we can literally do nothing about it; we have been simply stripped to the bone of police who have all been sent north & further have been told that there are no soldiers available, & we have virtually to admit as tactfully as possible to the aggrieved villagers that the King's Govt.cannot protect them -- I have rarely felt so angry, but what can we do.[176]

Kenneth Blackburne described the demoralizing effect on his own staff of the continuing disorders:

Haifa has had a terrible time with bombs and rioting -- among the casualties was the father of my Jewish District Officer in Tiberias -- so the poor fellow is in a very bad way -- one can hardly be an impartial District Officer when one's father has been knifed and stoned to death by Arabs!.... I am afraid there is now no end to this until we get a political solution and that will not be for another nine months at least -- so we have a depressing time in front of us. The partition Commission do not seem to be much good. They keep on sending me quite futile questions to answer and my impression is that they realise that they have an impossible job in front of them and that they really do not know what to do! However although I can foresee no proper improvement, I do not think that things can get very much worse if we can keep all the troops that we have got now. We ourselves are very well protected as we have a picket every night on the hill at the back of the house and a Lewis gun on the roof of the Kirkbrides' house![177]

Even in near-war conditions, there were still junior officers who could admit that despite the muddle, the violence and the frustration, there were occasionally satisfying and even exhilarating moments in Palestine. The voice is that of Ivan Lloyd Phillips:

It is all very worrying sometimes, but on the other hand it is fun & I do enjoy it. I've never been so excited & thrilled in all my life -- I wouldn't

have missed Palestine just now for anything. Ordinary matters of administration are going by the board these days & Public Security (or the lack
of it) is the one overriding question with which we have to deal. I like
Gaza very much & I also like the Arabs. I know I'm pro-Arab in sympathy
as most of us are -- though I can see too the Jews have got a good many
legitimate complaints. We have of course for the last 18 years tried to
accomplish the impossible & it remains to be seen how we can "wind
ourselves handsomely" out of this.[178]

Summing up, he added:

It would be stupid to pretend that this country is a bed of roses or that life
is particularly amusing or enjoyable! However it is very good for one I
suppose & when I am living quietly in the Cotswolds I shall be very glad
that I came here! The state of the country is getting very much worse &
large rebel bands infest the whole of the Southern District & Gaza has
been simmering like a boiling kettle.... I still don't regret coming to Palestine a bit, though I hope I shall get to know it better in happier days.[179]

Despite a near-collapse of British administration in much of southern
Palestine, and in non-Jewish parts of the Jerusalem District, some officials
managed to carry on with an almost normal social life. A young member of
the Survey of Palestine later recalled:

Nearly all the stations on the railway had been burnt, so all now had military guards, and because trains were being blown up, a military trolley
preceded them. After one or two of these had blown up, Arab detainees
were carried on them, as hostages or potential martyrs.... The police station at Beersheba was raided for arms, after which all the posts in that district... were closed, being indefensible.... While all this was going on, the

Italian cruise ship Roma anchored off Jaffa on 13th September and 700 tourists came ashore, mostly heading for a day in Jerusalem. In fact, we all continued our social lives much as usual. One day I was playing tennis at the Tabitha Mission in Jaffa when bullets started whining overhead. As the court was surrounded by high walls, we ignored them and played on.... As Jaffa seemed no longer a place in which to linger in comfort, I removed east of Tel Aviv to Sarona.... I handed over the flat in Jaffa to the owner's agent. Next day he was detained inside at gunpoint while raiders removed all the furniture....[180]

The security situation in Palestine was now complicated by a Jewish Revisionist underground military group, known as the Irgun Zvai Leumi ("National Military Organisation"), an even more secretive group than the Haganah, devoted to the extreme views of Ze'ev Jabotinsky, disavowed by mainstream Zionists in 1935, calling for a Jewish state on both banks of the Jordan. The Irgun's terrorist retaliation campaign against Arabs included placing bombs in public places, some of which exploded inflicting heavy casualties among mostly Arab civilians. Further adding to the polarization of Arab and Jewish communities, the British authorities began to request Jewish volunteers to help in selected offensive counter-insurgency operations, thus giving quasi-official approval to the Haganah, the majority clandestine military force of the Jewish community in Palestine. The Haganah itself, though split between moderate and more activist factions, was evolving into a national and relatively non-partisan clandestine Jewish army. As such, it wished at this point to distance itself from the Irgun and its deliberately provocative activities.

Ivan Lloyd Phillips wrote to his father:

The country is just crawling with troops at the present moment... violence & sabotage, battle, murder & sudden death continue unabated as before.... At the moment there seems no way out: I am convinced that the London Conference will fail -- both Arab & Jew are too intractible & intransigent ever to come to an agreement, & one rather trembles to think of the solution which H.M.G. threaten to produce, rather like a rabbit out of a hat, in the event of a deadlock. I am inclined to think that Titus was the only man who ever made a show at governing this country, though his methods were summary.[181]

Undaunted by security problems, Miss Emery carried on at the English Girls' School in Haifa, reassuring her family that

School goes on again as usual. Last week, after the bomb, some of the girls got a bit hectic & started spreading wild rumours: but it's all fizzed off again now. On Monday morning there was a lot of firing outside during my Scripture lesson. Most of the girls looked sick with fright and attention to the matter in hand was nil so I dictated some notes to calm their minds. We heard afterwards that three people were killed....[182]

Convinced that its hitherto relatively restrained security measures had failed, yet reluctant to upset Muslims elsewhere in the Middle East and the Empire, especially India, by too harsh a repression of the Palestine Arabs, the Palestine Government havered, but continued officially to pursue a policy of minimum force. The result was a renewed wave of murder, highway robbery, thefts and other crimes, and the abandonment by British authorities of police posts and administrative offices in many outlying districts.

By mid-summer the authorities decided on a shift to the offensive. An unconventional counter-insurgency campaign was launched with the formation of several Special Night Squads under the singular leadership of a charismatic Army officer, Colonel Orde Wingate, among whose eccentricities was a passionate pro-Zionism born of the religious tenets he had absorbed as a member of the Plymouth Brethren. Composed of British officers and men and an elite group of Jewish supernumerary troops, the hard-hitting Special Night Squads drew on an effective intelligence network and actively sought night combat with the rebels, harrassing them wherever they had sought safety, whether in the hills or remote villages. Ultimately much feared and admired, the Special Night Squads were effective far beyond their numbers, appearing by stealth after forced night marches to take the war to the guerillas, thus denying them territory and support, as well as reassuring intimidated villagers. In addition, a country-wide permanent night curfew was imposed outside the cities, allowing troops to isolate guerilla bands and re-establish control over wide areas of the countryside that had virtually been given up to the rebels. After the crisis over Hitler's demands on Czechoslovakia had abated with the signing of the Munich agreement at the end of September 1938, troop reinforcements poured into Palestine, ultimately numbering nearly 20,000, and some 2,900 British policemen were also added in 1938. Systematically, villages and neighbourhoods were cordoned off and searched for arms and wanted men. By November 1938 Sir Harold MacMichael ceded virtually dictatorial powers to the military, placing both police and local administrators directly under military command, and enforcing at last the draconian security legislation that had for some time been on the books, but largely unenforced.

As the counter-insurgency gathered momentum in the autumn, so too did reports of misconduct by British personnel, deliberately exaggerated by German and Italian propaganda, now actively spreading accounts of supposed British atrocities against the Arabs. The suppression of the insurgency nonetheless went on, a campaign of attrition with few dramatic successes, but continuous pressure on the Arabs. Constant patrolling, searches for guerillas and their arms, as well as exemplary, harsh military sentences on individuals and the levying of collective penalties against villages harbouring rebels, ultimately had their effect. In addition to purely military measures, administrative control was reinstated in villages that had been given over to rebel influence. Arab resistance was ultimately broken: British authority was successfully re-imposed throughout most rural areas, and within the cities including Beersheba and the Old City of Jerusalem.

Mrs Teague reported to her anxious family in England that the sheer number of troops was reassuring: "true the place has a warlike air, and bullets are singing round the sky at all hours of the day and night. You can't see the trees for the soldiers, and a policeman is draped round every pillar box. It's lovely. We have never felt so safe before." [183]

The technical commission charged with elaborating a detailed partition scheme arrived in Palestine at the end of 1938, provoking renewed Arab demonstrations, but the overwhelming British military presence allowed it to make its pro forma investigation, travelling about the country with a heavy military escort.

The day before yesterday was the second anniversary of the beginning of the disturbances here, and the situation is really worse now than it was then -- what a country! The partition Commission is arriving here on the 28th and the rumours are that their arrival is to be celebrated by an intensification of rebel activity all over the country, as if we hadn't enough to cope with already! However we're looking out for squalls!.... I think most of the local villagers and people are beginning to feel they've had about enough.... Of course if things do ever get normal again we simply shan't know what to do with ourselves! [184]

As the threat of a European war became clearer, the British Government began to take anxious account of the strategic importance of Palestine, and of Britain's vital military bases, oil reserves and communications arteries elsewhere in the Middle East. The Government concluded even before the Partition Commission had departed for Palestine that it would be impossible to impose partition over Arab objections. The Commission finished its work in August, but did not formally present its findings to Parliament until November; by then it had long been known in London and Jerusalem that the Commission would recommend abandoning partition altogether. Partition was officially rejected as impracticable in a White Paper issued on 9 November, and it was then announced that a conference would be held in London early in 1939 with representatives of the Jewish Agency, the Palestine Arabs and neighbouring Arab states in an attempt to agree on a future policy for Palestine, including the issue of immigration. The British government announced that it would reserve the right to impose its own solution in the absence of an accord between the parties attending the conference.

The London Conferences, for they were separate meetings between British officials and delegations from each of the disputants, opened with great ceremony and an address on 7 February by the Prime Minister, Neville Chamberlain, against a background of increasingly grim international news. It rapidly became clear to all participants that the British Government, preparing for the war that now loomed closer, was anxious to modify the Mandate with the strategic aim of strengthening Britain's position in the Middle East; and, in actively seeking the good will of the Arabs of Palestine and the neighbouring countries, was preparing to construe much more narrowly the pledges it had made to the Jews and to the League of Nations. The calculation was simple: Arab friendship could not be taken for granted, and had to be cultivated. The Jews, hardly candidates for cooperation with the Axis powers, had no option but loyalty to Great Britain. The Arabs, feeling they had the upper hand, held out for maximum concessions from Britain, adamant in their refusal to accept what in their view were mere palliative solutions to their grievances in Palestine. Since Anglo-Arab as well as Anglo-Jewish talks ended in deadlock, the Government drew up its own proposal, drastically cutting back Jewish immigration and land purchases, and providing for an eventual independent unitary Palestine state. The Jewish delegation refused to accept the Government scheme, and left the conference; the Palestine Arab delegation in its turn attempted to impose conditions that the British Government found unacceptable, leading to a formal termination of the talks on 17 March. Two days earlier, German troops had marched into Prague, establishing a so-called Protectorate over Bohemia and Moravia, in violation of the accords Hitler had concluded with Britain and France at Munich. Italy invaded Albania in April, and the Berlin-Rome military Axis was proclaimed in early May.

The British Government announced in a new White Paper published on 17 May that a Palestinian state was to be established in which Arabs and Jews would share authority, a process that was envisaged as lasting for a decade. The grant of full independence was made contingent on the restoration of public order, and the establishment of good relations between the Arab and Jewish populations of Palestine. For a five-year period beginning in April 1939, a maximum of 75,000 Jewish immigrants would be permitted to enter Palestine, after which time such immigration would depend on Arab consent. Illegal Jewish immigrants who were not deportable because of their refugee status would be deducted from the annual Jewish immigration quotas. It was also laid down that the High Commissioner would be empowered to regulate land sales in Palestine so as to avoid the dispossession of Arab farmers.

The White Paper was bitterly denounced by Jews of all political persuasions as a betrayal of the Mandate that would leave the Jews in the lurch at the moment of their greatest need. The Arab Higher Committee attacked the White Paper for granting any special position to the Jewish National Home, and again demanded a complete cessation forthwith of all Jewish immigration to Palestine. The British Government submitted the White Paper policy for the approval of the League of Nations, as it was bound to do by the terms of the Mandate. After considerable debate, the Permanent Mandates Commission rejected the White Paper policy as not in conformity with the Mandate; but before the League Council could render its final decision, war was declared, the Council never met and the legality of the White Paper was left undetermined. Great Britain, which had maintained its fragile authority in Palestine only by military suppression of the Arab rebellion, and with the tacit support of the Jewish community in the building of the National Home, thus found itself in the unenviable position of having profoundly alienated both populations in Palestine. The Jews remained unalterably opposed to the White Paper, the Arabs far from reconciled even to drastically curtailed Jewish immigration. Thus, on the eve of world war, "the mandatory ruled in Palestine without the consent of either section of the population, and the government was gradually transformed from one that by and large was benevolent into one that was increasingly autocratic."[185]

"There seems so little peace for this wretched land that was the birthplace of the Prince of Peace," wrote Heather Teague to her parents in England.[186]

chapter 4 ~ **Varieties of War 1939–1945**

In a harshly worded debate in the House of Commons, the Colonial Secretary, Malcolm MacDonald, reiterated the Government's determination to enforce the immigration and land purchase stipulations of the White Paper despite any opposition they might encounter from Jews or Arabs; the Government's policy was thereupon approved in the House of Commons by a small margin. In Palestine itself, Jewish youth groups expressed particular bitterness at the official British response to the years of self-disciplined restraint that had characterized the Jewish community's reaction to Arab attacks. For the first time in the history of the Mandate, there were acts of sabotage by Jewish extremist groups against British government buildings in Tel Aviv and Jerusalem, where bombs were placed at the Law Courts and the Palestine Broadcasting Service offices. To the frustration of the administration, the Jewish quasi-government subsequently refused cooperation with British security forces in rounding up the perpetrators. Collective fines and curfews that were then imposed only added to the tensions between the Jewish community and the British rulers of Palestine.

The High Commissioner allocated 10,350 immigration certificates to Jewish immigrants for the period ending 30 September 1939, including 5,000 for refugees. The Jewish community responded with defiance, declaring that any British attempts to stop Jewish immigration were null in both law and morality. Whatever the responsibility of policy-makers in London, it was the High Commissioner himself, Sir Harold MacMichael, who bore the brunt of Jewish anger over immigration. A colonial civil servant with a distinguished career in the Sudan and Tanganyika, an Arabist and classical scholar impeccable and cool in demeanour, described even by one of his colleagues as "a loveable bit of inhumanity"[187], he seemed to embody the very archetype of the British proconsul most likely to goad the Jewish community into rage. Their bitter feelings against MacMichael were in due course to lead to harsh *ad personam* accusations of bias, obstructionism, and, in a famous poster, complicity in murder. The mildest criticism of MacMichael and his colleagues of the Palestine administration charged them at least with that "lack of imagination which was often so deadly that it could be mistaken for active wickedness."[188] The Arabs for their part referred to MacMichael as "the man of the Palace"; and in his self-imposed isolation within Government House he remained something of an enigma even to his colleagues. The distance and mutual distrust between all the people of Palestine and their rulers increased significantly in the MacMichael years. "So the government was severed from the governed," Edward Keith-Roach recalled. "All parties thought their own thoughts and went about their own affairs and the cleavage became almost complete."[189]

In their continuing efforts to facilitate the exodus from Europe, the Jews had the cynical and self-serving cooperation of the Third Reich, Poland and Rumania, each anxious to expel as many Jews from its territory as possible, and embarrass the British Government in the bargain. The Polish and Rumanian governments both pursued active anti-Semitic domestic policies with the aim of excluding Jews from lucrative occupations and professions, encouraging them by all means to leave as rapidly as possible, and suggesting that mass, summary expulsion would be an option if other methods of significantly reducing their Jewish populations proved insufficient. The diplomats of both countries kept up a drumfire of representations in London urging the British Government to admit more of their unwanted Jews, either to Palestine or anywhere else in the British Empire. The quasi-Fascist regime in Hungary also joined the increasingly strident chorus, maintaining that if the British persisted in helping Nazi Germany get rid of its Jews, then Hungary and other East European countries with similar "Jewish problems" would inevitably be compelled to adopt German methods for offloading their surplus Jews. Years of relentless German anti-Semitic propaganda also had their effect: it was increasingly obvious that a world which found it unappealing to absorb a few hundred thousand largely middle-class Jews from the Reich would refuse absolutely to welcome millions of mostly impoverished Jews from further East. For Zionists and for many other Jews, the logic of the situation was ineluctable: masses of Jews were unwanted in their own countries, and were unlikely to be admitted in any numbers to North or South America, the vast continents of Asia, Africa or even Australia. Palestine, in which Jews had been promised "a National Home", to which admission was to be "as of right and not on sufferance", was therefore the sole remaining plausible place of asylum.

The desperate position in which European Jews now found themselves proved a business opportunity for many individuals, beginning with corrupt foreign consuls in major Central and East European cities, who for handsome remuneration were willing to supply dubious visas and landing permits to "tourists", mostly with alleged South American destinations. In open collusion with the Polish, Rumanian and Hungarian authorities, a host of smugglers, ship brokers, captains, shadowy middlemen of all kinds then took over, participating in the highly lucrative clandestine traffic that brought thousands of Jews to Palestine waters, many after voyages that began in sealed trains departing after nightfall from stations in Warsaw, Bucharest or Vienna. Refugees and would-be migrants in Central and Eastern Europe who had literally nothing further to lose put their remaining funds in the hands of agents, many affiliated with the increasingly militant Revisionists, who organized the traffic, obtaining transit visas, passports and other sometimes forged documents, bribing officials and chartering trains to bring the Jews, often after long roundabout voyages, at last to ports on the Black Sea or the Aegean. There, again frequently under cover of darkness, they were herded aboard small, grossly overcrowded vessels for the

attempted run to the Palestine coast: on occasion the local authorities themselves would at the last minute pack more scores or hundreds of passengers
aboard already dangerously overloaded craft, ranging in size from fishing
vessels and small yachts to rusting obsolete cargo ships and tankers.

The conditions aboard these barely seaworthy "little death-ships" were
unspeakable: crammed to near foundering, invariably lacking adequate supplies of food and water, with broken-down and usually filthy sanitary facilities. The vessels and their often ill and malnourished passengers presented a
picture that horrified British consuls at ports along the immigration route
routinely compared to the slave trade. Despite concerted efforts by British
diplomatic officials and the Royal Navy to stop the traffic, the movement of
transports inexorably continued, and German and Italian propaganda
broadcasts ceaselessly hammered at the insidious theme that the British
Government was in fact conniving at the wave of immigration it was only
pretending to discourage. The British authorities in London and Jerusalem
observed with growing alarm that the object of the White Paper policy -- to
enlist Arab and Muslim sympathies in Britain's cause -- was rapidly being
defeated as unauthorized clandestine Jewish immigration to Palestine
increased despite all efforts to combat the traffic.

Convinced that upward of 5,000 illegal immigrants had landed in Palestine since May 1939, and with thousands more reported en route, the Palestine administration announced as war approached that no quota whatsoever
would be issued for the next immigration period, ending in March 31, 1940.
The Jewish Agency's official response to that announcement was a warning
that the Jewish community would inevitably continue its efforts to land as
many Jews as possible in Palestine, whatever the cost. The British authorities
were well aware that their countries of origin would refuse to accept
refugees turned back off Palestine, that it would be impossible to imprison all
those who managed somehow to land, and that the supply of refugees and
would-be migrants from Central and Eastern Europe was overwhelming.

Until and well beyond the outbreak of war, the authorities in Jerusalem and London felt they had no option but to combat illegal immigration by all means, a dilemma with no solution and no end until after 1941, when the Nazi occupation and the decision to exterminate, not expel the Jews effectively sealed off all escape routes from what would become the killing grounds of Eastern Europe.

"We listened in to the White Paper broadcast, which surely is better than the Arabs expected," wrote Dr. E.D. Forster in Hebron, adding "I'm sorry for the Jews, I must say, but I cannot believe that the outlined policy is anything but just."[190] Most of the Palestine Arabs, however, following the lead of the Mufti and other exiled members of the Arab Higher Committee, rejected the White Paper in its entirety, refusing to agree to any modification of their original national demands, and objecting particularly to the provision that 75,000 Jews be admitted legally to Palestine over a five year period. From his exile in Beirut, the Mufti, who continued to enjoy the loyalty of most Palestinian Arabs, declined to issue orders ending the rebellion, thus leaving the Government no choice but to maintain its refusal of permission for him to return to Palestine. The sole Palestine Arab faction that wholeheartedly endorsed the White Paper policy, the Nashashibis, failed to rally the majority of Palestine Arabs behind their campaign to support the British Government in its efforts to meet Arab aspirations. The Mufti and his followers on the Higher Committee meanwhile continued to attack the White Paper and stir up anti-British feeling, with the active assistance of the widely heard Arabic broadcasts of Radio Berlin. Despite lingering resentment at the rough methods the British had ultimately used in quelling the Arab rebellion, the White Paper did succeed in depriving the extremists of their following: attempts to organize an Arab strike protesting the White Paper fizzled out, and most organized Arab guerilla forces disbanded or melted over the frontiers to Syria and Lebanon. Although acts of violence by scattered Arab individuals or small groups persisted in Palestine, mostly aimed at individuals in the course of inter-communal feuds, and punitive British Government operations were mounted in response, the country was at relative peace for the first time in years. Once the world war broke out Palestine proved a tranquil island, and a secure base for British military forces and support personnel from the entire Middle East.

For British soldiers, policemen and other functionaries of the Crown in Palestine, the White Paper meant the potential opening of a new front: after years of attempting with mixed results to cope with the Arab rebellion, they were now compelled to contemplate a clash with the Jewish community as well in its angry defiance of British authority. However Jewish opposition might manifest itself, it seemed that both official and unofficial contacts with the Jewish community were bound to be strained. And yet inevitably the picture was mixed: some contacts, at least on the local level, persisted with a degree of apparent cordiality. Writing to his father, Ivan Lloyd Phillips described one evening in Galilee, dining at the Regimental Mess of the Leicesters and then going on with a few of his fellow-officers to a small dance at the invitation of the local Jewish community. Lloyd Phillips was relieved to find that "fortunately most of them talked English & some of the girls were quite pretty in a metallic sort of way, but usually they make themselves up too badly." He had a conversation with "one dazzling ash-blonde - - quite natural I think - who had arrived not so long ago from Berlin; she was very interesting on the subject of Hitler's concentration camps & her family had apparently had a pretty awful time." "One can't help being sorry for the Jews & admiring their tenacity & their amazing powers of work," he added, "but still in this present impasse I know my own personal sympathies are Arab which makes it difficult in one's official duties."[191]

Meeting in Geneva in late August 1939, the international delegates to the last pre-war Zionist Congress expressed in strong terms their official opposition to the White Paper policy, but the moderates at the Congress prevailed in their argument against adoption of an official anti-British policy. At the final session of a Congress cut short because war was now only days away, Dr. Weizmann assured the British Government of the Jewish community's loyalty to the Allied cause. "Above our regret and bitterness are higher interests," he declared. "What the democracies are fighting for is the minimum... necessary for Jewish life. Their anxiety is our anxiety, their war our war."[192]

For British military officers in Palestine planning war strategy, neither Jewish nor Arab loyalty could be taken entirely for granted. In a summary report to the Secretary of State for War, the General Officer Commanding in Palestine, General Sir Robert Haining, wrote that the Jewish Agency "were wise enough to realize that they were in no position to adopt a whole-hearted policy of non-cooperation or active opposition to the British Government by whose authority alone they exercised their powers as a political body." He warned that the peace of Palestine could not be assumed, and urged that no troops be withdrawn from outlying areas: "the pressure must be maintained uniformly and consistently to ensure that the present improvement in security becomes a permanency."[193]

General Haining's exhortations were not given much credence as far as the Jews were concerned: despite their loathing for the White Paper policy, their anguished speeches, demonstrations, protests and strikes, even their stirring up of potentially damaging anti-British sentiments within the American Jewish community, the Jews of Palestine would not, it was firmly believed, employ violence against the mandatory authority and its officials. They would fight the White Paper with propaganda, evasion, political pressure, but not with arms. British officials also altered their assessment of the alleged far-ranging power of "world Jewry", that phantom influence that in the days of the First World War had loomed large in official calculations of the costs and benefits of pro-Zionist policies. The Jews in 1939 were revealed as helpless in the face of the Nazi menace, and forced to rely entirely on the strength of the Allies for their survival. In the context of total war, the mortal danger to East European Jews was simply not a high priority issue, nor was removing any significant number of Jews from that danger ever a serious policy option. Maintaining Arab good will by strict enforcement of the White Paper and above all its immigration restrictions was, by contrast, deemed critical to Britain's entire strategic position in the Middle East.

To reinforce its precariously reasserted control over the Arab population of Palestine, the British Government relied on a variety of confidence-building measures. Police posts that had been abandoned at the height of the Arab rebellion were reoccupied: military and civil officers made themselves visible, and conscious efforts were made to build bridges to the Arabs in order to enlist their sympathies in the war effort. A British police sergeant recalled that "although we had been virtually 'at war' with the Arab people of Palestine, over this vexed question of Jewish Immigration, there was a wealth of good feeling between us and even though some of us might be shot and killed, there was no personal animosity and the local Arab Youth Club invited us to play football against them. It was not a bad match, but they were fitter and I think younger than we were and they beat us by five goals to two. There was no unpleasantness in the game." Once war was declared, the campaign to attract Arab allegiance toward the Allied cause was accelerated. At an Army Band concert in the main square of Jenin, presided over by the Assistant District Commissioner and the District Officer, with coffee and sweetmeats for all the notables of Jenin and its outlying villages, an Arab shopkeeper said to the same sergeant: "last year you were blowing up our houses and shops, and now you're courting us with your band concert."[194]

With the final winding-down of the Arab rebellion there was a noticeable decrease in tension within Palestine. Sydney Burr, the insouciant policeman, reported that "the war has made little impression on this country & if it is ever discussed is treated as a joke", adding "we have not had a killing in this area for over a week now."[195] He described a resumption of traffic on the roads, Jewish buses plying their routes without armoured car escorts, and social events including polo matches, drinks and parties at the Jewish colony of Natanya where the British police "dance with the maids of the village & fight with bumptious little army subalterns till late in the morning." Dorothy A. Norman wrote to her family listing multiple engagements, including tennis matches with officers from the Sherwood Foresters, bathing parties on local beaches, and an invitation to a cocktail party "seething with people" aboard a British warship in Haifa port. In the hectic atmosphere of the weeks immediately preceding the war, Ivan Lloyd Philips attended a large Army party in Haifa to welcome the new Brigadier of the 16th Infantry Brigade, and was struck by the brilliant illumination of three Royal Navy destroyers and other ships in the harbour, the numerous lights of Acre in the distance, and the crowd of Army wives as well as officers in attendance.

The British authorities expected the Jewish community to give the war effort its undivided loyalty and energies, subordinating all other interests. But for the extremists within the Jewish community, opposition to the White Paper and its policies remained paramount: their continuing terrorist activities, always disowned and sometimes deplored in strong terms by the Jewish Agency and other official Zionist bodies, claimed victims among all communities. Wherever one was, even in times of relative peace, violence was never far away in Palestine. On the very eve of the declaration of war, Mrs Heather Teague experienced at first hand the consequences of a Jewish terrorist bomb placed in the Jerusalem offices of the Palestine Broadcasting Service. The explosion took the life of a young colleague and friend, a South African Jewish woman, whose random death was felt with deep shock:

I had passed my First Aid Certificate thing and was attending a lecture on home nursing at the Government Hospital when a purler of a bomb explosion rattled the windows. Everyone gave a weak smile, and pretended it was a roadmaking blast. Seven minutes later there was another; we still pretended, but I had a curious tense feeling. Another two minutes, and there was a colossal bang. We still continued with our lecture. Presently some of the class signalled to me that a man was calling to me from the road. I rushed down. Mae Weissenberg, the woman I work with on the children's hour, had been hurt, and had asked for me to come to her. Her husband was away in Tel Aviv. I went. Her legs, from the knees down, were pretty badly smashed up. They had placed three bombs in the P.B.S., one under her announcing desk, one in the hall, one in the control room. She was very brave, very quiet and showed no sign of hysteria at all. It was difficult to believe she was so badly shattered. I stayed with her until she went into the operating theatre. At the last moment her poor wretch of a husband rushed in.... We waited and waited. Oh! what a wait. She was in there an hour and a quarter. The injuries were worse than they had at first supposed.... About 11 I telephoned the night sister. She was doing well - had been conscious and sent her love to us. At two the telephone rang. She was worse - could we come up. We staggered out on one of those heartbreaking night rushes - trying desperately to beat time. She was dead when we got there - shock. It was a peaceful beautiful face lying on the bed. But she was only 25, and my heart is bitter -- bitter against the inhuman swine who must have known what they were doing and to whom, unless the time on the bomb went wrong.... If you have never seen a Jewish funeral you cannot understand what an appalling day that was. I can never forget it. She was a South African by birth - young, intelligent, gay and charming. Nobody knows what faction placed the bombs, but it looks pretty certain it is a Jewish Revisionist one.... It took only 24 hours to shovel her in to that weird last trump Jewish cemetery on the hills above Jerusalem.... Mae Weissenberg's death has been a great shock. She was such a loveable personality; and her asking for me quite got me on the raw. How lonely she must have been in Jerusalem when I was nearest to her bar her husband.[196]

Arab rioting to protest Jewish immigration, Jaffa,
October 1933: the Police being forced back by
stone-throwing rioters

Sir Arthur Wauchope and aides, Stewart Perowne and
Edward Keith-Roach at the opening of Haifa Harbour,
October 1933

Hearing of the Peel Commission, Jerusalem, 1936

Scots regimental band playing at opening of Scottish
Church bazaar, Jerusalem, 1937

British Police poster advertising a dance in aid of Lord
Mayor of London's Relief Fund for victims of the Blitz,
Haifa, 1940

Sir Arthur Wauchope with his aide de camp,
Lt. the Hon. H.C.H.T. Cummings-Bruce, at the
gates of Government House, Jerusalem, 1937

Sir Harold MacMichael taking oath of office as High
Commissioner, Government House, Jerusalem, 1938

The Chief Justice of Palestine arriving to open the Law
Courts, Russian Compound, Jerusalem, March 1938

Officials and wives at the British war cemetery,
Jerusalem, 1935

Mrs Saunders and Lady Tegart arriving at Lydda with
their husbands and other officers of the Palestine
Police Force, December 1937

Showing the flag: Highland regimental pipe band
marching through Jerusalem, ca. 1940

Arab and British spectators at a race meeting outside
Jerusalem, 1940s

Lady Mountbatten visiting St. George's Cathedral,
Jerusalem, January 1943

After the alarms and violence of the preceding three years, the actual coming of world war to Palestine was almost anti-climactic, deceptively quiet: "we heard the declaration of war & Chamberlain's speech on the wireless this morning & I also heard H.M. this evening. There is really nothing to say; the tragedy is so vast, it is at present impossible for us to contemplate it, but one wonders rather vaguely what the world will be like when the holocaust is over & even how many of us will be there to see it. But for the last year it was plain it had to come & we have now made some preparations.... What a crazy world it is -- I wonder if we shall ever be the same again."[197]

The British community in Jerusalem had scheduled a party for its children, an event that was mounted despite troop movements, rumours and dark forebodings: "just after war was declared the Club threw an evening party for all the kids in Jerusalem - old and young. They had a charade, songs etc. at 7 p.m. followed by a stand-up supper and a dance!" For Mrs Teague, the coming of war meant the abrupt loss of a competent and congenial German nursemaid: "I am, of course, without a nurse. Hitler saw to that. She has returned to Germany much to the children's (and I think her own) sorrow."[198] Reporting the unusual quiet, Ivan Lloyd Phillips wrote that "in Tiberias everyone is being as good as gold at present, & the Arabs are actually going into Jewish shops again. It is of course only a truce, & after the war everything will flame up again, but sufficient unto the day!" Surveying the world situation, he exclaimed, "What a fantastic mess we are all in & how different the world would have been if only Hitler had been to Balliol!"[199]

The day after declaration of war, a British coastal patrol vessel opened fire on the ship *Tiger Hill* as it landed 1,400 illegal immigrants from Poland, Rumania, Bulgaria, and Czechoslovakia on a beach near Tel Aviv, probably the first hostile shots fired by British forces after the German attack on Poland. The Germans for their part continued to promote by all means the movement of Jews out of the Reich, as well as from certain areas occupied by the Wehrmacht. Thus throughout the autumn and winter of 1939-40 the

145

wretched ships kept sailing from Black Sea and Aegean ports, organized by the Jewish Agency and the Revisionists, sometimes in competition, occasionally even in conflict, and their well-paid, unsavoury accomplices from the Polish, Rumanian and Balkan underworlds. The official British reaction was denial that the swelling traffic represented a genuine refugee movement; it was instead characterized as an organized political invasion, in which the Zionists, especially the Revisionists, cynically manipulated the refugee crisis to bring disciplined groups of their young, trained militants into Palestine. The role of Adolf Eichmann's office in organizing the transports lent some credence to another concern: that among the bona fide refugees and other immigrants were bound to be numbers of enemy agents infiltrated for the purpose of carrying out espionage and sabotage in Palestine. Increasingly desperate British efforts to stop or at least slow the traffic led to repeated, if polite clashes between the Foreign Office and the Colonial Office, each accusing the other of lack of zeal or efficiency in pursuing the White Paper policy. The authorities in London had scant appreciation for the difficulties of the Palestine administration in sealing even the land frontier with Syria, where Arabs and Jews collaborated in a profitable trade, smuggling across illegal immigrants who had infiltrated down through the Balkans. Despite urgent instructions issued by the Foreign Office to its representatives in Rumania, the Balkans, Turkey and Greece urging governments to stop Palestine-bound traffic through their territories; and to Liberia and Panama to forbid use of their country's flags to register immigrant vessels, the traffic went inexorably on. The Rumanian and Hungarian governments turned a blind eye to British protests because the traffic suited their policies and enriched a whole class of officials, and because British embarrassment was not unwelcome, especially to regimes trying to curry favour with the expanding Third Reich.

Upon the outbreak of war, it was announced by the mandatory authorities that no refugees from Germany or from German-occupied territory were henceforth to be admitted to Palestine. In addition, despite doubts as to the legality of the procedure in international law, the Admiralty instructed British naval forces to intercept ships carrying illegal immigrants, if necessary outside Palestine territorial waters, alleging the necessity to examine their holds for enemy contraband. Several ships managed, despite reinforced coastal patrols, to land passengers on the Palestine beaches. Even when some of these were apprehended, it rapidly became clear that deportation of illegal immigrants to their countries of origin was simply not feasible, especially after the immigrants and refugees began to arrive without passports or other official identity papers that would enable the British authorities to ascertain which nationality they held prior to their departure for Palestine.

Flailing about for plausible deterrents, the Palestine Government promulgated new emergency regulations: ships engaged in the transport of illegal immigrants were liable to forfeiture; exemplary fines for owners, masters or agents were prescribed; and the illegal immigrants themselves were subject to heavy fines and imprisonment, penalties that were irrelevant and immaterial to penniless refugees. The ships came on: the *Libertado*, under the Uruguayan flag, with 343 passengers; three Greek cargo vessels carrying a total of 3,000 passengers, the *Atlantic, Pacific* and *Milos*. By the time the *Atlantic* reached Crete on 16 October 1940, having run out of food, fuel, and all water, there were cases of typhoid aboard. On 28 October, while the ship was still immobilized at Heraklion, Italy attacked Greece; at last, having been deserted by her crew, the passengers of the *Atlantic* themselves took over, eking out the remnants of fuel provided them by demolishing the wooden superstructure and consigning that to the furnaces. At last, with her passengers near starvation and all fuel gone, the *Atlantic* was towed into Limassol on 12 November, with conditions aboard that the Governor of Cyprus reported as "indescribably shocking" and dangerous.

The *Milos* and *Pacific* were intercepted off Palestine and brought into Haifa harbour: their passengers were detained on board pending transfer to a Messageries Maritimes liner, the *Patria,* confiscated from the French, which was to carry them all to internment on Mauritius. On 20 November, a General Strike to protest the deportation decision was proclaimed by the Jewish community in Palestine, and Sir Harold MacMichael announced that after the war those deported would neither be permitted to remain in Mauritius nor to be admitted to Palestine, and that the same treatment would be meted out to any further illegal immigrants.

On 24 November, the *Atlantic* too arrived in Haifa, and her 1,800 passengers and a further 800 from the Athlit detention camp were transferred aboard the *Patria.* But in pursuance of the Jewish Agency's determination that no Jewish immigrants should be deported from Palestine, a Haganah underwater team was detailed to explode a bomb against the hull. The saboteurs grossly miscalculated the amount of explosive required, and instead of immobilizing the ship the device tore out its bottom. The *Patria* rapidly heeled over and sank, drowning over 200 of her passengers. The Jewish community, many of whom had seen immigrant ships docked in Haifa port, and had witnessed the sinking of the *Patria,* were universally outraged by the High Commissioner's subsequent declaration that the survivors, all of whom had been transferred to Athlit camp, would nonetheless be deported from Palestine, and never be permitted to re-enter. When the London Zionists denounced this decision as inhuman, the Colonial Office reacted with asperity, one official minuting, "The Jews have no sense of humour and no sense of proportion."[200] The Cabinet, meeting in London during one of the worst weeks of the Luftwaffe's bombing campaign, overruled Sir Harold MacMichael and decided that the survivors of the *Patria* should be allowed to stay in Palestine "as a special act of clemency": in future all other illegal immigrants attempting to enter Palestine would be interned on Mauritius or elsewhere.

General Archibald Wavell, British Commander in Chief in the Middle East, strongly protested against the Cabinet's decision, claiming it would have a deleterious and immediate impact on relations with the Arabs, and that serious future consequences could be anticipated if it were perceived in the Arab world that "Jews have again successfully challenged decision of British Government and that policy of White Paper is being reversed." Wavell too was overruled, and the Cabinet's decision, one of a long series in which recommendations from Jerusalem were countermanded in London, remained in force.

In Palestine, however, the clemency decision was strictly interpreted by the High Commissioner, so that those *Atlantic* passengers who were not yet on board the *Patria* before the explosion that sank her were to be deported as previously decided to Mauritius. On 9 December, overcoming considerable passive resistance including refusals to pack their belongings or to dress, 1,580 of the *Atlantic* passengers were turned naked out of their barracks at Athlit camp, bussed to Haifa port and embarked for Mauritius, amid allegations of brutality by British police and military units. One of the policemen present was quoted as saying, "You try to move a group of people who don't want to be moved. You have to use *some* force."[201] A subsequent report by the Inspector-General of Police admitted that the operation had been "a distasteful task", but the exigencies of war prevented a full-scale inquiry that might have settled the Jewish Agency's contention that the police had used excessive and deliberate violence.

The steamship *Salvador*, with 380 Czech and Bulgarian Jews, left Varna after the Bulgarian authorities confiscated all passports to prevent any repatriation; when she reached Istanbul on 7 December, the *Salvador* was delayed for four days during which diplomatic attempts were made to persuade the Turkish authorities on one pretext or another to prohibit her passage through the Dardanelles and into the Aegean. The *Salvador* finally left Istanbul on 11 December, but a gale drove the ship on to rocks, causing her to sink almost immediately, and drowning 200 of her passengers, including 70 children. The head of the Foreign Office Refugee Section, T.M. Snow, wrote that "there could have been no more opportune disaster from the point of view of stopping this traffic."[202]

The *Patria* and *Salvador* sinkings had indeed some effect in curtailing the flow of immigrant ships; but the greater obstacle to refugee movement was a change in German policy, which by early 1941 had shifted towards deporting Central European Jews to Poland rather than facilitating their emigration. Between 1941 and 1944 virtually no illegal immigrants succeeded in reaching Palestine, as the Germans efficiently sealed possible escape routes from southeastern Europe.

In February 1940 the Palestine Government moved to implement the land transfer stipulations of the White Paper, promulgating regulations that divided Palestine into three carefully demarcated zones: in one, Jewish land purchases were prohibited entirely, in a second restricted, and in the third free of restrictions. Both the Jewish Agency and pro-Zionist M.P.s protested the new regulations in vain; the High Commissioner in Palestine was equally unmoved by strikes and violent demonstrations by Jewish crowds in Tel Aviv and Jerusalem. Though there was public rejoicing among Arabs in Jaffa, the Mufti for his part was not satisfied, restating his conviction that all land sales to Jews should be prohibited throughout Palestine. Jewish feeling about land acquisition in Palestine, though it ran high, was a mere fraction of that over immigration: land issues, it was felt, could be resolved in due course, but time was rapidly running out for the Jews of Europe, and escape had become a matter of life and death.

After the initial shocking realization that Palestine too was at war, a flurry of panicky hoarding and some financial distress, the several communities settled into acceptance of the situation, and even some inter-communal cooperation, especially in the citrus industry, which had experienced an immediate severe drop in employment. An abrupt slump in the building trades was within a short time succeeded by the mobilization of resources for military projects, and Palestine rapidly built up a substantial war-based economy, with military-related manufacture, repair and construction absorbing all available manpower. Although the provisions of the Mandate precluded introducing conscription, vigorous efforts were mounted to recruit both Jews and Arabs into the British armed forces. One British Jew later recalled that Hebrew University students, though seething with resentment over the White Paper policy, were successfully shamed into enlisting in the British armed forces by the Rector, Leon Roth, who described his own experience as a student at Oxford in the First World War: "'Initially there was no conscription in England, and we thought to continue our studies. We thus found ourselves in much the same position as that in which you are now placed. But more and more of our fellow-students joined the forces, and we came to feel that we had to choose between being scholars or gentlemen. We chose to be gentlemen and not scholars. I know, of course, that all of you prefer to be scholars rather than gentlemen.' It was highly effective."[203] The Zionist leadership pressed strongly for Palestine Jews to be mobilized in their own units, participating fully in the Allied war effort; the British official view, however, strongly urged by the authorities in Jerusalem, was that conceding such participation might give legitimacy to Jewish post-war claims, and in any event reinforce Arab nationalist suspicions of British motives, thus strengthening the hand of the pro-Axis elements among the Arabs. A separate Jewish Brigade Group was to be permitted only at the very end of 1944.

The British had always been ambivalent about Jewish armed forces, at one point in the Arab rebellion arming Jews as members of the Jewish Supernumerary Police, knowing that they were simultaneously members of Haganah, and recruiting them for the Special Night Squads led by Col. Orde Wingate. In those years, when Arabs caught with arms were routinely prosecuted, and some hanged, the authorities had known of the organized Jewish defence units of the Haganah, whose arms acquisitions, training and even maneuvers had been winked at as long as they were reasonably discreet. In the wake of the White Paper, however, it was thought necessary to make an example of the Jews as well, and in October 1939 Moshe Dayan and other Haganah men caught on training maneuvers were arrested, tried and sentenced to long terms of imprisonment. Both Jerusalem and London authorities were determined, neither for the first nor the last time, to be seen to be impartial in their treatment of Arabs and Jews, and to avoid at all costs the vividly imagined catastrophe of setting the entire Muslim world against Britain by any display of favouritism to the Zionists. At the same time, the Jewish Revisionist faction, for its part, announced it was suspending terrorist action for the duration of the war, and appears to have concluded its own private truce with the British authorities, exchanging information with British security units in return for such concessions as the release from imprisonment of leading Revisionists. These included Abraham Stern, a charismatic teacher and poet, who led an extremist splinter group, known as Lehi ("Lohamei Herut Israel" or Fighters for the Freedom of Israel) that seceded from the Irgun later in 1940, and became notorious to the British as "the Stern Gang". The Irgun organization at this stage financed its activities by systematic extortion from well-off members of the Jewish community, but desisted from these activities after a Government warning in the summer of 1941; Irgun members had earlier that year participated in clandestine activities on behalf of the British forces.

Barbara S. Thompson, wife of the Senior Medical Officer to Palestine Railways, arriving in Haifa after a long journey in the autumn of 1939, came through a Europe that seemed "largely at a stand still, the 'phony war' as it was called," but set immediately to work helping to organize canteens for the British armed forces, arranging dances and receptions for the increasing numbers of troops coming through Palestine, which rapidly became the principal rest and recreation centre, as well as supply depot for the entire Middle East. She recalled one dance in a large marquee on the beach, at a low point in the war:

The heat and the humidity was terrible, somewhere around 90°F. The soldiers were soaking wet with sweat, their faces deep in gloom, their thoughts far away. They were angry. It was the time of the Dunkirk evacuation. We had had the news over the wireless... We did our best to cheer them, but with little effect; we danced like automatons.[204]

The relative insulation of Palestine from the wider conflict ended when Italian bombs aimed at the oil installations fell on Haifa in the summer of 1940, and stray aircraft bombed Tel Aviv in September. These raids claimed civilian and military casualties, but did not significantly erode the sense that Palestine was a privileged enclave, safer than elsewhere in the Middle East. Ordinary life within the British community proceeded placidly enough: "since the last bad raid in September Miss Emery has had the school made a whole lot safer... In fact, we now are an Air Raid shelter on the ground floor.... In spite of air raids the school is as full as ever."[205] From his vantage point as a young district officer, Ivan Lloyd Phillips felt able to write that

in spite of all the troubles & difficulties I have been happier here than at any other station since I joined the service. This is an intensely interesting area, not least by reason of the great Jewish development here, & it is interesting to look back & to feel that for a short time at any rate one has governed this small area which has so profoundly affected the history of the civilized world. I'm terribly thrilled about my leave!![206]

The seemingly unstoppable German offensive in the Balkans and North Africa did, however, have a chilling effect in Palestine: "It seems awful to be so calm & peaceful here when they are having such a ghastly time in Greece & Lybia & London... at the moment one doesn't know what will happen next,"[207] wrote Miss Norman to her family in England, adding a few weeks later, "I've been getting my papers and things sorted out in case we should happen to be evacuated this summer.... I'm proposing to have my things more or less in readiness so that I wouldn't get into a frightful muddle."[208] In British-dominated Iraq, a pro-Axis coup in May 1941 abetted by the Mufti was suppressed by forceful British military intervention, and the Mufti fled from Baghdad to Iran, later proceeding to Rome and Berlin, where he spent the remainder of the war actively engaged in pro-Axis activities. By July, the alarm was past, and Miss Norman could write that she had been "canteen-ing" twice a week, dancing with British soldiers: "The canteen has a dance twice a week, & I've been going to them since term ended. It is excessively hot, & one never pauses to take breath; but I'm incidentally improving my dancing quite a lot, & the men do enjoy coming to them. Last time I found myself dancing with a youth from a village some six miles from where we lived a year or two ago & he was simply thrilled to hear that I'd once cycled over to rub brasses in the church & knew what the village looked like."[209] "Jerusalem seems packed these days," Ivan Lloyd Phillips reported, "but everyone is much more optimistic about things."[210] When his wife arrived in Palestine, they undertook engagements that included within one ten-day period a tour of a Jewish colony, cocktail parties with the British military, "various people" coming in to meals, a dance given by an Australian army medical unit, teas for "my Arab District Officer & his wife" and "a number of my Jewish constituents" including the local Mayor, and ending with a week-end in Jerusalem and a stay at the King David Hotel.[211]

In early 1942, however, continuing German military successes in North Africa, and a series of staggering defeats for Britain in the Far East, including the loss of supposedly impregnable Singapore, led the War Office to enter into an informal, deniable and secret alliance with the Haganah, sending officers from Special Operations Executive (SOE) to Palestine, where they trained selected Jewish personnel in guerilla tactics, and equipped them with arms, radios and explosive devices, to be used for delaying and then sabotag-ing an anticipated German invasion. The advance of Rommel's Afrika Korps to the Egyptian frontier in the summer of 1942 led to the evacuation to Palestine of several departments of Middle East headquarters from Cairo. At this low point in British fortunes, one British official recalled being invited by a wealthy Arab lawyer to a large cocktail party in Jerusalem:

> And between the time of the issue of the invitations and the date of the party things looked worse and worse for the British forces in North Africa. It was quite clear that Moghannams were under heavy pressure from their friends to cancel the party - but they decided to risk it. I've never indulged in propaganda but I let loose a story and I saw it go round the party, and it was a true story. A chap called Wilkinson in Barclays Bank had been transferred from Jerusalem to Alexandria about three weeks before and that very morning he had sent a telegram asking for his golf clubs to be sent to him! And I told this to a group and I could see it go round, and their expressions said - Well, those British, perhaps they aren't finished after all.[212]

Although the first mass transports of Jews from Germany to Poland had begun in the autumn of 1941, it was not until the Wannsee conference of 20 January 1942 that the scope and methods of Hitler's final solution for the Jews were established. At that conference, representatives of the many state and Nazi party organizations concerned with the concentration and eventual extermination of the Jews exchanged detailed technical information as to how the immense project was to be organized and accomplished. A trickle of Jewish refugees, mostly those who could finance their attempts at escape, continued nonetheless to flow to the Iberian peninsula and down to the Black Sea ports. On 12 December 1941, a group of Rumanian Jews fleeing the murderous policies of the Fascist regime under General Ion Antonescu bought passages on a converted yacht, the *Struma*, for some $1,000 apiece, and set sail from Constantsa on the Black Sea, making for Palestine. There were 769 of them packed onto a vessel with a capacity for 100 passengers, and shortly before the *Struma*'s departure the ship had been stripped by Rumanian officials of most of its provisions; the same officials relieved the passengers of their remaining few valuables. Breaking down frequently, the *Struma* struggled finally into the Bosphorus, and was towed by a Turkish tug to the port of Istanbul, where she lay for more than two months, while increasingly frantic negotiations among the Jewish Agency, the Foreign Office, the High Commissioner in Palestine and the Turkish authorities attempted to resolve the fate of her wretched human cargo. While futile attempts to repair the engines were undertaken, the passengers were not permitted to disembark, and conditions aboard the *Struma* steadily deteriorated, with numerous cases of illness overwhelming the most primitive of sanitary arrangements.

The Jewish Agency's plea that the refugees aboard be admitted to Palestine was rejected out of hand by the High Commissioner and the Colonial Office; some members of the Foreign Office, moved by the suffering of the passengers, made efforts to arrange that at least the children aboard be permitted to enter Palestine. This effort foundered on the Turkish government's refusal to let the children proceed overland from Turkey, and the unavailability of alternative maritime transport. Impatient at last of the negotiations and delay, the Turkish authorities had the *Struma* towed beyond Turkey's territorial waters towards the Black Sea, where on 25 February she blew up and sank rapidly. It was never ascertained whether she struck a mine, was torpedoed, or simply foundered in the rough seas.

One of her passengers survived, a young man who was rescued after some twenty-four hours in the sea. He and one woman in advanced pregnancy who had earlier been permitted to land at Istanbul became part of a group of twenty Jewish refugees stranded in Turkey. When it was proposed a few weeks later that these individuals should on compassionate grounds be admitted to Palestine, Sir Harold MacMichael expressed his firm opposition: the refugees were nationals of Rumania, a country at war with Britain, and no exception whatsoever should be made to the principle that enemy nationals were not to be admitted to Palestine. The Jewish community in Palestine blamed the British administration entirely for the disaster: posters appeared all over Palestine proclaiming that Sir Harold MacMichael, "known as High Commissioner for Palestine", was wanted for murdering the drowned passengers of the *Struma*. The virulent anti-British feeling was heightened by increasing knowledge of the true dimensions of the catastrophe overwhelming Jews trapped in occupied Europe. Indeed, the *Struma* episode destroyed "the last vestiges of the special relationship between Britain and Zionism inaugurated by the Balfour Declaration."[213] MacMichael's refusal to contemplate admitting the two *Struma* survivors to Palestine was felt as the last straw.

In this refusal, however, MacMichael was again overruled, this time by a newly appointed Colonial Secretary, who was anxious to pacify the wave of fury in Palestine and elsewhere, particularly the United States, over the *Struma* sinking: both *Struma* survivors were ultimately admitted to Palestine. When MacMichael was next in London for consultations, he conceded that there was now a clear danger of a Jewish uprising over the issue of refugee immigration; and in an effort to avoid another fiasco a slight modification of official British policy on refugees was agreed by the Cabinet. Jews who had somehow succeeded in reaching wartime Palestine would be detained, and if successful in passing security checks would subsequently be permitted to remain, but no effort would be made to facilitate in any way their journeys to Palestine, and there was to be no intervention on behalf of those who might be stranded in Turkey, even if the Turkish Government threatened to deport refugees to Nazi-occupied Europe. The Foreign Office nightmare, a flood of refugees headed for Palestine with German connivance, was never realized: by early 1942 the gates had closed, and escape from Europe was almost impossible.

From the British point of view, both in Palestine and London, the entire Jewish refugee question was an irritating, tiresome distraction at a time of increasing peril to the Empire, and refugee exigencies and tragedies took place in a psychological universe far from the experience or knowledge of officials. The military struggle with the Axis was straining every nerve, and the diversion of even the small naval and military forces needed to deport arriving refugees to Mauritius or other colonies was felt as an imposition, a continuing drain on manpower and shipping that were always in desperately short supply. Moreover, the ceaseless barrage of complaints and attacks, often *ad hominem*, from the Jewish Agency and the Zionist offices in London and New York, also took its emotional toll. In Palestine, a British official remarked: "One cannot help having the greatest admiration for the Jews in their industry, their boundless enthusiasm, & their loyalty to each other: it is strange that so intelligent & gifted a race should as a whole be so completely devoid of tact which has made their relations with both British & Arabs increasingly difficult -- it is simply incredible how they manage to rub you up the wrong way!"[214] The great mass of Palestine Jews, for their part, simmering with rage since the White Paper was issued, now conceived an implacable hatred for the British administration and all its works.

Although various Jewish military organizations, including the Haganah and the Irgun, continued their clandestine cooperation with Special Operations Executive and other elements of the British military, the breakaway Stern group refused any truce with the British, and embarked on a campaign of terror including selective assassination, bombings and bank robberies. The Stern group devoted special efforts, dismayingly successful, to find and kill Jewish police and intelligence agents working for the British. Stern was himself eventually killed by a British policeman, and most of his followers arrested; but in 1942 several escaped and continued to pursue their campaign of terror and extortion, condemned by the Jewish Agency but never successfully extirpated. On 11 April 1942, at a Zionist conference in New

York, David Ben Gurion and his supporters overrode the gradualism of Chaim Weizmann's pro-British policy to promulgate the so-called Biltmore Programme. The Programme was an explicit call for a Jewish common-wealth in Palestine that went far beyond the Balfour Declaration, and that Ben Gurion foresaw with unsentimental clarity would most likely have to be accomplished by force of arms.

By the autumn of 1942 the scope of the Nazi war against the Jews had become amply apparent, and on 17 December the Allies released an official statement announcing that "from all the occupied countries Jews are being transported, in conditions of appalling horror and brutality, to Eastern Europe... None of those taken away are ever heard of again."[215] So efficient and rapid was the machinery of mass murder that the survival of more than a minute fraction of the Jewish community in Eastern Europe seemed unlikely. Most of the Palestine Jews were convinced that if there had been a sovereign Jewish state, no matter its size, a welcoming refuge could have been available to Hitler's victims: however few might have been rescued, they would certainly have been more numerous than the remnant that might be left by the end of the war. The Palestine Jews were corresponding-ly strengthened in their determination to press on with plans for statehood, plans that put them on collision course with British aims in the Middle East. The British Government for its part, both in England and Palestine, "could not see the connection between the tragedy overwhelming the Jews in Europe and the intensification, indeed the transformation of Zionism."[216]

One British officer in Palestine recalled that during his time there he

was able to meet and learn quite a lot about the Jews and their aspirations in Palestine and I became friendly with quite a number.... The older Jews, who had actually helped to plan and build Hadera, more than fifty years before, were, generally speaking, very moderate in their views and their children, mostly born in Palestine, were not particularly politically ambitious. They had worked hard, often under heart-breaking conditions clearing swamps and making a hitherto malarial district, into a beautiful, healthy and fruitful township surrounded by orange groves and other agricultural pursuits. They had succeeded and were rightly proud of their achievements. The newcomers, however, who had come to Palestine from Europe after Hitler's rise to power, were of an entirely different type. Many were openly belligerent towards the British and accused the government of having a Gestapo working in the country against them.... I had always had sympathy towards the Jews who were non-political Zionists and just wanted to settle in Palestine and live the religious lives as Jews had done two thousand years before. But I consistently failed to see how the political Zionists who claimed Palestine, as of right, arrived at their conclusions. Around Hadera of course being wholly Jewish, I was able to discuss the subject freely and I know I was regarded as an 'Anti Semite" because I would not agree to the claims for a Jewish National Home in a country already populated by the Arabs...."[217]

After the British victory at Alamein in the winter of 1942 had removed the threat of a German invasion of Palestine, the Jewish Agency and most Palestine Jews increased their opposition to such government measures as controls over industrial production and supply, war taxation, and any attempt by the Palestine authorities to interfere with the supply and training of the clandestine Jewish armed forces. One British officer described coming by chance upon a group of Jews engaged in target practice, a clearly illegal activity, and how one had attempted to bribe him to forget what he had witnessed. When he refused the bribe, but nonetheless turned a blind eye to the episode, that led to a friendship with one of the shooting party, who "was so pleased that I would not accept any bribe that whenever I met him he would always want me to stay and share a bottle of wine with him." The ambivalence of the same officer in enforcing Palestine law was expressed in his further remark: "there was of course justification for the Jews to want to practice in the use of firearms, for at that time Rommel's Army was standing at the threshold to Alexandria and the situation in the Middle East looked black for the Allies. Some of the Arab youth were boasting of which Jewish girls they were going to take for their pleasure as soon as the Nazis arrived. Rice and flour had been stored and cattle earmarked for slaughter, for a feast to welcome the German victors, who never quite made it."[218] But other British officers commented on the disparate treatment Jews and Arabs received when caught violating arms regulations: during the Arab rebellion more than 100 Arabs were hanged for possession of arms, but Jews so apprehended were often released after relatively mild sentences.

In late 1943 there was a spectacular series of trials in Jerusalem of British military personnel and Jews involved in an extensive and systematic arms procurement operation that had been conducted with the collaboration of mostly Beduin Arabs. The primary source for this large traffic lay in the British and other arms dumped in the North African desert; but there was also evidence of organized and widespread theft from British weapons and ammunition stores all over the Middle East. The defendants were convicted and received long prison terms. Acting subsequently on information of arms caches and a secret training camp in the Jewish settlement of Ramat Hakovesh, British police and troops raided the colony and were stunned to be met with ferocious resistance by the women as well as men of the settlement. By the beginning of 1944 the Jewish authorities no longer troubled to deny the existence of stockpiled arms within the Jewish community, but stoutly maintained their right to self-defence and their refusal to let the Mandatory authorities have any information about the size or location of the arms caches. In January 1944 the Irgun announced it was ending its self-declared truce with the British, and by October that year had bombed four police stations and a series of British government office buildings throughout Palestine, refraining from attacking any military targets as long as the

British were still fighting Hitler. The Stern faction, not similarly restrained, made an unsuccessful attempt in August on the life of Sir Harold MacMichael, though his term of office was coming to an end. In November they accomplished the murder in Cairo of Lord Moyne, British Minister Resident in the Middle East, a personal friend of Churchill's and a member of the British War Cabinet. This deed led to the reimposition of the near-martial law regulations that had last been promulgated during the Arab rebellion of 1936-39. With the cooperation of the Jewish Agency, which strongly repudiated the Stern group and the Irgun, the British authorities were able to arrest and deport over 200 suspected terrorists, and no new acts of terrorism were committed in Palestine until after the Allied victory in May 1945. A further calming influence in Palestine was the appointment of Lord Gort, the much-admired former Governor of Malta, as High Commissioner to succeed MacMichael; it was hoped that Gort might have the same effect on both communities in Palestine as his widely respected military predecessor in a happier time, Lord Plumer.

For His Majesty's servants in Palestine, both civil and military, life went on much as it had done earlier in the war. By late 1942, private cars had been banned from the roads, Palestine had two meatless days a week, and flour, bread and sugar were all rationed; nonetheless, compared with the wartime austerities of England, Palestine living was easy. Local foodstuffs were plentiful and varied, could always be supplemented from the flourishing black market, and featured fresh fruits that were appreciated as a particular delicacy, having long disappeared from the English diet. Although prices had risen, all ranks serving in Palestine received a cost of living allowance in at least partial compensation, and most officers were in a position to patronize the restaurants, clubs and cafés that were plentiful, especially in Jerusalem and Haifa. Military office hours were from 8.30 a.m. till 1.00 p.m., and again from 4.00 till 7.00 p.m., with one half-day off per week, leaving time in the afternoons for tennis or other sports activities. Civilians, whether with

Government or business concerns, had roughly comparable hours. All had to make an effort to adjust to certain local customs, which some found irksome:

> I gradually acquired a general supervision of the finances of the station and, in going through the accounts, I found that we were paying what seemed to me extortionate sums for the hire of cars.... On making enquiries at the garage... I found that our office clerk... enjoyed a "rake-off" of 10/- per day per car. On extending investigations in other directions, I realised that this practice was almost universal. Stationery, newspapers, furniture, office supplies of all kinds - whenever the order was placed by one of our staff, commission was paid to him as a matter of course. I suggested to my chief that we should pole-axe the whole system.... Long years of living in the East told him that any such decree would cause a major revolution among the staff, so I had no choice but to watch the system flourish.[219]

Jerusalem was a lively venue for cosmopolitan social life, offering a variety of social engagements for higher civil and military ranks, centred primarily on Government House and the King David Hotel. The King David, which boasted the amenities of a first-class European hotel, maintained in its high-ceilinged public rooms with their cinema-palace Orientalist decor an atmosphere of glamour and opulence especially appreciated in wartime. With a smoothly running cosmopolitan staff presided over by an unflappable local manager, Mr Hamburger, the self-consciously grand hotel was a meeting place for English, Arabs and Jews who could afford its prices and cared to participate in the lively society of its celebrated Bar and dining rooms, or the Saturday *thés dansants*, in which officers and their friends gathered as a matter of routine. Officers on leave, those who were attached to the Palestine administration, travellers and camp followers of all kinds, wives, girl friends,

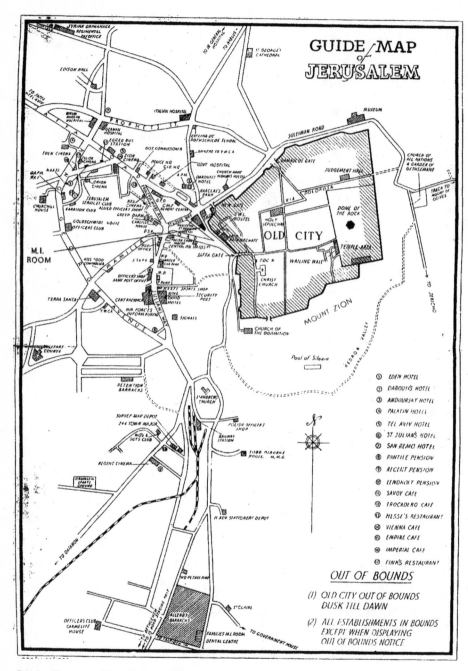

British military map of Jerusalem, ca. 1947

notables and civilians all met in the rooms and manicured garden of the King David with sufficient frequency to feel part of a cosy enough club, something of an island, recalled as a "never-never land"[220] by one officer. Another remembered the King David with affection:

> Its two top floors were then occupied by the G.O.C. Palestine and his staff, so that the number of bedrooms available was severely limited and the demand for them prodigious. The manager did wonders in the way of sardine-like packing, but the waiting list never seemed to grow less. On the ground floor were the restaurant, lounge and bar (all densely populated) and behind a particularly lovely and peaceful garden. The K.D. was the great meeting place of the city.... I never haunted the King David with quite the regularity that so many British officers found necessary, partly because the price of drinks was a salutary deterrent. A dance was held there every Saturday night, to which congregated the youth and beauty of Jerusalem. One or two of these I attended as a looker on....[221]

For others posted to Jerusalem or Haifa, the cafés and cinemas offered recreation and a welcome alternative to military facilities:

> There were half a dozen or so good cinemas in Jerusalem, where we saw films not many weeks later than they had first been shown in London. There was a kind of convention that officers should occupy the most expensive seats. These took the form of something resembling a sawn-off horse box, containing four chairs, right at the back of the cinema. Unless one were in a party of four, one had to share the box with whoever had bought the remaining seats. There were occasions when I and another man were the unwilling intruders upon love's young dream, averting our eyes and sealing our ears with whatever discretion we could assume, but feeling that we were all too physically adjacent.[222]

Advertisements from The
Palestine Police Magazine,
ca. 1944

For British officers, the musical life of Palestine was a revelation. The
large number of refugees from Germany and Austria had brought with them
the taste and standards of Berlin, Vienna and other cities of Central Europe:
both as performers and audiences for the frequent concerts given all over the

country by the Palestine Philharmonic Orchestra, they raised musical expectations to the highest European levels. Even in smaller places, there was music-making of a sophisticated sort, a feature of Palestine life much commented upon in British reports:

> I took her to a Concert of the Palestine Orchestra (entirely Jewish) which happened to be on that night at the Armon Hotel. It was entirely Mozart programme including the Overture to the "Magic Flute" & the "Jupiter" Symphony. It really was a first class show; simply grand. In spite of being completely unmusical & knowing nothing about it, I love listening to it... I stayed to lunch [in Nazareth] with the Tours but had to leave early as I had to go to a Concert (orchestral) given by one of the Jewish Colonies in the Jordan Valley -- entirely Bach & Haydn. Considering these people are simply agricultural labourers & only practice in their spare time it was really a most remarkable performance. The cultural level of the Jewish settlement is very high indeed - such a contrast to their neighbours at Arab Samakh & makes one realise how difficult this job really is![223]

For another officer, the concerts of the Palestine Philharmonic Orchestra were events not to be missed. The orchestra regularly played to sold-out houses throughout Palestine, and Major Law recalled, "I don't think I ever saw a single empty seat," adding that "the Jews are, of course, an extremely musical race, but I was glad to notice so many non-Jewish folk in the audience -- officers and men of the British, Greek, Czech and Polish armies. Every concert was to me sheer delight, even though I know nothing of music. It was no less a delight to hundreds of others who were spending a time of often dreary exile."[224]

The tedium of wartime posting to Palestine was compounded for other ranks by low pay and the relative geographic and social isolation of some military establishments.

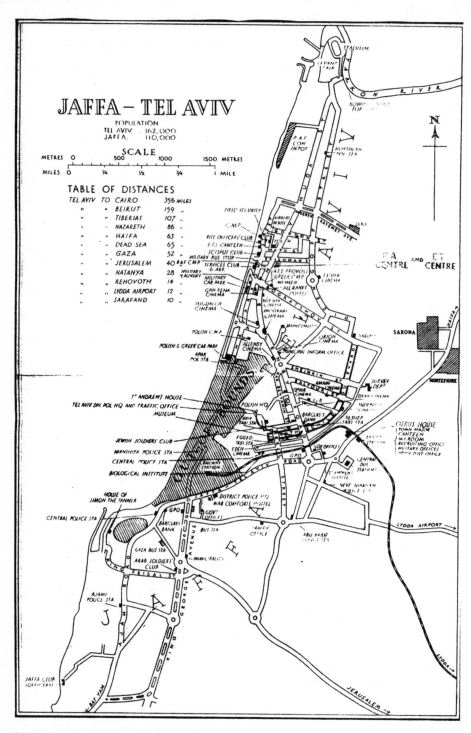

British military map of Jaffa and Tel Aviv, ca. 1947

Our destination was a place called Gedera in the Judean hills. When we arrived at the camp groups of Jews and Jewesses were putting the finishing touches to the roads. We looked at the latter appreciatively for they all wore the briefest of shorts. But if we had any ideas on the subject we were doomed to disappointment for the Jews of Palestine would have nothing to do with British soldiers. Even though Britain was fighting Germany where a good many of them had come from, it still made no difference. We were to find out in due course that the Arabs to whom the country really belonged appreciated us far more, except perhaps the itinerant traders of Haifa. The camp was completely isolated. The nearest village was called Rehovat... the only way to get there was to walk and chance a lift by a truck belonging to another regiment... [225]

British and other Allied troops were, however, allowed leave, and in the major urban centres canteens and clubs were established to provide entertainment and places for troops to meet the locals. Inevitably, enterprising prostitutes of several nationalities were also available in Palestine, some inspected by local military medical authorities, others entirely unregulated. In efforts to keep venereal diseases under control, troops were instructed to visit the nearest P.A.C. (Prophylactic Ablution Centre), several of which were available in each town, after meetings with the local prostitutes. With thousands of troops on leave or on station in Palestine, relations with males were also, if less openly, available from among the locals, and certain venues became well known for facilitating these encounters, notably the beach front in Tel Aviv. One soldier later recalled that "it was in the oldest city [Jaffa] that I was introduced to the oldest profession," and described the incident as follows:

Madame Rose's establishment was in Jaffa and it was three o'clock in the afternoon when we arrived.... the fact that the girl, a Spaniard, could speak a little English decided me.... If there's anything calculated to put a man off, unless he's a sex maniac, it is this cold-bloodedness and the lack of preliminaries. What feelings I had disappeared.... I grabbed up my jacket and left hurriedly.[226]

Leave in Palestine was especially welcome after the rigours of desert campaigning and the exoticism of other stations: one officer described a brief liberty spent largely on the friendly premises of the Jaffa Club, bathing, meeting friends for tea on the club veranda, then returning to Tel Aviv and a "damn good" dinner at the Scopus Club, consisting of steak and chips "washed down with Carmel Hock", a local wine.[227] Writing to his sister in England, a soldier on furlough from the Eighth Army expressed an unusual British reaction to Tel Aviv, positive admiration:

the countryside [near Natanya Leave Camp] reminded me of Devon, with the cliffs and the sea below crashing against the large rocks. The camp itself was situated by the sea and was an ideal place.... Plenty of amusements and to suit everyone's taste; tennis courts, library and canteens and reading rooms dotted about the camp.... On Monday we arose at six thirty, and after having breakfast, proceeded to the bus which was going to take us to Tel Aviv, which is considered the most modern city in the Middle East... ten years ago, there was barely a building there. Most of the population originally came from Russia, and they are quite a nice set of people to mix with. They arrange Service Clubs for the Forces and they do make them welcome, and do their utmost to entertain them. They have special afternoon teas and a cabaret show. We went practically all around the town, and saw the wonderful buildings they have recently built there. During the day, we spent most of our time along the promenade; in the evening we had a few drinks and at ten we started back on the bus to our camp....

Taken on a tour of a nearby kibbutz, the same soldier described its features in some detail, but remained puzzled by the local version of tea:

> After the tour around the farm we went into the dining-hall for tea, which consisted of a glass of milk and a plate of dates. Very nice of course, but not so filling to us, but I suppose the climate they always live in makes them so they do not eat as much as we do. I must say the hall was very well built... And so we said goodbye to these delightful people who are trying to make Palestine a rich country.[228]

When hostilities came to an end in Europe, the full dimensions of their loss became apparent to the Jews of Palestine, and their resolve to bring into the country those of the survivors as they could hardened into a campaign that was to bring them rapidly into renewed clashes with British forces in Palestine. Shortly before his resounding defeat in the General Election of July 1945 that was to bring Labour to power, Winston Churchill had written in weary disgust over Palestine, "this very difficult place", that he was "not aware of the slightest advantage that has ever accrued to Great Britain from this painful and thankless task" of administering the Holy Land.[229] Even as he wrote, evil omens abounded: the Arabs of Palestine were sunk in internecine feuding, able to agree only on resistance to Zionist claims, but incapable of presenting any alternative to the leadership of the Mufti, whose intransigence mirrored that of the extremists on the Jewish side. A split between Britain and the United States over Palestine now seemed inevitable, despite exhausted Britain's financial dependence on her American ally. The relative peace of Palestine was rapidly coming to an end. Miss Norman in Haifa had prophetically written in April, "we've not been treated to any bombs lately thank goodness. Still, I shouldn't be surprised if we aren't working up for a bit more trouble. Some country, this!"[230] The Irgun and even the morally outlawed Stern organization now joined forces with the

Haganah to promote accelerated Jewish immigration into Palestine. On 14 May 1945 pamphlets were distributed in Jerusalem warning the population against coming near British government offices. A mortar bomb campaign against British police posts in several parts of the country kept both the police and the general population on edge.

In the night of 31 October, there were coordinated sabotage attacks by the Haganah and its allies on railway lines and other public property all over Palestine, two police vessels in Haifa were destroyed and an attempt made to blow up the Haifa oil refineries as well. Troops of the 6th Airborne Division were sent to reinforce the Palestine garrison. On 13 November, Foreign Secretary Ernest Bevin gave a free-wheeling interview to a group of journalists in which he warned the Jews that Palestine was not the solution to the problem of Jewish refugees, and added that the Jewish displaced persons left in Europe should not try to push to the head of the queue. Deeply offended, the Palestine Jews declared a general strike, and rioting took place in Tel Aviv accompanied by attacks on Government buildings and stoning of troops, to which the 6th Airborne Division eventually responded with gunfire. There were deaths and other casualties among the Jewish rioters, and British soldiers were also wounded. The High Commissioner, Lord Gort, resigned for health reason early in November, and was succeeded by another soldier, General Sir Alan Cunningham, who took up his post on 21 November. Even as an Anglo-American Commission appointed to re-examine the tangled Palestine issue was proceeding to its task, the Haganah blew up a British coast guard station. British troops who traced the attackers to two nearby settlements came under fire, which was returned, again with deaths among the Jews. The anti-British mood among Palestine Jews intensified, and as usual ordinary police and soldiers bore the brunt of hostility expressed verbally, by social ostracism, and in continuing random assaults. On 27 December, police posts in Jerusalem and Jaffa were attacked, and ten British troops and police killed.

Writing to his father, Ivan Lloyd Phillips said

I'm terribly busy & these are anxious times here, but all the same I quite
enjoy the thrill of all the excitement; & wondering what will happen next
- much as I should like to go to those parts, I think a West Indian island
might seem rather dull after the tempo of life in Palestine! On the other
hand it would be a great relief to get away from Jews! - Palestine would be
almost ideal if there were only the Arabs & ourselves here!![231]

But of course Palestine was not destined to be "almost ideal" for any of its
three communities, all of which were now girding themselves for the armed
struggle to come.

Official programme for the
arrival of Sir Alan Cunningham
in Palestine

PROGRAMME

FOR

THE ARRIVAL AND RECEPTION

OF

HIS EXCELLENCY

LIEUTENANT · GENERAL

SIR ALAN CUNNINGHAM

K.C.B., D.S.O., M.C.

HIGH COMMISSIONER AND COMMANDER-IN-CHIEF.

21st NOVEMBER, 1945.

chapter 5 ~ **Endgame: 1945–1948**

Visiting Jerusalem during the war, Olivia Manning put into the mouth of a fictional character views on Palestine that by 1945 were doubtless shared by many in the British community:

> Ideal climate this, never too hot, but awful place, everyone hating every-
> one else. The Polish Jews hate the German Jews, and the Russians hate
> the Polish and the German. They're all in small communities, each one
> trying to corner everything for themselves: jobs, food, flats, houses. Then
> there's the Orthodox Jews -- they got here first and want to control the
> show. The sophisticated Western Jews hate the Old City types with their
> fur hats and kaftans and bugger-grips. See them going round on the Sab-
> bath trying the shop doors to make sure no one's opened up on the quiet.
> All they do is pray and bump their heads against the Wailing Wall. Their
> wives have to keep them. Then all the Jews combine in hating the Arabs
> and the Arabs and Jews combine in hating the British police, and the
> police hate the government officials who look down on them and won't
> let them join the Club. What a place! God knows who'll get it in the end,
> but whoever it is, I don't envy them.[232]

With the accession to power in July 1945 of the Labour government, in which the Zionists had originally reposed great hopes, British Palestine pol-icy became the preoccupation of Ernest Bevin as newly appointed Foreign Secretary. Zionists who relied on Hugh Dalton's statement, just before Labour took over, that "it is morally wrong and politically indefensible to impose obstacles to the entry into Palestine now of any Jews who desire to go there", were rudely shocked: Bevin was persuaded by his Middle East experts that the solution to the problem of Jewish survivors left in Europe was reintegration in their home countries, not their immigration en masse to Palestine. He was moreover adamant in opposition to any Jewish state, "because of its disruptive impact on the Arab world and, in turn, on the British Empire."[233] Unswerving in his attachment to these twin concepts, Bevin was characterized in most Zionist circles as coarsely anti-Semitic, and was recognized as a formidable obstacle to the attainment of Zionist aims. His consistent opponent and critic in Parliament was Winston Churchill, whose long attachment to Zionism had after the assassination of Lord Moyne been transmuted to disenchanted withdrawal, tempered with his perennial concern for imperial priorities and the primacy of the American alliance. Churchill considered Palestine a tiresome and costly distraction from major policy concerns, and cautioned against British involvement in the continuing Arab-Jewish conflict, which he characterized as "wars of mice". Britain, he said, should "as soon as the war stopped, have made it clear to the United States that, unless they came in and bore their share, we would lay the whole care and burden at the foot of the United Nations organisation."[234]

In August 1945, President Truman requested the admission of 100,000 Jewish refugees to Palestine, a number he had obtained from the postwar report of Earl G. Harrison, a former United States immigration official, who made his calculations after surveying the grim conditions in which displaced persons were housed under military guard in camps throughout the Allied occupation zones in Germany. The British government responded with a proposal for a joint Anglo-American Committee of Inquiry to study the refugee problem, conceding two cardinal points: that Palestine should be the focus of the Committee's inquiry, and that its report should be presented within 120 days. The British anticipated that the Committee's study would conclude that the refugees could not be absorbed in Palestine alone, but should be shared out among other countries, including the United States. Bevin and his colleagues still hoped, despite all evidence to the contrary, that it might be possible to establish a bi-national state in Palestine, in which Britain would retain a significant strategic presence. The Committee worked from January to April 1946, and concluded unanimously that the 100,000 refugees should immediately be admitted to Palestine, and a bi-national state established in which neither Jews nor Arabs would be the majority. The Committee's report was almost immediately rendered nugatory by President Truman's welcoming the admission of the 100,000 to Palestine but offering no practical assistance in their absorption, and Prime Minister Attlee's announcement that Britain would not proceed to implement any of the Committee's recommendations until after the "private armies" of both Jews and Arabs in Palestine had been disbanded. "In dealing with Palestine", it has been remarked, Ernest Bevin "was dealing with a problem that had no solution," and in the context of a failure of communication the more lamentable because it encompassed all the parties to a deteriorating conflict.[235] In Palestine itself, few British officials had illusions about the probable outcome:

> I'm awfully fond of the fellaheen - but more & more I'm realising that I'm violently anti-Zionist (I'm not anti-Jew) & that is why I feel I shall not be able to stay over long in this country. To my way of thinking the writing on the wall is plain; the Jews are going to get their country sooner or later - which I think is morally wrong & imperiallyunwise - nevertheless it may now be inevitable after 25 years of drift & pious & rather ineffective well-meaning! One must wait till the new Commission reports; but I'm unhappy about the future of Palestine & cannot but feel that merely through charity of heart coupled with woolly thinking (a fatal combination!) we have made a most tragic mistake - with untold consequences - in the Middle East.[236]

On 23 April 1946, an Irgun force attacked a police station at Ramat Gan, escaping with British weapons, but leaving behind one of the wounded attackers, Dov Gruner, later condemned to death by a British military court. Two days later, some 25 Stern group members penetrated an encampment of the 6th Airborne Division in Tel Aviv and killed seven paratroopers in the car park before withdrawing. This incident brought the young British soldiers close to mutiny, and a day later a few dozen troops retaliated, breaking windows and assaulting several residents in Natanya and Beer Tuvya. The High Commissioner, however, refused to impose any of the severe penalties on Tel Aviv, including collective fines and blowing up buildings, requested by the 6th Airborne's commander, instead imposing a night-time curfew on cafés and restaurants. The incident cast a pall over the entire British community in Palestine. "All the British Community here are sad at the death of the paratroopers last Thursday," wrote Miss Burgess from Jaffa. "We are hedged around by curfews and Jaffa & Tel Aviv are out of bounds to all troops. The Jews are so silly. It is only the youngsters, (many of them girls) who attack. The older people are so pleasant and sensible."[237]

By this point, all parties to the Palestine conflict were enraged: the Jews because it was clear that the 100,000 might not be admitted after all; the Arabs, who felt that they were unfairly being forced to compensate for the massacres European Christians had perpetrated on the Jews; and the British, incensed at what they perceived as the ingratitude of both Jews and Arabs, and fearful that any gesture to one or the other would embroil British troops in a squalid endless guerilla struggle with no certain outcome. Despite their official condemnation of terrorism, the Jewish community were virtually united in refusing to reveal the whereabouts or identities of terrorists, a non-cooperation with alien authority deeply rooted in Jewish historical memory. British police and troops, baffled and frustrated by this display of solidarity, were infuriated by the disparity between the Jewish Agency's public pronouncements and their knowledge, gleaned from having broken the

Agency's cypher, that there was in fact coordination between the Agency's officials and senior officers in the Haganah, if not both Irgun and the Stern group. The Jewish community was moreover unanimous in furthering immigration to Palestine by all means, and was systematically engaged in arming for the inevitable clash with either the British or the Arabs or both. The Arabs, though still riven by intra-communal strife, were also preparing for war. And the British for their part hoped that under their new, no-nonsense General Officer Commanding, Lieutenant-General Sir Evelyn Barker, they could firmly restore order before the situation deteriorated further. The stakes were high: senior British military officers had concluded that Haifa should replace Alexandria as the centre of British defence in the eastern Mediterranean, and were persuaded that with a determined, serious effort Jewish resistance could be crushed or at least neutralized. Arms searches and selective arrests did little, however, to improve the security situation, and certainly had no effect on Jewish morale: British plans were often known before any troops or police moved, and the results of each raid were correspondingly meagre. As Spring came to Palestine, and crowded immigrant ships kept appearing on the horizon, the signs for an easing of tensions were not propitious.

By June, after a series of Anglo-American exchanges of increasing acerbity over the issue of the 100,000, Bevin aroused widespread hostility by remarking at the Labour Party conference that the United States wished to see 100,000 Jews in Palestine because they "did not want too many Jews in New York". British diplomats were appalled at Bevin's gaffe, which came just as the United States Congress was about to vote on a loan to Britain, and further envenomed an already strained atmosphere in relations between the two countries. In Palestine itself, two Irgun men captured in a raid on the Sarafand army camp were sentenced to death, and the Irgun announced that it would retaliate if they were hanged. British plans to pre-empt such a development by mounting a comprehensive security sweep to disarm the

Jewish community and arrest its military leaders were meanwhile revealed to the Haganah, which had extensively infiltrated much of the British administration, either directly through Jewish staff or through the Jewish girl friends who were sent as agents to establish relationships with vulnerable British troops and police. The full text of secretly photographed British documents detailing the planned operation was publicized in wall posters and by the Haganah's illicit radio, while most of the individuals to be sought went into well-prepared hiding places. The Irgun, Haganah and the Stern group, not always in concert, proceeded to accelerate their anti-British sabotage, blowing up trains, bridges and railway installations throughout Palestine. The Irgun escalated its independent campaign, brazenly kidnapping five British officers from their club in a Tel Aviv hotel, and keeping them in hiding for four days, treating them well but releasing them with a warning of worse to come if the sentence against the two Irgun men were carried out. "Very dreadful news of the capture of the five British officers in Tel Aviv," Miss Burgess reported, "there was a curfew all next day and we had no Jewesses at all at school. It is a dreadful business and the authorities don't seem to be very bright in dealing with the offenders."[238]

The authorities did try: on Saturday, 29 June, in the long-awaited operation named "Agatha", troops and police proceeded to arrest Jewish community leaders and to search in selected locations throughout Palestine for clandestine arms. Although many officials of the Jewish Agency were arrested, including the head of its Political Department, Moshe Shertok, the operation failed of its object, most of the senior Haganah leaders handily escaping and all but a few Jewish arms depots remaining undetected. It was now clear that in the absence of a determined, large-scale and indiscriminate military operation, Soviet or Nazi style, Jewish resistance to British policies would not be broken. Such an escalation of the violence, targeting the entire Jewish community of Palestine, was not however to be contemplated: quite aside from its heavy military requirements and the distaste of the

British public for any such move, the international repercussions of a violent repression would have been disastrous.

With what even then seemed singularly bad timing, the moral and tactical aspects of the operation quite aside, the Irgun chose 22 July, shortly after the Anglo-American Committee's report had been published, to blow up the wing of the King David Hotel which housed the offices of much of the Palestine administration. Whether or not adequate notice was given, or other precautions taken to spare lives -- a subject of lingering controversy -- the fact was that over ninety British, Arabs and Jews lost their lives in the explosion. Ivan Lloyd Phillips was in the hotel that day, and much later recalled

> sitting in the bar of the King David when up it all went, fortunately I and my family were not hurt but the thing that struck one so much was not only were so many of my own friends in the British administration killed, but my own driver, he was an Arab,... was killed... and later that day... I was asked to go to the mortuary...I think perhaps one of the most searing episodes of my life, this awful spectacle, I think there were ninety-two people killed, laid out.... Jews, Arabs, British and one got this awful example of a collective wickedness.[239]

Shortly after the bombing itself, Lloyd Phillips wrote to his father in cold anger, describing his narrow escape and the events that followed:

> Was in Jerusalem on business, in the King David.... I thought of going then to see Bob Newton in the Secretariat, but finally decided I would first go & have a pink gin in the Bar before I did so: & that saved my life. I walked back to the Bar, which also adjoins the Secretariat wing, got my drink & settled myself down in a chair by a window; fortunately open. I had been in the Bar about five minutes & had half finished my drink when

suddenly there was the most appalling roar (there was no other word for it) from under one's feet. Everything went completely black & there was the noise of smashing glass & wrecking furniture & through the blackness one could feel the atmosphere was full of smoke & dust. Looking back now, I realise how quickly I must have thought. I knew I was perfectly all right & unhurt & then from above came the most terrifying sound I have ever heard: the sound of falling masonry, & we could only assume that we were about to be crushed to death. I realised the only thing to do was get out through the door, across the hall into the garden, & I wondered if I should have time to do it. I certainly got out all right into the Hotel garden without even a scratch & as it happened the building didn't crash in over the Bar: it was the Secretariat wing which I had heard falling. I made my way through the garden amidst crowds of screaming orientals (an unedifying sight!) & round to the front of the hotel to see how the car & driver had fared. The car was badly smashed; a large piece of King David radiator was lying in the driver's seat, but the driver was no where to be seen, so I assumed he had managed to get to safety. The Secretariat wing was an awful mess & the enormous pile of rubble (knowing how many human beings it must have contained nearly made me sick) but there was nothing which I personally could do so I walked back to the Pollocks - completely white from head to foot in dust & plaster. Later in the afternoon I rang up the hospital about casualties & found my poor driver was amongst them.... For most of this week I have felt most dreadfully upset & haven't been able to settle down to anything... the awful shock of all these people being killed - all of whom I knew very well -- is just appalling. On Tuesday I went to my driver's funeral in Lydda from where he came. He was a Moslem. I feel his loss dreadfully.... On Tuesday I had to go to the Military Cemetery at Ramle to represent the Chief Secretary at the funerals of the 13 military victims, & for the rest of this week we have done nothing at all.... Considering, we are really awfully well, all of us -- but it will be grand when I leave Palestine never to have to speak to another Jew again - they have murdered too many of my friends.[240]

Feelings of loss and sadness predominated over those of anger in a private letter written by Sir John Shaw, Chief Secretary of the Palestine Government, to Richard Crossman, MP:

In the terrible event of the 22 July I lost nearly 100 of my best officers and old friends. I have been in Palestine off and on for 11 years: these people meant a lot to me, not only the British officers by any means, but also the loyal and faithful Palestinians including several Jews. My own police escort who had been my inseparable companion and friend for 20 months, my own Armenian chauffeur, and many other humble persons of this type were among the dead. I helped to dig out their stinking putrefying bodies and I attended about 14 funerals in 3 days. In these circumstances I find the niceties and refinements of political argument and discussion rather hard to digest...[241]

Miss M. K. Burgess, from her lodgings in Christchurch Hostel in the Old City, heard the blast, and wrote to her family enclosing a sketch of the

most dreadful thing.... 5 stories has been sliced off as with a knife.... Now there is literally not sufficient men to carry on the government. If you look at the list of the Secretariat in the Telephone Directory, only 4 are left! No one is likely to want to come out to the govt. here, & it can't be done without a knowledge of Arabic & Hebrew. Never have I heard of such a city of mourning. Anglican, Orthodox, Armenian, Moslem & Jewish funerals are going by all day long.... Added to all the horror, we have had a week of sirocco with a temperature of 78.5° F in the shade. With 36 still beneath the ruins, the Public Health Dept. have had to wake up! We went to one lot of funerals in Mt. Zion cemetery. The shops are shut most of the time & the streets are lined with silent crowds. As the coffins went by, there was silence from all the Arab crowds (No Jews!). Their sympathy with the British is very real.... The Arab hatred of the Jews is at boiling point. So what will happen now, no one knows. This is such a wonderful land, it is awful to think of all the strife which defiles it.[242]

Immediately after the King David Hotel bombing, the general commanding in Palestine, Sir Evelyn Barker, issued a non-fraternization order to British troops, forbidding them to have "social intercourse with any Jew" in order to punish the Jews "in a way the race dislikes as much as any, by striking at their pockets and showing our contempt for them." This intemperate public order, promulgated in the heat of rage, was exploited by Zionist propagandists as yet another egregious example of British anti-Semitism, on a par with Bevin's remark about Jews pushing to the head of the queue. The international furore over Barker's order came to overshadow the horror of the bombing itself, and fuelled the increasing tendency, skilfully heightened by Zionist publicists, to regard the British as a thoroughly compromised, hostile occupying army in Palestine.

Writing privately to an Army friend, General Barker conceded that the King David Hotel bombing had been unforeseen:

What we all thought was a fair possibility, happened, but we didn't see it, as you know, taking the line it did as we always banked on the fact that they wouldn't blow up their own people. The Irgun have become quite ruthless and there is very little to choose between them and the Stern Gang. As you may imagine the Arabs are furious at having so many of their own people killed, and the situation out here at the moment is fairly explosive. Another ship with 2700 illegal immigrants on board is due at Haifa in a few hours; we are going to try and prevent them being landed and if possible have them returned, but you know as well as I do what the chances of that are! I am afraid HMG does not look on the local situation with the same eyes as we do out here, and I think it is a good move HE having sent Shaw home to put our case to them personally. Actually he was on the verge of a breakdown as the result of this latest outrage and losing so many of his old friends. I will not weary you with the details of it.... The fact that they were dressed as Arabs was what made things difficult and no one realised what was up until the event occurred. The weather is keeping quite lovely and everything would be so pleasant were it not for these troubles. We gave a dance in the Mess a little time ago which seems to have been a great success and everyone enjoyed themselves. There were about 100 people there. I have had a deck tennis net put up on the lawn and the old boys get a certain amount of exercise on Sunday afternoon.[243]

Acting on information that the King David Hotel bombers had absconded to Tel Aviv, the British army cordoned off the entire city on 30 July, imposing a four- day curfew during which each neighbourhood was thoroughly searched. Hundreds of suspects were arrested, but none of the major figures sought was apprehended; Menahem Begin, head of the Irgun, eluded the surrounding troops by hiding for several days in a secret compartment of his own house.

By the end of the summer, in an effort to drive a wedge between the Jewish extremists and the Jewish Agency, proposals were floated that Palestine might be ruled for a transitional period as a trusteeship, in passage to ultimate self-determination.

A new Colonial Secretary was appointed, who to the intense frustration of the British military in Palestine ordered the release of most of those arrested in the Tel Aviv sweep, and the easing of such repressive measures as curfews and house-to-house searches. General Barker was reprimanded for his non-fraternization order, which was permitted quietly to lapse. Although the military continued to grumble at this policy of "appeasement", the general relaxation of tension was welcomed, and official contacts were resumed between the British government and the Jewish Agency. This relative détente was to be brief.

Alarmed by reports that thousands more unauthorized immigrants were en route from Europe, the administration strengthened the Royal Navy blockade of Palestine, and it was announced in mid-August that illegal immigrants would henceforth be interned in Cyprus or elsewhere pending an ultimate decision as to their fate.

A subsequent Jewish protest march in Haifa led to battles with soldiers ringing the port, casualties on both sides and much bitter feeling, augmented when frogmen of the Haganah managed to sabotage with limpet mines the two British vessels used to transfer Jewish immigrants to Cyprus. Moreover, the organizers of Jewish immigration now decided that resistance would be offered to all Royal Navy attempts either to board their ships or to transship the passengers. British sailors were at first disconcerted, then outraged to be confronted with bottles, showers of slops, and attacks with fists, sticks and fingernails, not least from women and teenagers.

Unprepared for the spirited resistance they encountered, the sailors were at first intimidated and demoralized by assignments they had not encountered in wartime. Special courses and team competitions were organized to teach naval boarding parties how to deal with their increasingly unpleasant and violent tasks. In these as in the security duties of troops and police, there were ambiguities in instructions: at no time were British sailors permitted to use their overwhelming advantage in firepower to crush opposition or cause large-scale casualties aboard the immigrant vessels, rusting hulks that were easily outmanoeuvred by modern warships.

Plans for a conference in London to discuss the fate of Palestine limped forward, fatally handicapped by a boycott of both the Palestine Arabs and the Zionists, and the absence of the United States. In early September, one of the few British detectives who was an expert in counter-terrorism, Sergeant T. G. Martin, was gunned down on a tennis court in Haifa, and incidents of sabotage on the railways and oil pipeline were reported from several areas. In a laconic report on "rather a disturbed week here", Ivan Lloyd Phillips described the assassination of the Area Security Officer in the bombing of his house in Jaffa:

> I knew him very well... he had been into my office the morning he was killed; he was due to leave both Palestine & the Army next week & he already had his boxes packed... The Jews blew up the house at 8.15 p.m. & we heard the bang as we were sitting at dinner here in Ramle... Then on Friday came the attack on the branch of the Ottoman Bank in Jaffa.... The news of the London Conference is depressing: everyone is rejecting everything: I'm very pessimistic about the future: I can only see an endless vista of unrelieved bloodshed....[244]

Arriving in Jerusalem to take up an assignment replacing one of the British officials killed in the King David Hotel bombing, Sir John Fletcher-Cooke described the Holy City as "at war with itself". On his first morning of duty, setting out to walk to his office at the King David Hotel, he came under fire: "as if to protest my arrival, there was a prolonged burst of small arms fire from the Arabs in the Old City... and within seconds this fire was returned by Jewish snipers." Forced to take cover, Fletcher-Cooke began crawling though an open culvert by the roadside. Later he recalled that

> It was a lovely sunny autumnal morning. Occasionally I would turn over on my back in the drain to rest for a moment and study the blue sky above me.... I looked up into one of these trees where something had caught my attention. This turned out to be half a human corpse which

had remained impaled on the tree since the explosion had occurred some four months earlier... My report about this gruesome relic was my first official act in Palestine.[245]

And yet Miss M. K. Burgess spoke for many in the British community when she wrote home: "I have just been reading some Daily Telegraphs. They all make Palestine a much more sinister problem than it feels when you live on the spot. Here we take incidents & refugees as a matter of scenery -- although yesterday's bank affair in Jaffa was rather close scenery."[246] She was referring to an armed bank robbery, one of several mounted by the Irgun and Stern groups to replenish their respective treasuries. Shootings, mining of roads and railways, bank raids and selective assassinations went on throughout the autumn of 1946. After one roadside bombing that caused casualties to his men, the commanding officer of the Argyll and Sutherland Highlanders erupted in a furious statement to a group of journalists, referring to Jews as "a despicable race", and all but daring higher military authority to reprimand him for his outburst. Having thus given further credence to the Zionist view, assiduously propagated in the American press, that the entire British military and civil establishment was anti-Semitic, he was duly relieved of his command.[247]

With the multiplication of terrorist incidents and the steady increase in casualties, British personnel began to live increasingly behind barbed wire, in heavily defended security enclaves that the Jewish community scornfully referred to as "Bevingrads". "Congratulations!", Teddy Kollek was quoted as telling a British officer, "you have finally succeeded in rounding yourselves up."[248] One officer recalled,

My life and work in Jerusalem, like those of every other Government Officer, were severely circumscribed. Armed guards accompanied me to my Jewish dentist for treatment; armed guards patrolled the main shopping area for an hour or two on certain days, which were the only times we could visit the shops and the banks; and travelling outside Jerusalem was only permitted with armed escorts... except in a few predominantly Arab areas where there was little risk of encountering Jewish terrorists.... There was not much private entertaining in those days and apart from the occasional dinner at Government House or with Gurney, I rarely left the Hospice in the evenings....[249]

Security precautions included an extensive pass system, prohibitions on individual or even small group travel, and watchful wariness about possible road mines, with the knowledge that there was no complete defence against determined terrorist attacks. "On Wednesday I went to Jerusalem for the day... but was glad to get away from the place: it is a mass of barbed wire & restrictions & everyone very jumpy - hardly surprising in view of the bombs & shooting they have been experiencing there lately," wrote Ivan Llloyd Phillips.[250] For some British civilians, however, life still retained some semblance of normality, and letters home were deliberately reassuring:

The real excitement of this week - apart from terrorist activities -- has been trying to destroy an enormous hornet's nest in the garden... We have got curfew passes so as to be able to be out after 6 p.m. and on Wed. four of us went to practice carols at St. George's. It was quite exciting coming back past all the patrols & barbed wire, & showing our passes.[251]

There were other excitements at more exalted levels. Anglo-American relations sank to a new nadir when President Truman, responding to election-year pressures from party colleagues and his Republican opponent, despite the urgent pleas of the British Government issued a public statement on the eve of Yom Kippur endorsing the Zionist position on partitioning Palestine, and calling again for large-scale, immediate Jewish immigration to the country. The British Government and the Arabs were furious. Richard Crossman expressed the views of many in and outside the British Government when he wrote: "why should these people from a safe position across the Atlantic lambast my country for its failure to go to war with the Arabs on behalf of the Jews? America was not prepared either to receive the Jews from Europe or to risk a single American soldier to protect them in Palestine."[252] But the Colonial Secretary, determined to reduce tensions in hopes of Zionist participation in the next phase of the London conference, released Jewish Agency and other leaders from internment. In exchange, the Jewish Agency formally dissociated itself from violence, and undertook to deny terrorists any support. The London conference was doomed to failure: the Jews and the Arabs had hardened their positions. The Arabs would not budge from the line they had taken in 1939 and were adamant in opposing partition, or a bi-national state that might be a prelude to partition; they were willing to accept only an Arab state in Palestine. The Jews maintained their boycott of the conference, in the absence of a proposal on the agenda for a Jewish state. Chaim Weizmann's plea for a specific repudiation of violence, made to the Zionist Congress that convened in Basel in December, was narrowly defeated, and he was eased out of power.

British Government officials struggling with the Palestine problem over the winter months of 1946-47 did so against a background of widespread malaise at home: unprecedented winter cold had profoundly affected rail transport, crippling segments of the economy and plunging ordinary people into a real sense of crisis, their patience exhausted with austerities harsher than those endured in wartime. Britain was involved in the wrenching decision to quit India. There was a growing awareness of military and financial impotence to deal with multiple simultaneous emergencies, heightened by ceaseless pressures from the Soviet Union, which threatened British interests in the Middle East through heavy-handed interventions in Iran, Greece and Turkey. The Foreign Office kept hoping for an Arab state in Palestine that could stabilize Britain's position in the Middle East and cement Anglo-Arab friendship, while the Colonial Office still thought some version of partition might meet Zionist aspirations without totally alienating the Arabs. The consensus among senior British military officers was that Palestine should be kept permanently as a strategic base and an anchor of British interests in the Middle East. When the London conference ended in irreconcilable deadlock, with the bald announcement that the British Government now proposed to refer the entire Palestine question to the United Nations, the assumption was that the Zionists could not obtain a majority vote in the United Nations to uphold partition. "We are not going to the United Nations to surrender the Mandate," announced the Colonial Secretary in Parliament.[253]

In Palestine, security continued to erode despite the presence of over 100,000 troops and police, four times the number at the height of the Arab rebellion eight years earlier. "Jerusalem is still like a fortress & every week there seems to be one building less," wrote Miss Burgess. "How we wish things would settle down. It could be such a lovely country if the people in it were different."[254] With Tel Aviv and large parts of other urban areas off limits to troops, morale was low, and the sense of constant menace heightened by the ubiquitous roadside mines, against which no British vehicle could be adequately armoured. When a British military court sentenced two Irgun raiders to heavy terms of imprisonment and a flogging, the Irgun retaliated by kidnapping a British officer from a hotel in Natanya and three British sergeants, abducted at random elsewhere in Palestine, and giving each the same punishment of eighteen strokes of the cane. The High Commissioner thereupon remitted the flogging sentence on the second Irgun defendant, causing outrage throughout all ranks in the British military, who had hoped that exemplary punishment of Jewish terrorists would have a salutary effect on security. The nerves of ordinary troops and police were frayed, after months of confinement to quarters, of being assailed by shouts of "English bastard" or "Nazi" when searching for arms and suspects in Jewish areas, of ceaseless alerts; and above all a pervasive sense of political drift and imperial humiliation. Irgun posters appeared all over Palestine, appealing "as soldiers address soldiers" to the British rank and file, playing on their weariness of war and distaste for police action. The posters assured the troops that the Irgun's operations were not directed against them personally, but against "a regime of treachery and oppression" trying to crush a movement of national liberation, and asked individual soldiers to reflect on whether they had left home and joined the Army in order to participate in "oppressing the Jews in their homeland" and putting down a "revolt of free men".[255]

Higher ranks too felt an erosion of morale, embarrassment and foreboding over the turn of events in Palestine. "Yes, we are in an upset here!" Ivan Lloyd Phillips admitted in a letter home.

> After three more of these perishing Jews had been sentenced to death by a Military court there was further likelihood of kidnapping by terrorists, so for the time being, I've left my house & am living in Police H.Q. at Gaza behind simply masses of barbed wire and Bren guns: pretty dreadful.... I go up every day to see the house & look at the garden & generally have tea up there.... The Jews have now committed their final crime: they have made me very uncomfortable!!![256]

Beginning in January 1947 the pace and intensity of terrorism increased, with virtually daily incidents: mines on roads and rails, raids on army installations of all kinds, and the bombing of District Police Headquarters in Haifa with over 100 casualties. Later that month a British judge was abducted by the Irgun while presiding over a case in the Tel Aviv District Court. In a separate incident, a British businessman was also taken into custody: both were held as hostages until word came that the High Commissioner granted a stay of execution to Dov Gruner, the Irgun member who had been imprisoned since the raid on Ramat Gan police station in March 1946, so that he might appeal his death sentence to the Privy Council in London. Flaying the Labour government in Parliamentary debate, Winston Churchill paid tribute to Gruner's fortitude, but cited his case as an instance of the government's craven vacillation and un-British behaviour in Palestine. Churchill asked rhetorically what all those troops were doing in Palestine, what was the point of their staying on, and at last called on the government to divest Britain "of a responsibility which we are failing to discharge and which in the process is covering us with blood and shame."[257] The Gruner case became a cause célèbre, with tension mounting in all communities in Palestine as his appeal went to London. The Irgun had made it very clear that there would be retaliation for any hanging of Irgun members.

Flicked on the raw by criticism of what was widely perceived as British weakness, senior military officers, determined in the words of Field Marshal Montgomery not to "tolerate insults to British rule from a lot of gangsters", decided to clear the decks for punitive action by ordering that no more military families were to be sent to Palestine. On 30 January the High Commissioner ordered that "non-essential" British civilians and dependents be evacuated from Palestine within three days, an operation that caused much grumbling from those it was designed to protect, many of whom had lived through worse situations, and in any event did not wish to be labelled "non-essential". Codenamed "Operation Polly", the evacuation began three days later, when the evacuees were efficiently collected at the Sarafand military camp and flown out to Egypt, most of them en route home to England. The British community in Palestine was thus almost overnight transformed into the all-male and largely military society it had been at the beginning, when Allenby's army of occupation metamorphosed into Occupied Enemy Territory Administration, OETA. For some civilians, the abrupt scramble to safety seemed panicky, undignified and unwarranted:

Barbed wire and anti-vehicle obstacles in
Jerusalem, 1947

Searching the rubble for victims of King David Hotel
bombing, July 1946

British civilians and government officials are
escorted to their offices by military and police
convoy, Jerusalem, 1947

A Bren gunner of the Highland Light Infantry on guard
duty in the Old City, Jerusalem, 1948

A British sentry looking through a barbed wire
screen at the New City, Jerusalem, 1948

British soldiers and illegal
immigrant ship after landing
at Haifa, 1947

Arab women and donkeys walk by soldier of
the Highland Light Infantry manning a Bren gun
in Jerusalem street, November 1947

Young resident unimpressed by British troops
occupying a Jewish neighbourhood, Rehavia,
Jerusalem, August 1947

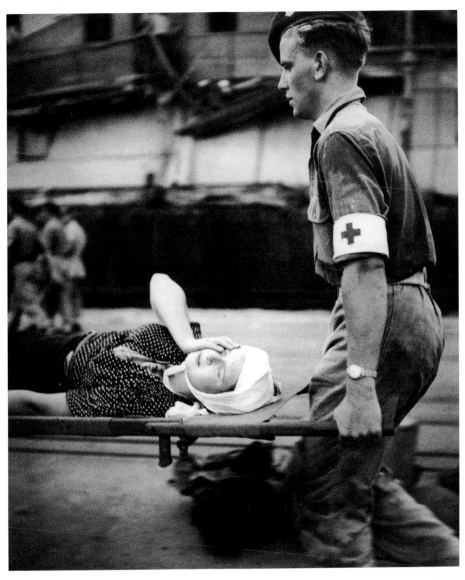

British medical orderly removing passenger
from immigrant ship, 1947

British soldiers escort a
wounded Jewish immigrant
after landing at Haifa, 1947

Medical rescue team aiding
survivors shortly after the
bombing of the British officers'
club at Goldsmith House,
Jerusalem, March 1947

Jewish immigrant ship, the S.S. Herzl, guarded
by British troops at dockside, Haifa, 1947

"Operation Polly": a British
officer parts from his family
as the evacuation convoy forms
in Jerusalem, February 1947

Rescuers search for victims of the Ben Yehuda
Street bombing, Jerusalem, February 1948

The Old City wall and Tower
of David, seen from "Bevingrad"
fortifications in the British
security zone, Jerusalem, 1948

I am amazed and appalled, as everyone is, by the apparent lunacy that has hit our governors - local or in England, I can't say which - paralyzed in a stupor of ineffective surrender. The Jews rebel, so lock up the British; the Jews rebel because some of them are displaced persons, so lock up the British and turn their wives into displaced persons; you can't find the criminals to lock up (though they number a few thousands), so lock up the British instead. That seems to be roughly the policy. I can't help feeling the alternative expedient should have been tried first -- a wire ring round the centres of disturbance, which are well enough known, and martial law inside. The opposite policy, of scuttle, can only bring the British government and British people into contempt, and more than anything else will convince the Arabs that they must protect themselves, as before, by armed rebellion.[258]

Others, though regretting the abandonment of tasks and friends - "We shall close school tomorrow morning. Poor children, I wonder what they will do?"[259] - reacted with a measure of relief at leaving, and even pleasure at the whirlwind of military efficiency. Leaving her post in Jaffa, Miss Burgess reported:

What a marvellous time we are having at the expense of the British taxpayer! We left Jaffa this morning & are now being looked after by the army in royal style. I understand now why important people get through so much and never seem tired. Everything is arranged for them and they never suffer the exasperation of tickets, visas, porters etc.... We have had a frantic week end clearing up the school & house & packing our own belongings.[260]

Houses in Jewish quarters of Jerusalem were now requisitioned for the use of British personnel, an action that further increased tensions with the

Jewish community, which in its turn declined officially to cooperate with British anti-terrorist investigations. Most of the remaining British community continued to feel betrayed by the admission implied in "Operation Polly": that Great Britain could no longer protect her own nationals in a British-administered country swarming with troops and police.

> Today was the great and lamentable emigration of the families. What a culmination of 25 years of British administration for a British Government to proclaim publicly that it cannot be responsible for protecting its own women and children! Now the remaining population, men or women, are being required to retreat behind the barbed wire. I hope to be left undisturbed in St. George's where a number of women and clergy are residing, protected by the odour of sanctity -- a more efficient agent, I trust, than the blunted bayonets and misdirected bullets of the British army. No-one has suggested putting a wire round Tel Aviv, because that, of course, would cause injustice to a "vast majority" of innocent people. Well, I am looking forward to coming home; not more than a month or so now, with luck. I have sent the shipping company a reminder that I want them to get me a passage.[261]

The High Commissioner now exercised virtually dictatorial powers, able to impose martial law at his discretion within any area of Palestine; moreover, the press was heavily censored and troops were authorized to search premises and individuals without warrant, arrest suspects, and impose collective fines and punishments. Despite all these powers, the administration was signally unable to reimpose its authority, and both Irgun and the Stern group stepped up the pace and intensity of their violence, while within the Arab community a number of shadowy groups pursued their own campaign of terror with selective assassinations, extortion and kidnappings. On 1 March, the British officers' club of Jerusalem was bombed by the Irgun, killing twenty British soldiers, and there were other explosions and British casualties in numerous other places in Palestine. The next day, the "Operation Elephant" was launched, which involved throwing a cordon around all of Tel Aviv, proclaiming martial law, and bringing ordinary life to a standstill. The total area cordoned off was some 10 x 5 miles and contained a population of just over 300,000 people, over half the Jewish population of Palestine. Although the imposition of martial law was a drastic measure, the results of searches were disappointing, and Major General Richard Gale, commanding the 1st Infantry. Division, reported that

Initially a rigorous curfew was imposed but this was soon lifted. I consider that no complete house curfew could be imposed for more than 48 hrs and in this case the continued imposition of a house curfew on such a large population was quite beyond the capabilities of the troops at my disposal. I therefore preferred to lift the curfew myself rather than have it broken under my nose as a result of having insufficient forces to guarantee its proper imposition. A task of this magnitude involving such a large civilian population cannot be undertaken effectively without some degree of co-operation from the people themselves.... This assistance could have been obtained either by the threat of, or the actual use of lethal force. It was on a just balance of a show of force and a co-operative approach to these bodies that I worked.... The operation was in my opinion successful. I consider it reached the peak of its success on Friday 14 Mar.[262]

But the authorities in London and Jerusalem were not similarly convinced, and Operation Elephant had no discernible influence on the Irgun campaign, which went on, doing its most spectacular damage on 31 March, when the Haifa oil refineries were sabotaged, setting off enormous fires that burned for weeks. On 16 April, Dov Gruner and three other Irgun members were hanged in Acre prison. Sgt Jack Denley of the Palestine Police later spoke of the powerful impact Gruner had made on him in the course of the year in which Denley had been one of his gaolers. He told an interviewer that Gruner had described being hounded all over Europe, and deciding once he had arrived in Palestine that

> this is where I stop running, I'm not going to run any further, he said. This is our place and this is where we will stay... and at that time I thought to myself we've got no chance, no chance to beat people like this, because most of -- lots of the Police had no real dedication and were merely doing their job, and doing very well mind you because it was an excellent police force, but to dedicated people like this, I thought we didn't have a great deal of chance to make any solution, it would have to be a government solution and not a solution by force.

Sgt Denley then recalled that when the death sentence was confirmed, Gruner had asked to see him and say goodbye.

> I put my hand through and he took both my hands in his, and said in different times you and I would have been great friends, and I walked out into the sunshine and Grant said something to me, oh I don't know what he said, I didn't take notice of him, I was -- tears were running down my eyes, very upset - that upset me because I don't think he -- something was in his personality so much impressed me, that was the point, it has never ever left me, and 29 years later I still remember it.

Sgt Denley added that despite all that happened he was sorry to leave Palestine:

> I loved it, I absolutely loved the place, I still go back there every year and I love the place still and had I not been there kicked out in 1948 when Mr.

Bevin said we're not going to hold the Mandate any longer I should still be there. I think, I shall stay there and retire, I should have retired at 55 and stayed on and lived there... I think it would have been a wonderful country if it had stayed status quo with the Arabs and the Jews -- I don't think they'd ever agree, but I think they would have agreed with the British to hold the balance, in fact people tell me it was better when we were there, you see now when I go back there, but they don't let anybody hear them.[263]

The incidents now came with increasing speed: on 21 April two condemned Irgun men committed suicide with grenades smuggled into the Acre prison; the next day the Cairo-Haifa train was blown up near Rehovot killing another five British soldiers and several civilians; the chief of the Haifa CID was assassinated in late April. The next month, the Irgun succeeded in blowing open Acre prison, a supposedly impregnable fortress, releasing a total of 251 convicts, including Irgun members, numerous Arab and Jewish common criminals and a number of lunatics. Five participants in the raid were arrested, and three promptly sentenced to death by a military court. This episode inspired a notorious full-page advertisement in the American press, written by Ben Hecht, a screenwriter and publicist who was a staunch supporter of the Revisionists, that caused profound outrage among the British in Palestine and was the subject of formal diplomatic protests in Washington. Addressing "my brave friends", Hecht wrote: "Every time you blow up a British arsenal, or wreck a British jail, or send a British railroad train sky high, or rob a British bank, or let go with your guns and bombs at British betrayers and invaders of your homeland, the Jews of America make a little holiday in their hearts."[264] A United Nations resolution calling on all the inhabitants of Palestine to refrain from creating by force or threats "an atmosphere prejudicial to an early settlement",[265] one of many United Nations resolutions ignored by all sides in Palestine, formed a background to the deliberations of the United Nations Special Committee on Palestine (UNSCOP), which arrived in Palestine in mid-June and spent five weeks in the country, soliciting Arab as well as Jewish views despite the official boycott by the Arab Higher Committee.

In late June there were abortive attempts in Jerusalem to kidnap a senior police officer, and then a government official, but most of the British community were wary and relatively safe in their wired-off cantonments. But on 12 July two British intelligence corps sergeants, who violated standard security precautions by going out in Natanya unarmed, after hours and in a group of two rather than four, were abducted by the Irgun and successfully hidden in a prepared cell, undetected from a massive search mounted by British troops and police, who repeatedly combed Natanya and environs. Six days later, a converted American river steamer renamed Exodus 1947, with some 4,500 Jews aboard, attempted to penetrate the blockade off Palestine, was duly confronted by destroyers of the Royal Navy and escorted into Haifa harbour. In a colossal blunder variously attributed to one of Bevin's "black rages", or the frustration of the Palestine administration which had failed to prevent the arrival in Palestine within the previous four months of some 11,000 unauthorized immigrants, it was decided to make an example of Exodus and her passengers. After a struggle resulting in several deaths, and casualties to over 100 passengers and some British sailors, Exodus was boarded and her passengers transshipped to two British transports, which instead of heading for Cyprus and internment sailed back to her port of origin, near Marseilles. With barely concealed delight in the discomfiture of the British, the French authorities offered to accept any passengers who might volunteer to leave the ships. As the days went by, some 120 Jews took advantage of this offer, but the vast majority stayed aboard, causing Britain exquisite embarrassment as the world's press converged on the spectacle, and Zionist publicists dilated with great success on the emotional theme of British inhumanity and callousness. The entire incident, painfully prolonged over nearly two months, was a public relations disaster of the first magnitude for the British authorities, and became the material for literary and cinematic exploitation that still resonates.

In another example of the fateful synchrony that seemed to multiply throughout the history of Britain in Palestine, the day the Exodus passengers arrived in France was also the day that three convicted Irgun members were hanged in Acre prison. The next day, 29 July, the two British sergeants were removed by an Irgun team from their hiding place in Natanya, hanged and suspended from trees in a eucalyptus grove nearby. An anti-personnel mine was placed underneath the bodies, which exploded as one of the sergeants was being cut down, injuring a British officer and adding to the horror with which the deed was viewed by almost all in Palestine and elsewhere. When the news came out, several units of British police ran amok in Tel Aviv in retaliation, storming a Jewish café, killing five Jews in the course of numerous assaults, and committing other acts of violence. No British policeman or soldier was prepared to identify the culprits and no criminal charges were subsequently brought. The High Commissioner, reporting to the Colonial Secretary, wrote that "such conduct on the part of a disciplined force cannot be excused", but then added in partial explanation that the mostly young recruits, after working for months under severe strain, were brought by the murders of the sergeants to "a pitch of fury which momentarily blinded them to the dictates of discipline, reason and humanity alike."[266] Ivan Lloyd Phillips commented

A dismal week here; which has demonstrated that political Zionism when carried to its logical conclusion will shirk at nothing - even the most cold-blooded & brutal murder - to attain its ends. Such is the measure of Jewish achievement. It's quite time I left Palestine: I never had any sympathy with Zionist aspirations, but now I'm first becoming anti-Jewish in my whole approach to this difficult problem; & it is very difficult to keep a balance & view matters objectively with a growing (a very real feeling) of personal antipathy. However I'm on the last lap now; & next month I hope I shall shake off the dust of this unhappy country for ever. I shall always be glad I've served in Palestine, but I have certainly no wish to stay.[267]

Inspiring widespread revulsion in Britain as well as Palestine, the sergeants' deaths focussed public attention as had no other single incident on the risks to British troops, and raised the concomitant question of why they were stationed in Palestine altogether. The Economist asked "why should British soldiers continue to be exposed to this kind of killing? Why should the British community bear the cost?.... The cost of Palestine to Britain is incalculable." Anticipating the deliberations of the United Nations committee, the newspaper went on, "partition... is in the best interests of the long-suffering British, and is, indeed, their last offer before they remove themselves lock, stock and barrel from an area which is a drain on their resources, a death-trap for their soldiers and a source of degradation, both to the men who are sent there and to the growing number of potential anti-Semites at home."[267] Preoccupied with their continued experience of harsh economic austerity, and the humiliations of financial dependence on the United States, the British public was indignant about the cost of Palestine in lives, treasure and prestige. If there had been any inclination by British authorities to give way in the wretchedly prolonged saga of the Exodus passengers, that was now foreclosed by the general anger over the deaths of the sergeants. The passengers were thereupon transported to Hamburg, in the British zone of occupation, and forcibly disembarked on German soil, to the accompaniment of resistance that necessitated the intervention of troop reinforcements. The violent scenes at the Hamburg docks, flashed all over the world, represented a propaganda defeat for Britain as total as it was predictable; and the images of women and children being led off to the waiting trains inspired in many quarters horror no less than the grisly, widely distributed photograph of the hooded sergeants hanging from the eucalyptus trees. The deaths in Palestine, the Exodus affair, continuing attempts to bring Jewish terrorism to London itself, all left their bitter residue in the public mood. There was corresponding relief and a certain grim satisfaction when the decision was made simply to walk away. "The British people would not tolerate a colonial war in Palestine."[268]

Events now moved rapidly. The UNSCOP report, signed by a majority on 31 August, recommended termination with all due speed of the British Mandate and the partitioning of Palestine into Arab and Jewish states, leaving Jerusalem for international administration. The partition scheme was firmly rejected by the Arabs, tentatively welcomed by the Jews, and faced Britain squarely with the dilemma whether she was going to enforce a proposed settlement that was violently opposed by one of the parties. The answer was no. Britain would withdraw entirely, demonstrating ostentatious neutrality in an effort to salvage something of her position with the Arab world: she would have no part in a scheme that would divide Palestine. On 29 November, surprising many observers, a two-thirds majority of the United Nations General Assembly voted for partition of Palestine; some days later the British Cabinet approved the policy of withdrawal, and set the date of 15 May 1948 for ending the Mandate and evacuating all British forces from the country. In the view of the British authorities, "there was only one way of remaining faithful to all her obligations, to the Mandate and to the United Nations, and that was by doing nothing."[269]

"Well," wrote R. W. Hamilton to his wife in England, "we spent yesterday afternoon...planning for chaos. I found it amusing, and a purely academic discussion. I can hardly believe that even a Labour government would walk out of the country without some authority to hand over to -- i.e. open the prisons and lunatic asylums, stop working the water supply, post-office and currency, and generally speaking invite civil war and chaos. Our department

[Antiquities] would be relatively easy: we would keep a skeleton staff financed by the endowment (safely invested abroad) and hand the keys and account books to the American Consul (if he would be simple enough to accept them)."[271] Dining in a small party at Government House in late October, Hamilton reported "we had something like an altercation over the propriety of Britain leaving Palestine to a vacuum; I said we had a moral obligation, as the primary inventors of the Mandate. Cunningham rather hotly denied it."[272]

W. G. Fitzgerald, Chief Justice of Palestine, writing privately to the former High Commissioner, Sir Harold MacMichael, expressed his dismay at what he considered a clear abdication of imperial responsibility:

The stark fact remains that I find myself a participant in what I can only regard as a retreat we may find it somewhat hard to justify in history. There is no doubt about it -- we are going. The decision undoubtedly has the concurrence of 99% of the British people and I accept vox populi: it is the manner of our leaving that worries me..... Whatever one may think of the rights and wrongs of either side, it surely is a new technique in our imperial mission to walk out and leave the pot we placed on the fire to boil over. The local reactions would interest you. Until a few weeks ago both sides refused flatly to believe it. Now the Jews are half convinced, but the Arabs just smile, put on the knowing look of the camel, and murmur 'so you say'. Despite all their blustering, the Jews are frightened. The genuine Zionists -- not Hitler arrivals -- will tell you openly it is the end of the dream.....I confess to a feeling, which does not appear to be shared by other officials, of sadness at this end of the Palestine journey. All that we did or tried to do seems to have gone for naught....[273]

Fitzgerald described a full case load in the courts, as both Arab and Jewish litigants rushed to have their cases determined by impartial British judges, "some consolation in an atmosphere charged with a sense of lost prestige," but he could not refrain from a cry of keen regret: "India, Burma, and now Palestine!"[274]

What was most galling to British officials schooled in the imperial tradition was the conviction that in the final months of the Mandate Britain was failing in the elementary obligation of a sovereign to keep public order. Arab-Jewish strife sharply accelerated following the United Nations vote, with reprisals and counter-reprisals following each other throughout the country. Sabotage, ambushes, snipings, bombs were a daily occurrence. British military and police were meanwhile under strict orders to "withdraw from the Arab-Jewish conflict, to concentrate on self-protection, not to get involved in any police action which could be interpreted as an attempt to enforce the United Nations decision."[275] British troops and civilians, now confined to their guarded quarters most evenings and almost all weekends felt a sense of claustrophobia to which John Watson, a twenty-year old airman stationed in a small forces broadcasting unit in Haifa, gave expression: "there is absolutely no news from this concentration camp!... what maddens me most is not being able to go out for walks alone, or in pairs - FOUR are needed to go anywhere on foot -- two in a truck in daytime. It's driving us almost mad and the result is a lot of friction in this camp of 15 people."[276] Watson, unlike many of his peers who were constantly carrying out security operations in which they were in danger from Jewish mines and bullets, expressed sympathy for the Zionist cause, and felt Britain should forthwith relinquish the Mandate: "the sooner we accept we have grossly mismanaged the mandate, acknowledgd defeat over the Palestine problem generally and decided to clear out of the country... the better."[277]

In the last months of the Mandate, some British troops cracked: there were casual assaults on Jewish or Arab civilians, incidents of vandalism, desertions, widespread thieving and corruption. British stores, rifles and ammunition were openly for sale in local markets, despite summary penalties for British soldiers who lost their rifles or were caught pilfering. Some British soldiers who deserted joined regular Arab units or criminal bands. Cash bribes from one or another side were a standing temptation to comparatively ill-paid and war-weary troops and police. Returning to Palestine in January 1948, a former Inspector-General of Police, John Rymer-Jones, reported with distress finding that all urban areas were "divided into small security zones. Syrian roving bands infested the countryside....Control of the country was visibly lacking. I won't describe the situation further. It's too shaming."[278]

Both civilians and officials were preoccupied with the practical business of surviving under siege conditions in Jerusalem: the main Tel Aviv-Jerusalem road was blocked by Arab forces, and not reopened by the Haganah until early April, by which time there was much distress in the city. Winding up schools, businesses, a museum or a Government department was difficult, depressing and sometimes simply chaotic, as the steady deterioration in public order meant wholesale criminality, with private cars the first objects to be stolen with brazen openness.

Some people think there will be a hectic scramble worse than operation "Polly", but no-one can do more than guess.... I think they will try to arrange for as many individuals as can be spared to drift home in advance of the final skidaddle; certainly that should increase the chances of getting one's furniture and books away. I should like personally to stay and hand over the key of the Museum to the Haitian or Hottentot who inherits it.[279]

Within the microcosm of the Jerusalem Girls' College, it became constantly more difficult to maintain either attendance or an orderly atmosphere, and as panic continued to increase among the Arab middle classes, there began a steady exodus of those who could afford to leave:

The school has had rather erratic attendance, owing to a general state of what they call "fear" in the town. Hardly any of the Jewish girls have come, & when they have it has been difficult to prevent any of the girls saying or doing anything that might be construed as antagonism. They are friendly enough as a rule: but feelings have been running very high, & many of their homes are hot-beds of violent political comment. This week-end, Miss Boyd, Ruth & I have been calling on various Jewish girls who haven't returned, they are mostly coming back -- in some trepidation -- tomorrow. Poor kids, what with the disapproval of many of their Jewish friends, unfriendliness or distant looks from Arabs in school, it's a miracle they want to come: but they do. Outside school in the town & country there have been endless acts of violence & each one breeds more. The last have mainly been Jewish: but really, both sides have been indulging & the front page of the newspaper is a series of headlines about Raids, Attacks, Bombs, Fires etc. However, one thing about Palestine is that things calm down as quickly as they burst up. Anyway, don't worry about me, for I spend most of my time in a very safe place.[280]

For Arthur Kirby, General Manager of Palestine Railways, the impending chaos was intolerable. He was a railroad professional who had kept the trains running despite sabotage of every kind, the defection of Arab and Jewish staff, and widespread pilferage as the security situation worsened. In an appeal to the Chief Secretary, he pointed out that the railroad had to be turned over to some plausible authority. Rolling stock, some of it from neighbouring countries, goods in transit, workshops, stations, every kind of equipment could not simply be abandoned. Kirby's responsibilities extended also to the ports of Palestine, and he found it inconceivable that some continuing provision should not be made for ships arriving at Haifa with vital cargoes such as foodstuffs. "There must, obviously, be some process of handing over", he wrote.[281] It was clear however that railroads and ports were not concerns of top priority in Jerusalem. Somewhat later, Kirby's urgent tone reflected the breakdown in public order throughout Palestine. Pleading for adequate military protection of railway equipment, staff and the headquarters building in Haifa, which was surrounded by Arab and Jewish snipers, he pointed out that the Palestine Railways also had to prepare documentation for the impending retirement of 6,000 loyal employees of all communities. "Unless the Railway staff has evidence that their interests are being safely cared for it is not likely that they will perform their duties loyally from day to day", he argued.[282] Clearly distressed by the seeming indifference of the Jerusalem administration to the critical situation of the railways, Kirby finally permitted himself a *cri de coeur:*

I have found myself in the position of having to beg for assistance to run an essential service and in effect the protection which is given to an essential service depends upon the skill of my advocacy in competition with the importunate demands of the scores of other people who are not operating essential services. The task of actually running the Railways is onerous enough without my having to spend a disproportionate amount of my time in having to deal with matters of detail concerning Military protection. If the situation is to continue as it has been during the last weeks I must make it clear that I cannot guarantee to keep the railways operating.[283]

For schools the continuing uncertainty was disastrous, with a steady flight of pupils and their parents:

we opened school on Monday & only about 17 out of 170 have ventured to come: while the Juniors had about 25 out of 60. All the schools in the country are facing the same problem & there was an emergency meeting of heads of schools on Friday to discuss plans for the future. The fact is that no Jewish pupils dare come at all in Jerusalem. Some do in Haifa. Most of the rich Arabs have beetled off to Egypt, TransJordan or Syria & Cyprus to be out of harm's way. The less well off have to stay but are all in a state of "flap" & keeping their children at home, & the question of producing the fees for the term weighs a good deal with those who don't know if they will be out of work or not in the near future & all this together has combined to empty the schools. Of course it's a vicious circle, for the schools now have to cut down staff & this makes more people out of work....our plan now is to run a term & ahalf with no Easter holidays & break up at the beginning of May before the change of Government. We shall have special Oxford & Cambridge papers set...& then have a very long summer holiday, hoping to start in more stable conditions next October. Still, it's all very unpredictable.[284]

The whole process of breaking up, saying farewell to colleagues and the work of many years, coupled with the sheer physical strain of going through files that often filled whole rooms, packing personal and official effects, was for most of the British community depressing and immensely wearying:

I am wrestling physically and mentally with the furniture problem.... I have been wading through piles of old knitting patterns, notebooks, linen, tennis balls, electric irons, photographic apparatus, albums, music, stationery of yours and Mummy's, in sundry boxes, endeavouring to organize and pack what I have not consigned to the same bonfire that is destroying our office files. I have perforce thinned out both yours and Mummy's apparent rubbish, and neither of you must complain; you will probably be surprised at what I have kept.... Now there is the unsold furniture: it either has to be abandoned or sent home. Sale here is almost impossible at present. I am going to get another lift-van anyhow, to take the books, one bed and so forth. I shall fill it as full as possible and then abandon the rest. Oh dear! How I hate all this..... The Museum garden is just beginning to look nice again. Cyclamens in vast bunches, lupins just beginning to open; lovely pansies, carnations, snapdragon, phlox, stocks, just painting the beds in front. But how melancholy everything is![285]

Stung to the quick by the seeming indifference of most Palestinians, including the Administration, to the impending fate of his beloved railway, Mr. Kirby wrote a strongly worded open letter to Arab and Jewish chambers of commerce, designed for publication in the local press:

Since I have been in Palestine I have neither seen nor heard any real public appreciation of the Railways, which have been taken for granted, or if not taken for granted have been regarded as a concern upon which to pour contempt or to level abuse and virulent criticism. The Railways have also been chosen as an easy target by political dissidents. During the many years of unrest in Palestine, bullets have been poured at railway staff honestly and conscientiously performing their duties as public servants, and bombs and mines have been used to wreck trains and destroy railway installations. Yet neither the railway management nor its loyal staff have flinched from a determination to keep railway services operating. I think it is important for the public of Palestine, whatever their race or creed, to realise the praiseworthy manner in which railway staff have taken trains out by day and by night in all weathers, fair and foul, in conditions which have been highly dangerous and usually with no personal defence against saboteurs, attacking and wrecking trains from hiding places, or large bands of robbers. I wonder if the average person in Palestine realises the heartbreaking task of railwayadministration and operating officers in keeping things going against the heavy odds? It has not been by just waving a wand that bridges have been repaired and the line made fit for trains within a few hours of destruction, nor has it been by taking thought that

locomotives wrecked by mines have been repaired time and time again so
that most of them, though blown up several times, are still working after
28 years of service -- and working efficiently.... An indication of what is
being done and of the loyalty of the staff is that even today, ten or more
trains operate each way daily between Haifa and Lydda carrying essential
supplies, while the railway between Lydda and Jerusalem is fully occupied in the conveyance of essential supplies and exports. ..... This is not
achieved without effort and suffering. We have no fewer than 50 personnel of the train crews absent from duty, some in hospital, suffering from
the effects of having been interfered with while trying to perform their
duty. Men have been killed while performing their duties. Running trains
are subject to attack and the principal marshalling depot is constantly
being fired over by snipers. Only a loyal staff would continue working in
such conditions..... It must be remembered that the railway administration, whether dealing with railways or ports, is a transport concern and
has no security forces of its own..... Finally, let me emphasize that so long
as the present Railway Management exists, it will endeavour to maintain
the railways and ports as fully as possible without fear or favour and irrespective of politics.[286]

John Higgins, a British travel agent on a short-term assignment to Palestine in order to close Cook's office, wrote home describing the blue skies of
Haifa, and said "it makes me mad that things are not normal. It must be the
most beautiful country in the world and here I am stuck in a British ghetto
unable to move. Would so love to prowl round."[287] His mood deteriorating
as the security situation worsened, Higgins observed that "all the military
and the police are concerned with now is looking after themselves and their
families. They let the Arabs and Jews shoot one another up without interfer-
ing." Complaining that "the British women here are the worst dressed ever.
Bombay lot would look smart in comparison", he was clearly unnerved by

the strikes, bombs and endless incidents. "Now I am trying all I can to leave as quickly as possible. I think I will be able to clear up by the end of this week but every day something happens to hinder it. Today there is a dock and railway strike. I want to get out quickly; it is hateful. This afternoon for the first time for a week I got out and went to the Zone at the top of Mount Carmel. It was glorious there. The blue sea 1,000 feet below, and we walked through the pine woods rather like those at Antibes, but it was horrid. You sort of suspected one of the Stern gang might pop out. I am thinking of moving my hotel tomorrow in view of the threat to blow it up."[288]

For Miss Norman in Jerusalem, however, aspects of the situation seemed downright exhilarating, and she adapted to siege conditions with a cheerful, almost Girl Guides sense of adventure:

Menu for Christmas dinner given by British Police, Safad, 1947

British Police

SAFAD TOWN STATION

PALESTINE

Christmas Celebrations
1 9 4 7

MENU

WISHING ALL
A MERRY CHRISTMAS
a n d
A HAPPY NEW YEAR

I must confess I feel most unwilling to do anything remotely like running away as so many of the rich Arabs have done & are doing. Nor do I want to risk not being here to run the school in October if there is anything to run. Its all extremely interesting anyway. We are laying in stores of essentials as far as possible, as there may be patches when shopping is out of the question. Also, food is going steadily up. At present there is plenty to buy & the Old City is full of food..... Black market is now called euphemistically Open Market & sugar is available in this "open market" which is to say almost every street corner at a price very little above rationed sugar ie about 10d a lb. I regret to say it is almost undoubtedly stolen or it would never be sold at the price, & I'm afraid we are waiving scruples & buying it for marmalade & for stores. The Old City is even fuller of ammunition than of food & every shop of whatever kind seems to have its quota. Bullets are 7 1/2 d each & big ones 1/6. Bombs are 6/ or 9/ according as you choose French or English. Revolvers & guns are a terrific price ranging from £10 -- £100. I have bought a bullet for fun but am glad to confine my attention to food. It costs at least £12 a month to live. Incidentally, it is still technically illegal to be in possession of arms but the police have stopped attempting to cope: at any rate in the Old City. It is surprising to find that I can still go anywhere in the town without anyone minding. The Old City is quite all right so long as you are obviously English which I apparently am. The Jewish quarters take no notice of me & I have to go up 3 or 4 times a week to Dr. Gutmann for treatment [asthma]. Also, I have passes for all the security zones: but the other day I walked up St. Paul's Rd (Army) through Zone C (Police) & back through Street of the Prophets (R.A.F.) & no one even wanted to see my pass. I felt quite sold! Madrigals continue on Fridays in the Bishop's House, & on Wednesdays we are having Lent discussions at St Georges which will be quite interesting. Next Wed. however the High Commissioner is going to speak to British Residents ...[289]

As all Government departments gradually wound down, the burden on those British officials still functioning at first increased; but as the Mandate's scheduled end came closer, it was apparent that even with minimal staff there was in fact little to do. The sense of letdown and humiliation was pervasive.

I will not give you my views in detail on the political situation here because it is odds on that any letter addressed to you will be opened in the post office by the Hagganah M.I. Personally, I am inclined to agree with the Jewish Agency that the sooner the U.N. Commission arrive here to negotiate the taking over of power, the better. It would be idle to pretend that British administration can function in present circumstances.... It is no exaggeration to say that most evenings Jerusalem is dangerous owing to cross fire. Every day one is faced with the violent death of some old friend. You will remember the grand old traffic policeman who used to dictate at the junction Mamilla Road-Julian Way. He was killed when the Stern Gang crashed the stolen armoured car from which they threw the Jaffa Gate bomb. Shitreet, my Jewish magistrate born in Tiberias, and whose mother tongue was Arabic, had his daughter and her English husband (N.A.A.F.I.) shot dead in the German Colony a few days ago. I fear, I greatly fear, that this will develop into a Spanish Civil War, and I pray God that it may not be so. It would be a tragedy if the great creative side of Zionism were to be destroyed now by violence; it would be an equal tragedy if the young Arabs were to be sacrificed as they were in the 1936-39 rebellion. I can say candidly that I do not feel any physical fear, but I am worried and depressed at the turn events have taken. We, or at all events the Home Govt. have failed somewhere. Our sacred trust in the Holy Land should not end thus. Enough of this: the issue must now be left to history. I have decided to stay to the end with the H.C. so that I can constitute a High Court for prerogative writs.[290]

Chief Justice Fitzgerald was not alone in his sadness. Other British officials too were depressed by the daily diet of isolation and multiple loss, not least of friends, treasured possessions and indeed illusions:

My room now looks so bare and bleak. I shall sleep tonight on a horrible broken-sprung settee....I have no cupboard, no chair, no table, no nothing but a chest of drawers and my trunk! I selected five books, which stand pathetically on the chest of drawers. I now realise that in spite of the absence of curtains I had made my room, with its bookshelves and writing table and bedside table, quite comfortable. Now it is like the cell of a prison, inhabited by a melancholic.[291]

Varieties of gallows humour were one way of coping:

We had a fairly quiet night but a lot of shooting this afternoon. It is funny once the shooting starts all the pie dogs join in and there must be as many here as in India.... Still no English mail has arrived. Don't know what the Post Office is doing. It makes one feel very isolated... the roads from the towns to the aerodromes are most unsafe. They could probably do with Herod back for a few weeks.[292]

Aware of the historic moment he was living through, Sir Henry Gurney, last Chief Secretary of the Palestine Government, kept a detailed diary of the last weeks of the Mandate, privately recording events and perceptions with an emotion quite at variance with his imperturbable public persona:

On this wet and cheerless day in Jerusalem -- it was snowing this morning -- all is quiet, because in this weather both sides prefer to remain indoors. But the nightly battle begins regularly about 8 o'clock, and continues sporadically till dawn. Two nights ago our windows were blown in by some monstrous explosions when some more Arab houses just outside the Zone were destroyed by Jews. The sky on these occasions is criss-crossed with tracers, yellow for the Arabs, red for the Jews. There is little sleep to be had, and one remembers that Jerusalem cocks have started crowing at 10.30 ever since the time of Peter...Consular cars are becoming quite a popular target for the robbers, as they are pretty sure to be good ones.... Two more British police deserted with 13 Sten guns last night. It is a tragedy that these men should forfeit their whole future for a handful of gold.... But out of 3,500 British police there have been only 16 possible cases of desertion in the last six months, and the temptations are great. No one envies them their task. The Army comes and goes and does a show and rests, but the British police are always on the job and have been for years....[293]

Arguing against the criticism that his Administration planned deliberately to leave chaos and bloodshed, to demonstrate the indispensability of the British and punish the people of Palestine for "their wickedness", Gurney wrote that he and his colleagues had been trying unsuccessfully for months to get the United Nations to take its responsibilities seriously.

His diary goes on to chronicle the daily problems resulting from the fighting in Jerusalem: massive telephone delays because most of the circuits were "either blown up or blown down"; a breakdown in postal services, with post office vans frequently stolen; the few remaining private cars held up at gunpoint; random shootings, bombings and bank robberies.

In a small convoy, he accompanied Lady Gurney and other British evacuees to Lydda airport on 24 March, passing en route the wrecks of recentlty ambushed buses, at least twelve Arab roadblocks "manned by Syrians and the wildest-looking ruffians all pointing guns", and coming under fire from a Haganah machine gun despite mounting "the largest Union Jack we could find".[294]

The remaining days of the Mandate meant, for officials such as Gurney, a long-sought opportunity to speak openly and with feeling about the burden Britain had assumed in Palestine:

Last December Mrs. Myerson, then the political head of the Jewish Agency in Palestine, told me that we British could not of course understand what it felt like to become an independent people and nation after 2,000 years of endeavour. I had to tell her frankly that it seemed a pity that so desirable an achievement should have had to be built upon a foundation of lies, chauvinism, suspicion and deception. She then departed for America and I have not seen her since. I have not done 27 years' Government service without recognizing the value of restraint and concealment of one's personal opinions, but in some circumstances only good can be done by exposing them. The choice of opportunity for frankness is not always easy to the politician, but with the Zionists we should have been frank 20 years ago and told them exactly where they stood so long as we were responsible for governing Palestine. In fact, the last 30 years in this country have seen nothing but fluctuations of policy, hesitations, or no policy at all. When Monty asked me here last year what was really wrong with Palestine, I said, "Merely a lack of policy with which nobody agrees." It is this continual surrender to pressure of one sort or another -- American Jewry or Arab rebellion -- that has made British policy in Palestine, with all its first-class administrative achievements, unintelligible to and mistrusted by both sides. [295]

In a further entry, Gurney mused on the essence of the Palestine dilemma:

The Arab feels as strongly about the freedom of his country as any American would if a Jewish State were proclaimed in New York, and is completely intransigent and wooden in the face of any argument or persuasion to recognise the hard facts. He has achieved, under the British Mandate, a prosperity and development that he never knew before, largely through the help of Jewish money, but he does not want these things at the expense of his liberty and of his country. He is easy-going to the point of indolence, disposed to cruelty and capable of only about one idea at a time. The idea is formed on emotion rather than from any rational thought; it is nursed and chewed over on innumerable occasions in coffee-houses and in the press, until it is firmly stuck and nothing on earth will shift it. Such is the conflict between Arab and Zionist.....the Arab knows the Zionist Jew a good deal better than most other people. He has had the opportunity to see through all the propaganda and all the smoke-screen, at the naked spectacle of Zionist aggression on his country as it really is. And it is this agression that, in his view, the British have been helping and encouraging since the Balfour Declaration of 1917.[296]

Writing to her family, Miss Norman admitted that "things have been rather noisy lately", what with mortar bombs -- "nasty things & quite indiscriminate" -- and steady sniping in the streets of Jerusalem, and then described the sudden death of a mission colleague in the course of a bright Sunday morning's walk to church:

We were walking down to church together for the 10.15 service... There was no one visible anywhere about: but suddenly there was a shot & Mildred fell down in the road. I knelt down beside her, & then, as the 'somebody' kept on firing, I lay down flat beside her & kept my head as low as I could while I looked to see if there was anything I could do for her, but she was so badly injured I thought she would die at once, & I fully expected to go with her. After what seemed a long time a policeman came running up the road shouting in Arabic to the snipers that we were English & they should stop firing, and by and by they did, and then the R.A.F. came out with a stretcher and fetched us in. As I was completely unhurt I could walk....Its been a great shock to us all as you can imagine, and cast a gloom over Easter. So needless. Musrara, from which the shots came is shocked to the core. I'm afraid it was some hot-head who was full of fury over all the mortar bombs sent over the night before, who took us for Jews and thought to retaliate. All the same, one can't really be sad for her. It was a quick & merciful end & she was getting on in age & had diabetes & every expectation of health deteriorating & for her it was a lovely day on which to go. Don't let this make you anxious about me. My guardian angel seems very active, & I expect there is more work in the world for me to do....[297]

Calmly proceeding with the business of winding down the Mandate administration, Sir Henry Gurney paused to reflect on the steadfastness of his colleagues:

In the Yemin Moshe explosion last week Stubbs had everything blown clean off his office table except the typewriter, which was hopelessly buckled inside..... A few nights ago a bullet came in at the open window and went through the picture behind his head. Is not some tribute due to people who do not seem to mind these things? I thought to-day that in spite of internal civil war in the country the Administration with its 30,000 Palestinian employeees and only about 200 British officers left carries on cheerfully. Only 6 weeks and a bit to the 15th May and to the end of their careers and all prospects for many of them. But the vast majority are still working loyally and doing what they can, at the mercy of events, and hoping. Like anyone else, they wonder what is going to happen to themselves, their wives, their children. They go to their work through bullets and bombs. I put this down as a tribute to the ordinary decent Arab and Jew and to the British who trained them. Many of them have already lost relatives, property and friends, but they go on...On the civil side we have really only one essential thing left to carry through -- the paying off of all the abolition benefits to our officers. This is a vast operation, involving over 20,000 computations and the payment of about £2 m. in cash over all Palestine in face of the risk of theft and attack. But to this at least we are pledged.[298]

The Jerusalem British community sent a committee to meet with Sir Henry Gurney to discuss their future. He told them that nobody was being officially advised to leave, since individual cases were so disparate. Some 100 British residents proposed to stay on after 15 May, and had made plans for emergency accommodations, mutual aid, rationing and evacuation if necessary. " It was naturally rather a depressing party", Gurney wrote.[299]

Random violence continued to claim civilian victims, and the general insecurity was heightened as ordinary criminals escaped almost daily from prisons. A junior Foreign Office official, arriving in Jerusalem to take up an assignment, commented on the eerie quiet of the city, "already smashed about by so much fighting, with shops and houses bricked up, others with the windows out, the main streets blocked by cement emplacements for the coming big battle, and everywhere barbed wire and control posts and troops permanently armed....the only noise is the noise of military movement. Elsewhere, there is the quiet, not of death, but of secrecy, preparation and hatred."[300]

Yesterday afternoon our Miss Thompson, who was acting Director of Social Welfare, was shot and killed in her car a few miles out of Jerusalem. She was to have left to-day and had gone to say goodbye to some friends. It seems that 2 Jews ran out into the road and poured bullets into her car. She was a wonderful person, who devoted herself to the people of this country and will never be forgotten by many of them....Several more prisoners escaped. Some now get away every day: yesterday's escapes from Acre include 5 British.[301]

"Every day now," Sir Henry Gurney wrote, "about 20 people are killed. Two bullets came quite close to-day; one going to the office this morning, and one outside the house to-night. These incidents become too numerous for words." He went on:

Since the Partition Resolution over 2,000 people have lost their lives because of it, and about 7,000 wounded. But no one is a whit better for it, or any less anxious to go on killing. It was a lovely spring afternoon, in which the Russian tower on the Mount of Olives stood sharp against a soft blue sky and the Mountains of Moab were etched with delicate, distant shadows. The mined wire of Yemin Moshe lay in the foreground as a dismal and sordid reminder of human degradation.....Fox-Strangways [reported that] at the Orient Palace in Damascus he had had the next bedroom to the Mufti. I wonder why the Arabs never object to their leaders living in comfortable hotels far from the scene: the same applies to the Jewish leaders in Tel Aviv.[302]

Gurney went on recording in the same even tone incidents of rail sabotage, continuing thefts of cars, "a big bang somewhere in the night", the near-critical shortage of oil in Jerusalem, and the coming necessity to ration electricity. Among other problems claiming his attention were the Jewish girls anxious to marry British policemen "in order to get out of the country", over fifty of them. And then, "summer almost came this afternoon, and as we came down from Government House at sunset, the sky, the towers of Jerusalem and the deep obscurities of the valleys had the colours of a Japanese print. A few red tracers floating across a very pale blue sky were like flowers blown in the wind."[303]

On 7 April, writing from Haifa, Arthur Kirby addressed a final appeal to the Chief Secretary, pointing out that incessant sniping and sabotage were claiming the lives of his railway workers, and that loyal staff were demoralized by the spectacle of British security forces not only refusing to intervene, but sometimes actively participating in the looting of railway assets. Older workers, who "always continue doggedly at work no matter what the conditions" were "becoming increasingly bitter at the absence of security measures to permit them to continue in their work." Conceding that centralised control of the railways had broken down, with telephone wires cut and equipment stolen all along the line, Kirby pleaded for cooperation: "I feel that if, even at this late stage, we could show some semblance of an attempt to provide some of the security measures which the men ask for we might be able to continue to operate until the end."[304]

In Jerusalem Gurney reported siege conditions: the water pipe-line was blown up, and water supplies for the Jewish quarters were becoming critically short. Sabotage on the rail line meant that fuel trains were not getting through, threatening a shutdown of electricity. With the departure of the British stenographers on 8 April, the remaining officers of the Administration were writing their own letters by hand. His sleepless nights were filled with the sound of explosions and heavy firing, and there were daily casualties within the so-called security zone. Thefts of cars were now so common that virtually all Gurney's officers had lost their vehicles. Elsewhere in Palestine, "the Railway, after all its gallant efforts, is now just about finished", a few trains still running with military crews. Gurney played five sets of tennis one afternoon "in an effort to dispel some of the funereal gloom."[305]

Again interrupting his narrative, Gurney set forth his apologia for the Mandate:

In the thirty years of its life the Mandatory Administration of Palestine, aided by Jewish finance, skill and enthusiasm, had transformed a poor and backward territory into a prosperous and progressive country equipped with all the services of modern western civilisation. For centuries under the Turks Palestine had lain neglected and forlorn, without roads, without water supplies, without a railway and almost without schools and hospitals. All the love professed by the three great monotheistic religions for Jerusalem had never furnished it with even a water supply. The Church of the Holy Sepulchre stood in danger of collapse. There were no telephones. The life of the fellahin pursued its slow round of dust, disease and debt. So had it been since the days of the Old Testament. Then suddenly, for the first time in its long history, Palestine awoke and became rich. First-class roads and water-supplies, schools and hospitals, electric power and agricultural research stations, ports and railways followed the inflow of Zionist capital to redeem the Holy Land. For some years the resources of the Administration remained modest; not until 1938 did revenue exceed £7 million, rising in 1947 to £25 million. The Administration's budget never equalled what the Jews raised from and spent on themselves, but was sufficient to provide first-class services and a judicial system unique in the Middle East for its freedom from corruption and other similar Levantine traditions. In this material field the British succeeded better than they knew. The Palestine Government, with its 450 British officers (apart from the Police) and 17,000 Palestinians was an efficient and up-to-date machine to which many hundreds of public servants, British, Jew and Arab had devoted their lives. But all the time, even as far back as 1920 and right up to 1947, there was the uncomfortable feeling that this great superstructure was built upon sand, because there could be no political agreement between Arabs and Jews as to the ultimate purpose of the Mandate. For thirty years the British Government worked for this agreement and for thirty years both sides rejected it....It is true to say that, in spite of all their efforts to find a bridge by which agreement could be reached, the British Government never had a Palestine policy of their own....From 1945 onwards terrorism was used by the Zionists as a political weapon, in spite of all the words of condemnation uttered against it and in face of the advice of the more mature Zionist leaders who saw in this deliberate campaign of murder and bloodshed the negation of the teachings of Judaism and of true Zionist aspirations. .... Many people [after the UN vote for partition in November 1947] began to recognize that the British had in fact never been anything but the stake-holders [in Palestine], concerned only to see justice done and to prevent both sides from gaining their ends by violence.....The blame for starting the actual fighting lay fairly equally with both Arabs and Jews.[306]

One "desperately busy" Saturday morning, Gurney wrote, "an insoluble problem came in every half-hour", including the evacuation of German and American citizens; the removal of Hadassah Hospital staff from besieged Mount Scopus; a breakdown in the water supply; clearing the railway of a bombed locomotive to permit passage of essential oil trains; deciding the future of Lydda airport and its foreign services; the maintenance of currency supplies and banking services; and urgent requests by both Arabs and Jews to rescue beleaguered units of their respective forces. Sniping and mortar attacks went on all day; yet another British official had his car stolen while breakfasting in the Club; more deaths by random fire were reported in the Zone.[307]

Toward the end of April, even the indomitable Miss Norman was required to leave Jerusalem and her school, which by then had very few pupils left. Writing to her parents from the comparative safety of St. George's Close, seat of the Anglican Bishop in Jerusalem, she reported "we had notice from Government to be ready to start from here on Wednesday early. Then we have one or two nights in a camp at Jenin & go on to Haifa probably on Friday. It will be Government convoy all the way & doubtless safe & slow as mass movements are inclined to be. We've spent a busy week packing up the school. Most of the property is now bricked up in downstairs rooms & a few of the most vital things are down here at St. George's."[308]

Despite the evacuation of virtually all British staff, the business of Government went on, and as the urgent tasks dwindled a sort of melancholic boredom set in:

> Next week's Gazette may be our last, as the Printing staff will not stay much longer. On the whole the loyalty and continued devotion of our Arab and Jewish staff in increasingly disheartening circumstances is remarkable. We have now only six British officers left in the Secretariat, but our Arabs, Jews, Greeks and Armenians are all working fairly cheerfully. One has the feeling that anything may happen at any time. The garden is now at its best, and I picked a large bunch of sweet peas yesterday. These are flowering among wallflowers, irises, cyclamen, stocks and violets -- all at the same time.....These days, beautiful though they would be under peaceful conditions are becoming terribly monotonous. The feeling that nothing you can do is likely to make much difference anyhow is fairly exasperating, but even more so when it is accompanied by lies and chicanery on the part of both the Jews and Arabs whom one is trying to help. Mail from London has now ceased, and we only get telegrams; though much too many of these, ...[309]

Reflecting on the paradox of the Mandate's continuing half-existence, Gurney wrote that "we are staying now merely to get out, and by staying on make getting out more difficult.... whereas until recently we were staying on to help the Army to get out, now the Army is staying on because for political reasons we are not allowed to go, although the Army wants us to. It is quite clear that the situation in Jerusalem is not appreciated in London."[310] He recorded the next day, "a ridiculous day," a cascade of new crises from early morning to evening:

The Railway headquarters were completely burnt down in the fighting at Haifa, and all records destroyed, which presumably means that all the final pay papers for the Railway staff have gone. This morning in Jerusalem the Accountant-General's office lost £18,000 on the steps of Barclay's Bank (Post Office pay), though whether through attack or collusion is not clear. Later came reports that the Haganah had taken over the Migration Department and had seized 1,500 unused British passports. Then Graves, Chairman of the Jerusalem Municipal Commission, came in to say he proposed to go on the 6th May and there was now no quorum for the Commission anyhow and who should sign the cheques. The 250 Arab prisoners at Latrun now seem likely to attain their liberty as soon as the warders are paid off on the 26th. Cable & Wireless now propose to remove their telecommunications unit to Amman on the 28th, which the Foreign Office say they favour. But they may not have appreciated that this will cut Jerusalem off from the outside world, as no landlines in Palestine are now functioning. This move of cutting off Jerusalem is an excellent one from our point of view, as we should get less nonsense to deal with.[311]

A day later, "the Government's authority is being flouted right and left by both sides, and what good this prolongation of these humiliating conditions does to anybody is hard to see." But Gurney nonetheless worked on, in the absence of his secretary writing all notes and letters in longhand; bidding farewell to officers; coping with wholesale disappearance of staff and materiel: "one of the last two Secretariat cars was stolen this morning, and a British constable killed, for the sake of his arms, in Mamilla Road this afternoon."[312]

The fiery destruction of Khoury House, the Palestine Railways headquarters in Haifa, was the last straw for Mr. Kirby, who in a final letter to the Chief Secretary poured out all his frustration and bitter anger:

the situation in which we now find ourselves would not have been anything like so bad if only I could have been given a warning to evacuate
essential documents, etc. from the Headquarters offices....I have been
expected to carry on the railway and ports under almost impossible conditions; I have taken upon myself risks and responsibilities which have
seldom, if ever fallen upon the General Manager of a Colonial Railway; I
have achieved more than could have been hoped for -- yet I am not,
apparently, thought to be sufficiently responsible or worthy of confidence
to be informed of operations which were so vitally to affect the work of
myDepartment and the welfare of the thousands of people who have
given their services loyally to the railways for many years. It is a fitting
culmination to the disillusionment which I have suffered during my
recent years of service in Palestine -- but I never expected the final disillusionment to be so catastrophic or severe -- nor did I expect such harsh
confirmation of the bitterly disappointing realisation that I can expect no
more from the Colonial Service and that, for my self respect, I must seek
retirement, and enter a new field of endeavour.[313]

Gurney went on methodically cataloguing the collapse in slow motion of
his administration and all public order: the Arab guard on his house was
reduced to one, when all were paid up to 15 May and the majority deserted;
the Jewish staff at Lydda airport walked out, taking with them essential bits
of radio equipment; almost all prisoners escaped from Acre prison, leaving
only some criminal lunatics; one young colleague was casually killed for his
money on the steps of Barclays Bank, another shot dead within the so-called
Security Zone; the director of the Labour Department, inspecting his bomb-
wrecked office, had his despatch case pilfered within minutes, and forthwith
decided to quit.

Gurney noted that he and his remaining colleagues were now in danger
from Arabs as well as Jews:

The trouble is that there are really no responsible Arabs to see. They always say it is necessary to refer the matter to Damascus or Cairo and then never produce an answer at all. There is certainly a growing anti-British feeling among the Arabs, largely as a result of Haifa and the refugees that have left there since the Jewish attack. Since Arab opinions are governed by emotions rather than facts, this tendency can very quickly spread and is another reason why the extrication of the Govt. and the garrison from an impossible position in Jerusalem becomes daily more pressing. It is not as though we could conceivably do any good by staying. All the bad hats of Arabia seem to be here.[314]

But certain government functions went on, including the final meeting of the High Commissioner's Advisory Council: "a handful of officials sitting in the ballroom of Government House by heaps of stacked furniture solemnly going through the rigmarole of passing legislation about the Transjordan Frontier Force".[315] Almost equally stolid in denial, the General Manager of Palestine Railways issued his final orders:

The intention of the Management is that the Railways will be kept in operation and handed over on the 15th May as a going concern. The severe loss of Khoury House, Headquarters, and the secession of Arab staff in Haifa will not interfere with this intention..... The Superintendent of the Line will make all arrangements for the continuity of traffic in the Haifa area and as far South as Hadera. He will also ensure an adequate system of documentation.....All the staff reporting for duty will be allocated to the best advantage, irrespective of the Branch in which they have hitherto been employed.[316]

The penultimate civilian convoy left Jerusalem on 28th April, about 100 British, including many heads of Palestine Government departments. "It was quite a bit of history, though it didn't look like it," Gurney recorded. "Air passengers in old mackintoshes are not a stirring sight. But this party represented the main body of the Government leaving Jerusalem, the Holy City, in the early light of a grey morning: policemen in blue in their green armoured cars: the parting of many friends and the finish, in some cases, of a life's work. The Press and the photographers missed it, and it all went off soberly and quietly, with handshakes and some rather studiously casual waves, hiding all kinds of thoughts and emotions. None of us would have had it otherwise; every sign of sentiment had been magnificently dulled."[317]

In his final official memorandum to the Chief Secretary, Mr. Kirby reported widespread looting and destruction of railway equipment, the theft of his own car at gunpoint by armed Jews, and a virtually complete breakdown in communications following the destruction of Khoury House and the collapse of telephone and telegraph services. "I fear," he concluded, "that any ordinary hand-over of the railways is now impossible... I hope to get some trains operating as far as Hadera or Benyamina today, but I fear that in present circumstances it will be almost impossible to reconstitute any stable administrative organisation before the end of the Mandate...." As to ports, Kirby was able to report that Haifa was continuing to function "very well in the circumstances" with Jewish staff, but that all contact had broken off with Jaffa. Appalled by the rapidly approaching vacuum in authority, Kirby proposed to request the Mayor of Haifa to take over remaining port and railway assets in the Haifa area.[318]

Another conscientious official, John F. Spry, acting head of the Department of Land Registration, made extraordinary efforts to safeguard and photograph the massive registry books documenting ownership of property throughout Palestine. Aided by loyal Arab and Jewish staff, Spry succeeded despite siege conditions in filming key documents going back to Ottoman times, and storing the irreplaceable original volumes under Red Cross protection in the Jerusalem YMCA building.[319]

By 29 April, Gurney and his remaining staff had removed to the comparative safety of the King David Hotel. The Government of Palestine had virtually ceased to function: "the Courts have stopped, and so has the Post
Office, except for urgent and official telegrams; nearly all our prisoners have
escaped, and the prisons are not functioning either." He described coming
into "our prison, the King David", where "Hamburger, the Manager, went to
great trouble to furnish rooms for us and provide a dinner according to King
David standards, which are as high as anywhere in the world. We sat down
to a seven course dinner, beautifully cooked and served, and decided that
this sort of thing, with the whole day in the office chair, would soon kill us.
But I am bound to say it is a not unpleasant form of prison for the time
being."[320] Ever the meticulous executive, Gurney described his administration's task: "to cut off the branch on which it was sitting. The branch must
hold until May 15th but must fall exactly on that day. Sometimes we did a
little too much cutting and the situation had to be restored by patching and
at other times we were in danger of being left with too much cutting to do at
the last minute. In the end, from the purely British standpoint, the whole
programme was completed accurately and precisely to an hour."[321] His
other preoccupations were to achieve a truce in Jerusalem, an object that
was only sporadically attained; and to find plausible authorities to take over
and maintain essential services, without incurring charges of favouritism to
either of the warring parties in Palestine.

Summing up his time in office, Gurney wrote:

In these last years the Administration's greatest handicap was that the
political direction of the two contending parties lay outside Palestine. We
were never able to bring the two sides together to a common table at
which the Government's authority could be used in mediation, because
the Jewish leaders were in New York and the Arab leaders in Cairo.
Whenever we attempted to come to grips with a problem, it slipped from

our grasp into the ring of domestic politics in the United States or into the mysterious arena of the Arab League, in neither of which could the Government of Palestine be itself a protagonist. The truth was that almost all our issues were international problems.... Britain's endeavours were throughout used in support of moderation and to persuade the League governments to resist popular clamour and seek a peaceful solution. But the clamour was as loud in their ears as the noise of the Zionists in election year in America. Finally, it should not be forgotten that the undertaking given by Britain to facilitate the establishment of a Jewish National Home in Palestine represented the only attempt made by any nation in history to help the Jews. It ended in ingratitude, bitterness and tragedy only because the Zionists wanted more than they had been given and turned against Britain in their determination to achieve their object. Meanwhile, those who have served in Palestine and have some acquaintance with its story are well content to leave their actions, their successes and their failures, to the judgment of history.[322]

Even as Gurney was writing that "the cleaners have left now and it is extraordinary what important people messengers and cleaners are -- when you haven't got them", the District Commissioner in Lydda, W. V. Fuller, was still engaged in his duties, which often involved trying to arrange local truces for humanitarian reasons. Going about his business unarmed, because "I felt that my best protection was the good-will & trust of the people in my District", Fuller would meticulously inform his Arab and Jewish District Officers each time he wished to cross the no-man's land, "a sniper's paradise", between Jaffa and Tel Aviv:

I then went alone in my car. Though it was a harrowing experience driving alone through a deserted area knowing that there were expert unseen gunmen all around, I just looked straight ahead trying to appear as nonchalant as I could. Both sides honoured the trust I placed in them. These were the only times when no shots were fired in No-Man's-land.... On the afternoon of 13th May the Army arranged a special ceremony for the lowering of the Union Jack at my office. It was pathetic in so far as there were no members of the public present to witness such an historic ceremony -- but it was very touching to me. At 6 p.m. that night I walked up alone to the flagstaff over my house, saluted the flag, and hauled it down for the last time.[323]

"Really the Arabs are rabbits," Gurney wrote in a rare display of exasperation, recording that most of the population of Jaffa had fled, that almost all the better off class of Palestine Arabs had discovered urgent business in Beirut or Cairo, and that "the remnants of the Liberation Army are looting and robbing. This is what the Palestine Arabs get from the assistance provided by the Arab States. Perhaps our warnings to the States not to indulge in such premature military action were not always strong enough. True it is that this ill-organized and stupid intervention, in defiance of all our protests, has cost the Palestine Arabs dearly, and one could almost say that it is all over bar the shouting and the re-opening of the Jewish road to Jerusalem." He added: "everything begins to have a very 'end of term' air. Cupboards full of files and maps and records that haven't been looked at for years suddenly come out into the light of day, and stand about waiting for some one strong enough to shift them. At 4.30 this morning, the sun came up behind the Old City, and all the towers and domes of the Mount of Olives and the Dormition sharpened into silhouettes. It is one of the world's most beautiful and most intriguing views. But in the Old City typhoid was diagnosed yesterday. We had been hoping to avoid this."[324]

On 10 May, Mr. Kirby wrote his handing-over memorandum to P.C.J. Baker,Superintendent of the Line, appointing him Acting General Manager until 15 May, and confirming arrangements to hand over the port and railways in Haifa to the Municipality. Even at this juncture, he instructed his successor to keep the trains running from Haifa to Hadera, and to try clearing the lines South, working toward Egypt those wagons of the Egyptian State Railways still trapped north of Lydda. Kirby himself left Palestine on 12 May, embarking on a civilian transport that carried most of the remaining Palestine administration back to England.[325]

The following day, Gurney assembled his remaining staff, some 100 of them, and bade them farewell:

> I gave them a short speech of thanks and said goodbye to them. Several were on the edge of tears, and all were genuinely sad. I said that by its very nature the Mandate could not last for ever, and the end had always had to come some time; they could be proud of belonging to the best administration Palestine had ever had -- which is true -- and that we should not forget them. All of them -- Jews, Arabs, Greeks and Armenians -- who have served us loyally and in many cases devotedly have had all they could do to carry on these last few months, but accept their fate with no recrimination and a friendly understanding. The Prime Minister sent us a particularly good message of thanks yesterday. The Palestine Post have published it under the heading 'Blaze of Glory'. They remain masters of the innuendo. The Jewish Press at the moment is surpassing itself, but no one takes any notice of it.[326]

That afternoon, he played tennis: "if anyone had told me three months ago that we should be playing tennis within three days of the end of the Mandate, I should have laughed at him. But in fact we have run out of work."

In Haifa, the last British Chief Accountant to Palestine Railways wrote a formal note to his Jewish successor, meticulously accounting for what remained of the Palestine Railways finance office:

In view of the termination of the Mandate you will take over charge of the Accounts Branch on 14th May 1948.... Keys of the Cash Office and the safes therein will be handed over to you against signature. The keys of the safe deposit boxes in Barclays Bank Haifa have already been returned to the Bank....You have already taken over the Ticket Printing and Stationery Office at Haifa East and also the remains of the Accounts Office at Khoury House.... Mr. Bate has handed you the key of the padlock of his desk. In the top drawer of the desk is a bunch of keys one of which is for the safe containing all duplicate keys and particulars thereof. There are also the keys of the Phoenix safe and of various cupboards. Inside the Phoenix safe are two spare motors for the Accounting Machines... and several sporting trophies -- football cups.....also an automatic pistol my own personal property which please hand over to the proper authorities.... I take this opportunity of thanking you most sincerely for your long and valuable service with the Palestine Railways and wishing you a happy and prosperous future.[327]

Gurney and his handful of officers were now engaged in final plans for the High Commissioner's departure: the Mandate was scheduled officially to end at midnight on 14 May. "We telegraphed London asking that our families should be advised, since we have had no mails from the outside world for three weeks; and referred the Colonial Office to Isaiah chapter 37 verse 32: 'out of Jerusalem shall go forth a remnant and they that escape from Mount Zion'."[328]

The Government offices at the King David Hotel now stood bare; with boxes and cupboards gone, the rooms began "to look once more as though they might belong to a hotel." The Police locked up their stores, worth over £1 million, and brought the keys to the United Nations representative, who initially refused to receive them, but then relented. When asked what he planned to do upon departure with the keys to his own office, Sir Henry

Gurney is reported to have told a visiting Jewish delegation, "I suppose that I shall just put them under the mat". This exchange may have given rise to the durable myth that, in the absence of a plausible recipient, Gurney did precisely that.[329]

The Palestine Government ended with exactly two cars left in Jerusalem, all the rest having been stolen. On the afternoon of 13 May, Gurney called formally on the commanding officers of the Highland Light Infantry, Suffolks and Warwicks, to thank them for their efforts. "The C.O. of the H.L.I. pointed to his casualty list." Very early on the 14th, as the sun came up over the Mount of Olives, the nightly shooting stopped, and the last British convoy formed outside the King David with its cargo of seventeen civilians in two cars and a bus, escorted by four Police armoured cars. The Union Jack was lowered, and the Red Cross flag raised on the King David roof.

In Allenby Square and along the route were tanks and troops, obviously out in strength and happy to be going. At this early hour only a few Arabs were about, and they waved us cheerfully on. At Kalandia airstrip and along all the road leading to it were more troops and guns, covering every danger point. This operation of withdrawal we had at one time thought would be thoroughly difficult. In the event, with the reinforcements we had and with the admirable organization that Brigadier Jones applied, the whole plan worked out completely smoothly and without a shot fired. At 8.oo the High Commissioner inspected the H.L.I. guard-of-honour at Government House, and left a few minutes later, the Red Cross having taken the place of the Union Jack. At Kalandia he said goodbye to us, and flew off to Haifa for the last ceremonies there. We then entered our Dakotas and flew to Ramat David, where our York picked us up and flew off at 11.oo for Malta and Heath Row. We landed at Heath Row on a perfect summer night at 11.3o. As we drove into London, the clocks struck midnight and the Mandate was ended.

We had thought out and planned this last day so often, that its historical importance had long given way in our minds to details of timing and
transport. Nothing was left to chance. This bare and naked narrative
leaves untouched the mountains of paper and telegrams that had been
devoted to it. In the end, like all well-organized operations, it all looked
very simple.[330]

The night before, the Palestine Broadcasting Service had come to an end
with a broadcast by the High Commissioner, in which he said: "the final
page in the history of Palestine and the British mandate in Palestine is
turned. On the morrow a new chapter opens and Palestine's history goes
on....if it shall be that by our going we bring eventual good to the people of
Palestine, none of us will cavil at our departure." There was a pause, then the
playing of "God Save the King". "In the silence that followed," Gurney
wrote, "you could think what you liked; the thoughts of most of us were
woven against a vast background of difficult problems solved and hard work
done, and our consciences were clear. But perhaps, at that short range, we
missed the full point of what was happening: a page of history was turning
over. "[331] Others who lived through the same historical moment left with
stronger feelings of regret, mixed with shame. H.M.O. Lester, Director of
Medical Services, after two years of heroic efforts to keep his department
functioning, experienced in the last weeks of the Mandate a collapse in
morale, the flight of his senior Arab staff, widespread looting and the casual
murder of medical personnel within hospital grounds and en route to their
duties. "During the last fortnight there was no administration" throughout
the health service, and communications with outlying hospitals and clinics
broke down completely. "When the end came on 14th May," Dr. Lester
wrote, "one felt a feeling of relief at leaving Palestine with a whole skin, a
feeling of disapointment at the collapse of a fine Service, and a feeling of
shame at leaving the Arab hospital staff in Jerusalem to wave their Red

Cross flags at the lines of armed Jews drawn up to take the zone. So the British left Palestine."[332]

Nigel David Clive, taking up his post as British Vice Consul in Jerusalem, wrote of the last day of the Mandate:

The arrival of three of the High Commissioner's servants made breakfast an advance on anything produced by the Suffolks. With two fried eggs inside me I went up to the roof to watch HE's forlorn little procession creep down St. Louis's Way and turn left at the Damascus Gate along the road to Ramalla and on to Haifa. At midnight he will embark and the mandate ends. His car, preceded by a little armour, passed at about 8.30 a.m. I think the early start must have been kept a comparative secret because there could not have been more than twenty Arabs outside the Damascus Gate, a handful of whom clapped childishly and one saluted. The salute was returned. This was how the seventh and last High Commissioner left Jerusalem. While realising that he might disagree, I felt that departure in some sort of blaze, of fire more probably than glory, would have been a more fitting end. As it was, he left waved away by three or four handclappings. Not with a bang but a whimper. An hour later the Cease Fire was broken properly. By midday the shooting included mortars and an occasional haversack bomb....[333]

When General Sir Alan Cunningham reviewed the small guard of honour at Government House, the military band played "Auld Lang Syne" as well as "God Save the King". A large armoured Daimler limousine, specially made for the Royal family during the Blitz and lent to the High Commissioner, bore him in safety to the airstrip from which he flew to Haifa, again reviewing troops before boarding H.M.S. Euryalus, which remained in Palestine waters until midnight. Withdrawing without designating a successor, the British had not so much transferred power as abandoned it. The United

Nations, caught up in red tape and politics, had intended to send out a secretariat to take over essential services, but only a handful of officials were actually on the ground, and it was finally armed Arabs or Jews who stepped into the vacuum, grimly battling for strategic advantage even as the last British troops departed.

"In the end," Cunningham wrote a few months later, "the British were blamed for not having handed over to anyone, whereas, in point of fact, there was nobody to whom to hand over." The true problem, at the conclusion as at the beginning of the Mandate, was that there were indeed those to whom to hand over; but the British could never quite decide who they should be. During the brief thirty years of the Mandate many thousands of British men and women had lived and laboured in Palestine, and not a few had died on its soil, many of them violently. Some of these individuals were inspired by their tasks, others served out routine tours of duty, marking off long arid days of tedium or anxiety. Especially in the last days of the Mandate, whether running the remnants of a railway, teaching a handful of pupils, organizing to the last detail the winding-up of a government, they kept at their assigned posts with a feeling of workmanlike pride. Sir Henry Gurney, Arthur Kirby, Dorothy Norman, and all those many anonymous policemen, soldiers, secretaries, doctors and others were not responsible for the conflicting promises, the wishful thinking, the sheer muddle of British Palestine policy. Ordinary individuals caught up in an extraordinary sitation, they persisted in their tasks becausefor them it would have been unthinkable not to do so. All their efforts were seemingly mocked by the Holy Land itself. Riven by ancient hatreds, blood-soaked and tragic, Palestine after a fleeting historical moment spewed its British rulers forth. Some departed with regret, most with a sense of failure; by the bitter end, virtually all were glad to get away.

"English domination in the Middle East meant both an opportunity and a responsibility," wrote Elie Kedourie. "That the opportunity was missed, and the responsibility shirked is perhaps not surprising, since whatever happens of peace or security men enjoy seems the result more of providential good fortune than of prudent exertion."[334] There was no lack of exertion by the British in Palestine; providential good fortune, however, was always in short supply.

Notes

All quotations from letters and memoirs preserve the original spelling and punctuation. Principal collections are cited as follows:
Private Papers Collection, Middle East Centre, St Antony's College, Oxford: StAP
Library, Rhodes House, Oxford: RH
Department of Documents, Imperial War Museum: IWM

Preface

1   Benny Morris, *1948 and After: Israel and the Palestinians* (Oxford, 1990), p.29

chapter 1 ~ In the Beginning

2   C.R. Ashbee, *A Palestine Notebook, 1918–1923* (London, 1923), p.276
3   Quoted in Nicholas Bethell, *The Palestine Triangle* (New York, 1979), p.360
4   Quoted in Palestine Royal Commission, *Report*, Cmd. 5479, 1937 (hereafter Peel Report), p.22
5   *Ibid.*, p.370
6   Edward Said, *Orientalism* (New York, 1979), p.226
7   Quoted, *ibid.*, p.37
8   V.G. Kiernan, *The Lords of Human Kind: European attitudes towards the outside world in the Imperial Age* (London, 1969), p.131
9   R.H.S. Crossman, *Palestine Mission: A Personal Record* (New York, 1947), p.3
10 See Kathryn Tidrick, *Heart-Beguiling Araby* (London, 1981, rev. 1989), pp.207–19
11 Bridget Blackburne to mother, 30 July 1935, Blackburne Papers, RH ""

12 Stewart Perowne to father, 26 May 1926, StAP
13 H.E. Bowman, Diary, 30 January 1921, StAP
14 Ronald Storrs, *Orientations: the Memoirs of Sir Ronald Storrs* (New York, 1937), p.357
15 *Ibid.*, p. 360
16 Crossman, *op. cit.*, p.131
17 Horace B. Samuel, *Unholy Memories of the Holy Land* (London, 1930), p.35
18 Crossman, *op. cit.*, p.123
19 *Ibid.*
20 *Ibid.*, p.130
21 H.E. Bowman, Diary, 10 June 1927, StAP
22 Owen Tweedy, quoted in Evyatar Friesel, "Through a Peculiar Lens: Zionism and Palestine in British Diaries, 1927–31", *Middle Eastern Studies*, vol. 29, No. 3, July 1993, p.424; and S. Perowne to father, 31 March 1926, StAP
23 G.E. Law, "Mediterranean Station", typescript memoirs, 81/8/1, IWM
24 Crossman, *op. cit.*, p.163
25 Sir Michael Hogan, quoted in Hadara Lazar, *Hamandatorim: Erets Yisrael, 1940–1948* (Jerusalem, 1990), p.86
26 Kiernan, *op. cit.*, p.131
27 Said, *op. cit.*, p.1
28 Kathryn Tidrick, *Empire and the English Character* (London, 1990), p.4
29 John Beames, *Memoirs of a Bengal Civilian* (London, 1990), p.221
30 Balfour in House of Commons debate on Egypt, 13 June 1910, quoted in Said, *op. cit.*, p.34
31 Tidrick, *Heart-beguiling Araby*, p.207
32 W.H. Deedes to Rose Deedes, 11 December 1917, StAP

33 Lord Milner to Bishop Hamilton Baynes, 1 April 1920, Milner MS. Dep. 47, Bodleian Library, Oxford
34 W.H. Deedes to Rose Deedes, 12 January 1918, StAP
35 Sir H. Gurney, Diary, 20 March 1948, StAP.
36 Edward Keith-Roach, *Pasha of Jerusalem* (London, 1994), p.53
37 Ashbee, Journal, 16 September 1918, *op. cit.*, p.20
38 John de V. Loder to mother, 4 May 1918, StAP
39 *Ibid.*, 7 June 1918, StAP
40 *Ibid.*, 14 September 1918, StAP
40 Kenneth Blackburne to mother, 21 July 1935, RH
42 Perowne, transcript of interview for Thames Television, 1978, StAP
43 R.F.G. Jayne to parents, 3 August 1930, 78/15/1, IWM
44 H.D. Myer to parents, 5 January 1919, StAP
45 Sydney Burr to parents, 29 April 1937, 88/8/1, IWM
46 J.C. Hurewitz, *The Struggle for Palestine* (New York, 1950), p.18
47 Quoted in C.R. Ashbee, *op. cit.*, p.7
48 Bernard Wasserstein, *The British in Palestine: the Mandatory Government and the Arab-Jewish Conflict 1917–1929* (Oxford, 2nd. ed., 1991), p.27
49 Covenant of the League of Nations, Article 22
50 *Ibid.*
51 The Peel Commission characterized the Jewish community in Palestine as a distinct "*imperium in imperio*". Peel Report, p.49
52 H.D. Myer to parents, 1 January 1919, StAP
53 Storrs, *op. cit.*, p.384
54 *Ibid.*, p.393
55 S.P. Emery, Diary, 26 October 1919, StAP
56 Storrs, *op. cit.*, p.390
57 H.D. Myer, letter to parents, 16 January 1919, StAP
58 Head of Palestine CID, quoted in Wasserstein, *op. cit.*, p.203
59 *Ibid.*, p.19
60 Storrs, *op. cit.*, p.404
61 Clara Struve Klingeman, Memoirs, StAP
62 Storrs, *op. cit.,*, p.442
63 S.P. Emery, Diary, 10 October 1919, StAP
64 Ronald Hyam, *Empire and Sexuality: the British Experience* (Manchester, 1990), pp.61,110
65 H.E. Bowman, Diary, 20 December 1920, StAP

chapter 2 ~ Irrepressible Conflict: 1920–1929

66 Bernard Wasserstein, *Herbert Samuel, a Political Life* (Oxford, 1992), p.257
67 H.B. Samuel, *op. cit.*, p.66
68 H.E. Bowman, Diary, 4 March 1924, StAP
69 A. Kermack, "Memoir of Judicial Service 1920–30" (1978), StAP
70 Interview with Mrs Philippa Keith-Roach, 18 February 1995
71 Bridget Blackburne to mother, 16 January 1937, RH
72 Heather Teague to parents, 25 August 1936, StAP
73 *Ibid.*, 16 October 1936
74 Poston interview with Thames Television, StAP
75 Interview with R.D.N. Bird, 30 September 1995
76 Helen Harrison, Diary, 13 April 1925, StAP
77 Poston interview with Thames Television, StAP
78 *Ibid*
79 See Thomas Hodgkin, *Letters from Palestine, 1932–36* (London, 1986)
80 H.E. Bowman, Diary, 1 March 1921, StAP
81 Hurewitz, *op. cit.*, p.25
82 Quoted in Royal Institute of International Affairs, *Great Britain and Palestine, 1915–1945* (London, 1946), p.42
83 S.P. Emery, Diary, StAP
84 H.C. Luke, Diary, 23 May 1921, StAP
85 "and prayed very well"; *ibid.*, 4 June 1923, StAP

86 Stewart Perowne, interview with Thames Television, StAP
87 Edwin Samuel, interview with Thames Television, StAP
88 A. Eisenberg, Committee of the Colony, Rehovot, to L.H.W. Nott, 12 May 1921,StAP
89 N. Nakhla, for Mayor of Gaza Municipality, to L.H.W. Nott, 26 June 1922, StAP
90 A.J. McNeil, Diary, 26 December 1923, StAP
91 *Ibid.*, 31 December 1923
92 Horace B. Samuel, *op. cit.*, p.91
93 *Ibid.*, p.191
94 Interview with R.D.N. Bird, 30 September 1995
95 Helen Harrison, Diary, 13 April 1925, StAP
96 Stewart Perowne, interview with Thames Television, StAP
97 Helen Harrison, Diary, 17 April 1925, StAP
98 *Ibid.*, 18 April 1925
99 *Ibid.*, 19 April 1925
100 *Ibid.*, 20 April 1925
101 *Ibid.*, 17 May 1925
102 Stewart Perowne, letter to father, 26 May 1926, StAP
103 Hector Bolitho, *Beside Galilee: a Diary in Palestine* (London, 1933), pp.105, 109
104 Jerome Farrell, "The Riots in Palestine, 1929", typescript, StAP
105 Amos Elon, *The Israelis: Founders and Sons* (2nd ed., London, New York 1981), p.157
106 S.P. Emery, Diary, StAP
107 H.B. Samuel, *op. cit.*, p.91
108 Stewart Perowne, interview with Thames Television, StAP
109 H.E. Bowman, Diary, 14 May 1922, StAP
110 *Ibid.*, 4 September 1929
111 *Ibid.*, 6 October 1929

chapter 3 ~ **Bowl of Scorpions: 1929–1939**

112 There is evidence that Hope Simpson reached his conclusions before investigation: see Friesel, *op. cit.*, p.430.
113 Quoted in Peel Report, p.73
114 Royal Institute of International Affairs, Information Department, *Great Britain and Palestine, 1915–1945* (London, 1946), p.45
115 Sir John Chancellor to son Christopher, 10 December 1929, Box 16/3 ffı5–28; Mss. Brit. Emp. s.284, RH.
116 Quoted in Bernard Wasserstein, *The British in Palestine*, p.15
117 R.F.G. Jayne, letters to mother, 24 July 1930, 15 August 1930, 78/15/1, IWM
118 *Ibid.*, 15 August 1930
119 *Ibid.*, 14 December 1930
120 Thomas Hodgkin, letter to mother, 6 June 1933, in *op. cit.*, p.36
121 Owen Tweedy, quoted in Friesel, *op. cit.*, p.424
122 C.G. Eastwood, Diary, 4 April 1933, Mss. Brit. Emp. s.509, 1/1A RH
123 *Ibid.*, 17 June 1933
124 *Ibid.*, 14 April 1933
125 *Ibid.*, December 1933
126 H.E. Bowman, Diary, 29 October 1933, StAP
127 *Ibid.*, 5 November 1933
128 S.J. Hogben, transcript of interview with A.H.M. Kirk-Greene, RH
129 Bridget Blackburne to mother-in-law, 27 October 1935, RH
130 D.A. Norman to family, 26 April 1936, StAP
131 Bridget Blackburne to sister, 27 April 1936, RH
132 Heather Teague to parents, 17 May 1936, StAP
133 D.A. Norman to family, 19 May 1936, StAP
134 Bridget Blackburne to mother, 27 May 1936, RH
135 Mabel C.Warburton to W.E Bickersteth, 14 June 1936, J&EM Box LXI/1, StAP
136 Heather Teague to parents, 24 June 1936, StAP

137 Kenneth Blackburne to mother, 5 July 1936, RH
138 R. Martin, "Reminiscences of the Palestine Police Force", Mss. Brit. Emp. s.514(1), RH
139 H.E. Bowman, Diary, 7 June 1936, StAP
140 S.P. Emery, Diary, StAP
141 Heather Teague to parents, 26 April 1936, StAP
142 H.E. Bowman, Diary, 22 August 1936, StAP
143 R. Martin, *op. cit.*
144 Sir A. Wauchope to H.E. Bowman, 19 September 1936, StAP
145 Hugh Blackburne to family, 8 May 1936, RH
146 R. Martin, *op. cit.*
147 Bridget Blackburne to mother-in-law, 23 November 1936, RH
148 *Ibid.*, 5 December 1936, RH
149 Bridget Blackburne to mother, 5 December 1936, RH
150 Kenneth Blackburne to father, 13 December 1936, RH
151 Kenneth Blackburne to mother, 18 October 1936, RH
152 E. Mills to Sir John Chancellor, 30 August 1936, Chancellor Papers, Box 17/4, f109; Mss. Brit. Emp. s.284, RH.2
153 Kenneth Blackburne to mother, 15 November 1936, RH
154 Kenneth Blackburne to father, 23 November 1936, RH
155 Peel Commission, *Report*, p.307
156 *Ibid.*, p.376
157 Winifred R. Coate to sister, 3 December 1937, J&EM Box LXI/2 StAP
158 Sydney Burr to parents, 19 December 1937, 88/8/1, IWM
159 *Ibid.*, 29 December 1937
160 Bridget Blackburne to mother, 10 March 1938, RH
161 Sydney Burr to parents, 24 February 1938, IWM
162 A. Morrison, "On the Road to - Anywhere!", 75/75/1, IWM
163 *Ibid.*

164 Lord Lloyd to Sir H. MacMichael, 18 March 1938, StAP
165 B.C. Gibbs, letter to fiancée, 6 April 1938, StAP
166 *Ibid.*, 16 April 1938
167 *Ibid.*, 24 April 1938
168 *Ibid.*, 25 May 1938
169 Sydney Burr to parents, 1 June 1938, IWM
170 B.C. Gibbs to fiancée, 12 April 1938, StAP
171 A.T.O. Lees to District Commissioner, Southern District, 25 October 1938, StAP
172 E.D. Forster, Journal, 19–20 August 1938, StAP
173 *Ibid.*, 5 November 1938
174 Major B.A. Pond, typescript memoirs, 78/27/1, IWM
175 Sydney Burr to parents, 5 February 1938, IWM
176 Ivan Lloyd Phillips to father, 25 July 1938, RH
177 Kenneth Blackburne to mother, 17 July 1938, RH
178 Ivan Lloyd Phillips to father, 31 July 1938, RH
179 *Ibid.*, 2 September 1938
180 John Loxton, typescript memoirs, StAP
181 Ivan Lloyd Phillips to father, 20 October 1938, RH
182 S.P. Emery, letter to family, 8 March 1939, StAP
183 Heather Teague to family, 20 October 1938, StAP
184 B.C. Gibbs to fiancée, 21 April 1938, StAP
185 Hurewitz, *op. cit.*, p.106
186 Heather Teague to parents, 10 June 1939, StAP

chapter 4 ~ **Varieties of War: 1939–1945**

187 Sir George Sanford, quoted by Sir John McPherson, interview with A.H.M. Kirk-Greene, 27 February 1968, Mss. Brit. Emp. s.487, RH
188 Christopher Sykes, *Crossroads to Israel* (London, 1973), p.212

189 E. Keith-Roach, *op. cit.*, p.223

190 E.D. Forster, Diary, 18 May 1939, StAP

191 Ivan Lloyd Phillips to father, 2 July 1939, RH

192 Quoted in Hurewitz, *op. cit.*, p.111

193 Haining to Secretary of State for War, 30 July 1939, StAP

194 R. Martin, *op. cit*

195 Sydney Burr to parents, 10 October 1939, IWM

196 Heather Teague to parents, 9 August 1939, StAP

197 Ivan Lloyd Phillips to father, 3 September 1939, RH

198 Heather Teague to parents, 16 September 1939, StAP

199 Ivan Lloyd Phillips to father, 3 October 1939, RH

200 Sir John Shuckburgh minute, quoted in B. Wasserstein, *Britain and the Jews of Europe* (Oxford, 1979), p.69

201 Nicholas Bethell, *op. cit.*, p.99

202 T.M. Snow minute, quoted in Wasserstein, *op. cit.*, p.77

203 Edward Ullendorff, *The Two Zions* (Oxford, 1988), p.66

204 Barbara S. Thompson, "Travels of Tatah, 1938–1945", StAP

205 D.A. Norman to family, 6 October 1940, StAP

206 Ivan Lloyd Phillips to father, 22 December 1940, RH

207 D.A. Norman to family, 20 April 1941, StAP

208 *Ibid.*, 4 May 1941

209 *Ibid.*, 14 July 1941

210 Ivan Lloyd Phillips to father, 11 August 1941, RH

211 *Ibid.*, 11 November 1941

212 Sir John MacPherson, interview with A.H.M. Kirk-Greene, 27 February 1968, Mss. Brit. Emp., s.487, RH

213 Wasserstein, *op. cit.*, p.155

214 Ivan Lloyd Phillips to father, 27 November 1939, RH

215 Quoted in Wasserstein, *op. cit.*, p.173

216 Christopher Sykes, *op. cit.*, p.240

217 R. Martin, *op. cit*

218 *Ibid*

219 G.E. Law, *op. cit.*

220 Christopher Holm, quoted in Hadara Lazar, *op. cit.*, p.118

221 Law, *op. cit.*, p.172

222 *Ibid.*

223 Ivan Lloyd Philips to his father, 17 December 1939, R.

224 Law, *op. cit.*, p.172

225 J.H. Witte, "The One That Didn't Get Away", typescript memoirs, 87/12/1, IWM

226 *Ibid.*

227 "The Second World War Diary of Capt. R. Askwith", typescript, 91/2/1. 13.9.42, IWM

228 J.H. Dunn to sister, 20 September 1943, 93/4/1, IWM

229 Churchill note of 6 July 1945, quoted in Bethell, *op. cit.*, p.201

230 D.A. Norman to family, 21 April 1945, StAP

231 Ivan Lloyd Phillips to father, 9 December 1945, RH

chapter 5 ~ **Endgame: 1945–1948**

232 *Olivia Manning, The Levant Trilogy: The Sum of Things* (London, 1983), p.507

233 Wm. Roger Louis, *The British Empire in the Middle East, 1945–1951* (Oxford, 1984), p.384

234 *Ibid.*, p. 386, from Parliamentary debate, 1 August 1946

235 Christopher Sykes, *op. cit.*, p.276

236 Ivan Lloyd Phillips to father, 9 February 1946, RH

237 M.K. Burgess to family, 28 April 1946, RH

238 *Ibid.*, 22 June 1946

239 Ivan Lloyd Phillips interview with Thames Television, StAP

240 Ivan Lloyd Phillips to father, 28 July 1946, RH

241 J.V.W. Shaw to R.H.S. Crossman, 2 August 1946, Crossman Papers, StAP

242 M.K. Burgess to family, 26 July 1946, RH

243 Lt. General Sir Evelyn Barker to Lt. General John C. D'Arcy, 29 July 1946, StAP

244 Ivan Lloyd Phillips to father, 15 September 1946, RH
245 Sir John Fletcher-Cooke, memoir, "The Compulsive Cuppa", StAP
246 M.K. Burgess to family, 15 September 1946, RH
247 Incident described in Bethell, *op. cit.*, p.280
248 *Ibid.*, p.323
249 Sir John Fletcher-Cooke, memoir, StAP
250 Ivan Lloyd Phillips to father, 8 December 1946, RH
251 D.A. Norman to family, 3 November 1946, StAP
252 Crossman, *op. cit.*, p.38
253 Creech-Jones statement, 25 February 1947, quoted in Louis, *op. cit.*, p.462
254 M.K. Burgess to family, 23 November 1946, RH
255 Irgun poster, 1946, Central Zionist Archives, Jerusalem
256 Ivan Lloyd Phillips to father, 17 January 1947, RH
257 Quoted in Bethell, *op. cit.*, p. 301.
258 R.W. Hamilton to wife, 2 February 1947, in *Letters from the Middle East of an Occasional Archaeologist* (Durham, 1992)
259 M.K. Burgess to family, 1 February 1947, RH
260 *Ibid.*, 4 February 1947
261 R.W. Hamilton to wife, 4 February 1947, *op. cit*
262 Maj. General R. Gale, GOC, 1st Inf. Div., "Report on Operation Elephant", Leray papers, StAP
263 Jack Denley, interview with Thames Television, StAP
264 Text quoted in Bethell, *op. cit.*, p.309
265 Quoted in Hurewitz, *op. cit.*, p.290
266 Quoted in Bethell, *op. cit.*, p.340
267 Ivan Lloyd Phillips to father, 3 August 1947, RH
268 Quoted in Louis, *op. cit.*, p.476
269 *Ibid.*, p.477
270 Bethell, *op. cit.*, p.351
271 R.W. Hamilton to wife, 7 October 1947
272 *Ibid.*, 29 October 1947
273 W.G. Fitzgerald to MacMichael, 8 November 1947, StAP
274 *Ibid.*
275 Bethell, *op. cit.*, p.353
276 John Wells Watson to family, September 1947, Watson Papers, IWM, quoted in Joanne Buggins, "The End of the British Mandate in Palestine: Reflections from the papers of John Watson of the Forces Broadcasting Service", *Imperial War Museum Review*, No.8, 1993
277 *Ibid.*, p.11
278 Bethell, *op. cit.*, p.353
279 R.W. Hamilton to wife, 11 December 1947
280 D.A. Norman to family, 14 December 1947, StAP
281 A. Kirby to Gurney, 17 December 1947, StAP
282 *Ibid.*, 20 January 1948, StAP
283 *Ibid.*
284 D.A. Norman to family, 25 January 1948, StAP
285 R.W. Hamilton to wife, 5 February 1948
286 A. Kirby, Letter to editors of Hebrew and Arab newspapers, presidents of Jewish and Arab Chambers of Commerce, 17 February 1948, StAP
287 John Higgins to wife, 19 February 1948, StAP
288 *Ibid.*, letters of 27, 28, 29 February 1948, StAP
289 D.A. Norman, letter to family, 22 February 1948, StAP
290 W.G. Fitzgerald to Sir H. MacMichael, 17 January 1948, StAP
291 R.W. Hamilton to wife, 23 February 1948
292 John Higgins to wife, 6 March 1948, StAP
293 Gurney, Diary, 15 March 1948, StAP
294 *Ibid.*, 24 March 1948
295 *Ibid.*, 25 March 1948
296 *Ibid.*, 27 March 1948
297 D.A. Norman to family, 28 March 1948, StAP
298 Gurney, Diary, 29 March 1948, StAP
299 *Ibid.*, 30 March 1948
300 Nigel David Clive, Diary, 28 April 1948, StAP
301 Gurney, Diary, 31 March 1948, StAP

302 *Ibid.*, 1 April 1948
303 *Ibid.*, 6 April 1948
304 A. Kirby to Gurney, 7 April 1948, StAP
305 Gurney, Diary, 15 April 1948, StAP
306 *Ibid.*
307 *Ibid.*, 17 April 1948
308 D.A. Norman to parents, 18 April 1948, StAP
309 Gurney, Diary, 20 April 1948, StAP
310 *Ibid.*, 21 April 1948
311 *Ibid.*, 22 April 1948
312 *Ibid.*, 23, 24 April 1948
313 A. Kirby to Gurney, 24 April 1948, StAP
314 *Ibid.*, 27 April 1948
315 *Ibid.*
316 General Manager's Circular No.14/48, 26 April 1948, StAP
317 Gurney, Diary, 28 April 1948, StAP
318 A. Kirby to Gurney, 28 April 1948, StAP
319 See Dov Gavish, "The British Efforts at Safeguarding the Land Records of Palestine in 1948", *Archives*, vol. XXII, no. 95 (1996), pp. 107–20
320 Gurney, Diary, 29 April 1948, StAP
321 *Ibid.*, 1 May 1948
322 *Ibid.*
323 W.V. Fuller, "Lowering the Flag", memorandum of June 1979, StAP
324 Gurney, Diary, 5 May 1948, StAP
325 A. Kirby, Note for P.C.J. Baker, Superintendent of the Line, 10 May 1948, StAP
326 Gurney, Diary, 11 May 1948, StAP
327 Note by W.D. Charlton, Chief Accountant, Palestine Railways to J.Beliavsky, MBE, Accountant, 11 May 1948, Kirby Papers, StAP
328 Gurney, Diary, 12 May 1948, StAP
329 See unsigned review in *Times Literary Supplement*, 15 April 1965, of Norman Bentwich, *Mandate Memories* and Christopher Sykes, *Crossroads to Israel*; also Walid Khalidi, "The Arab Perspective", in Wm. Roger Louis and Robert W. Stookey, eds., *The End of the Palestine Mandate* (Austin, 1986), p.132
330 Gurney, Diary, 14 May 1948, StAP
331 *Ibid.*
332 H.M.O. Lester, "The Department of Health, Palestine 1946-1948. The Decline and Fall", typescript memoir, RH
333 Nigel David Clive, Diary April–June 1948, StAP

Who Was Who

Blackburne, Sir Kenneth (1907–80). Marlborough and Clare College, Cambridge. Assistant District Officer, Nigeria, 1930; married 1935 Bridget Senhouse Constant Wilson; Assistant District Commissioner, Nazareth, Palestine, 1935; Acting District Commissioner, Galilee District, May–September 1938; withdrawn from Palestine because of death threats, and posted to Colonial Office, 1938; Colonial Secretary, The Gambia, 1941; West Indies, 1943–47; Director of Information Services, Colonial Office, 1946–50; Governor and Commander in Chief, Leeward Islands, 1950–56; Captain General and Governor in Chief, Jamaica, 1957–62; Governor-General of Jamaica, 1962, retired 1963. Published *Lasting Legacy: a Story of British Colonialism* (1976).

Bowman, Humphrey E. (1879–1965). Eton and New College, Oxford. Egyptian Civil Service, Ministry of Education, 1903–23; and Inspector of Education, Sudan, 1911–13. During First World War attached to Staff, Royal Fusiliers, in France, India, Mesopotamia. Director of Education, Iraq, 1918–20. Director of Education and Member of Advisory Council, Palestine, 1920–36. Between 1939 and 1945, special duty, Ministry of Information and Foreign Office. Published *Middle East Window* (1942).

Burgess, Mary K. (1919–). Leeds University, Honours degree in Geography. Taught in England 1939–45, then joined Church Mission to the Jews, and taught in English High School, Jaffa, from 1945 to

1947. After evacuation from Palestine in Operation Polly, taught at English Girls' College in Alexandria, then headed the Government Teachers' Training College in Kingston, Jamaica. From 1952 to 1957 served in Eastern Nigeria, helping to establish primary and secondary schools, as well as teacher training courses. Returning to England in 1957, she headed an independent school for girls in Exeter. Upon retirement in 1965, she was appointed Assistant Examiner for "O" level examinations under Cambridge University. She lives in Cornwall, where she is church organist, painter and bird-watcher.

Chancellor, Sir John Robert (1870–1952). Royal Military Academy, Woolwich. Commissioned in Royal Engineers in 1890, stationed in England, India, and then Staff College. Governor of Mauritius, 1911–16; Governor, Trinidad & Tobago, 1916–21; Governor, Southern Rhodesia, 1923–28; High Commissioner of Palestine, 1928–31. Riots of August 1929 and subsequent events shook Chancellor's faith in Government policy, and he left Palestine with disappointment and relief. He then served as chairman of several government committees, of the Royal Geographical, Royal Empire, Royal Africa societies, and was a Director of several companies.

Cunningham, General Sir Alan Gordon (1887–1983). Cheltenham College, University of Edinburgh, Royal Military Academy, Woolwich. Lieutenant in Royal Artillery, 1906. First World War in France, where won medals for gallantry. In Second World War was Division Commander, and in 1940 General Officer Commanding in East Africa, leading brilliant reconquest in four months of Italian East Africa. Commander 8th Army in North Africa, 1941; Commander, Staff College, 1942; Lt. General and GOC Northern Ireland, 1943.Promoted to General in 1945 and appointed seventh and last High Commissioner in Palestine, where he presided unhappily over winding down of the Mandate. In 1948 retired to Hampshire, where he was Deputy Lord Lieutenant and occupied various honorific military posts.

Eastwood, Christopher Gilbert (1905–83). Eton and Trinity College, Oxford. Home Civil Service, 1927; Colonial Office thereafter, Private Secretary to High Commissioner of Palestine, 1932–34; Secretary, International Rubber Regulation Committee, 1934; Private Secretary to Lord Lloyd and Lord Moyne, 1940–41; Principal Assistant Secretary, Cabinet Office, 1945–47; Assistant Under Secretary of State, Colonial Office, 1947–52 and 1954–66. Commissioner of Crown Lands, 1952–54; retired 1967.

Fitzgerald, Sir William J. (1894–1989). Trinity College, Dublin; served First World War, Durham Light Infantry, decorated; Barrister King's Inns, Dublin, and Middle Temple, 1922; Nigerian Administrative Service, 1920; Police Magistrate, Lagos, 1921; Crown Counsel, Nigeria, 1924; Solicitor-General and Attorney-General, Northern Rhodesia, 1933; Judge, Palestine, 1937–43; Chief Justice of Palestine, 1944–48; President, Lands Tribunal, 1950–65. He was

the last civilian official to depart from Palestine in 1948, leaving his official car on the quay at Haifa with the keys inside; and was one of the few old Palestine hands who after 1948 was always welcome at both the Israeli and Arab embassies in London.

Gort, sixth Viscount, Field Marshal, VC (1886–1946). Old Anglo-Irish nobility, educated Harrow and Sandhurst. Appointed Lieutenant in Grenadier Guards, 1905, then served in First World War, on staff and in combat on the Western Front, leading the 4th Battalion, Grenadier Guards. Repeatedly wounded, and awarded highest decorations for valour. Went on to Staff College and other senior assignments, and was appointed youngest Chief of Imperial General Staff and full General in 1937. Commander in Chief from September 1939 of the British Expeditionary Force in France, he organized the evacuation at Dunkirk after the French and Belgian collapse. Appointed Governor of Gibraltar in 1941 and Governor of Malta in 1942. As Governor, he became a local hero in helping the island withstand aerial bombardment and naval siege, organizing the feeding of a largely destitute population. He was promoted to Field Marshal in 1943 and in 1944 appointed sixth High Commissioner in Palestine. Well liked by all in Palestine, but became ill and had to resign after one year in office, dying soon after his return to England.

Gurney, Sir Henry L.G. (1898–1951). From Winchester, commissioned in 1917 in King's Royal Rifle Corps, and wounded in combat shortly before Armistice. Thereafter, University College, Oxford. Assistant District Commissioner, Kenya, 1921; then Secretary, to 1935; posted Jamaica, then Colonial Office, and again Kenya. From 1941 was Chief Secretary of Governors' Conference, Africa; Colonial Secretary of

Gold Coast, 1944; Chief Secretary, Palestine, 1946–48, where he won the admiration of his staff for his loyalty, clear decision-making and legendary imperturbability in crises. Appointed High Commissioner of Malaya in 1948, where a Communist-led terrorist campaign was approaching critical dimensions, he was killed in 1951 when his car was ambushed and he deliberately stepped into the road to draw fire away from Lady Gurney, riding with him, who remained unharmed.

Hamilton, Robert William (1905–95). Winchester, Magdalen College, Oxford. Chief Inspector of Antiquities, Palestine, 1931–38; Director of Antiquities 1938–48; Secretary-Librarian, British School of Archaeology, Iraq, 1948–49; Senior Lecturer in Near Eastern Archaeology, Oxford, 1949–56; Keeper, Department of Antiquities, Ashmolean Museum, Oxford, 1956–72; Keeper of Ashmolean Museum, 1962–72. Publications included works of Middle Eastern archaeological history.

Hodgkin, Thomas Lionel (1910–82). Winchester, Balliol and Magdalen Colleges, Oxford. Assistant Secretary, Palestine Civil Service, acting as Private Secretary to High Commissioner, 1934–36; after leaving Palestine and Government service was education officer in various trades union schools, then tutor and Secretary to the Oxford University Delegacy for Extra-Mural Studies, and Fellow of Balliol College, 1945–52; was also Director, Institute of African Studies, University of Ghana, 1962–65, Lecturer in Government of New States, Oxford, and Fellow of Balliol, 1965–70. Published numerous works on African history and politics.

Keith-Roach, Edward (1885–1954). After working for London and County Bank, 1902–08, joined the Mercantile Bank of

India in Bombay, 1908–14. In 1914, joined Lancashire Fusiliers as Lieutenant; promoted Major in 1915, posted to Egypt and Sudan. In Palestine from 1919, succeeded Sir Ronald Storrs and was District Commissioner, Jerusalem, 1938–43. Retired because of ill health, he published several books including *The Pageant of Jerusalem* and *Adventures among the Lost Tribes of Islam*.

Kirby, Sir Arthur F. (1899–1983). Educated grammar school, Marlow, then London School of Economics. Employed by Great Western Railway from 1917; then service with London Rifle Brigade and 2nd Rifle Brigade. Returning to G.W.R. after the war, he went through a six-year special training course. He joined the Colonial Service as Assistant Secretary, Takoradi Harbour, Gold Coast, in 1928; Traffic Manager, Gold Coast Railway, 1936; Assistant Superintendent of the Line, Kenya and Uganda Railways and Harbours, 1938; General Manager, Palestine Railways and Ports Authority, 1942–48, and Director-General of the Hejaz Railway; Superintendent of the Line, East African Railways and Harbours, 1949–50; Assistant Commissioner for Transport, East Africa High Commission, 1951–52; Acting Commissioner for Transport, 1952–56; General Manager, East Africa Railways and Harbours, 1953–57; KBE 1957; Commissioner of East African Common Services Organization, 1958–63; Chairman, British Transport Docks Board, 1963–67; Chairman, National Arts Council, 1967–71; President, Institute of Shipping and Forwarding Agents, Deputy Chairman, Royal Commonwealth Society; Chairman, Palestine Association; Member, Order of St John, and numerous charity boards, including Great Ormond Street Children's Hospital and Royal Society of Arts.

Lloyd Phillips, Ivan (1910–84). Selwyn College, Cambridge; Balliol College, Oxford.Colonial Administrative Service from 1934; Gold Coast, 1934–38; Palestine, 1938–47; District Commissioner, Gaza-Beersheba, 1946–47; Colonial Office, 1947–48; Cyprus, 1948–51; Commissioner, Nicosia-Kyrenia, 1950–51; Singapore, 1951–53; Commissioner-General's Office, 1951–52; Deputy Secretary for Defence, 1952–53; Malaya, 1953–62; Secretary to Chief Minister and Minister for Home Affairs, 1955–57; Secretary, Ministry of Interior, 1957–62; Secretary, Oxford Preservation Trust, 1962–65; Institute of Commonwealth Studies, Oxford, 1965–70; Chairman, Oxfordshire Playing Fields Association, 1966–77; President, 1977–84.

Luke, Sir Harry Charles (1884–1969). Eton and Trinity College, Oxford. Private Secretary to Governor, Sierra Leone, 1909; same in Barbados, 1911; various colonial posts, including Cyprus, until 1914. Political Officer on Army staff, Eastern Mediterranean, 1915–16; Chief British Commissioner in Georgia, Armenia, Azerbaijan, 1920; Assistant Governor of Jerusalem, 1920–24; Colonial Secretary, Sierra Leone, 1924–28, and then in Palestine. Acting for the absent High Commissioner in the summer of 1929, Luke was the senior British official when riots broke out, and was criticized in some quarters for insufficient appreciation of the seriousness of the disturbances. Appointed subsequently Lt. Governor of Malta, 1930; Governor of Fiji and High Commissioner for Western Pacific, 1938–43. In retirement he was for three years chief representative of the British Council in Caribbean. Wrote many travel books and a three-volume autobiography. Lived, in the words of Sir Ronald Storrs, "the most unwasted life of any man I have known."

MacMichael, Sir Harold (1882–1969). Magdalene College, Cambridge, First Class Honours in Classics and Arabic. Sudan Political Service, 1905; published books on tribes and on the Sudan; Governor of Tanganyika, 1933. Appointed High Commissioner of Palestine in 1938, he was the only High Commissioner to speak Arabic. Strictly enforcing Government policies, he was especially disliked by Jews, though his distant manner also alienated Arabs. In August 1944 an Irgun-Stern group attempted to assassinate him, after his term as High Commissioner was known to be drawing to a close, severely wounding his aide de camp and driver, and slightly wounding Lady MacMichael. He left Palestine shortly thereafter. In 1945-47 he worked on constitutional arrangements for Malaya, Malta, and East Africa. He wrote several books, including a two-volume history of the Arabs in the Sudan, and was a notable collector, not least of English pottery.

McNeill, Angus John., Brig. General (1874-1950). Harrow, then joined Seaforth Highlanders, 1895; Crete, 1897; Sudan, 1898; South Africa, 1899-1900; Staff, School for Infantry, 1904-08; served 1914-18 in France, the Balkans, Egypt, DSO and mentioned in despatches. In 1922-26 raised and then commanded British Gendarmerie in Palestine; after Gendarmerie disbanded, was Chief Stockbreeding Officer and head of the Government Stud at Acre until 1931, when retired. Continued to live on his farm in Western Galilee, undisturbed by Arab-Israeli wars, until his death in 1950.

Perowne, Stewart Henry, C.M.G. (1901-89). Haileybury College; Corpus Christi, Cambridge; then Harvard. Palestine, 1925-34, first as secretary to Anglican Bishop in Jerusalem, then in Education Department, where was a Lecturer at Arab

College. Private Secretary to High
Commissioner, 1929; various posts in
Nazareth, Jaffa, and Secretariat until 1934,
when posted to Malta; Aden, 1937–38;
seconded to BBC in charge of Arabic
programmes, returned to Aden in August
1939 to organize broadcasting service. Iraq,
1941–47, first as Public Relations attaché at
Embassy, then Oriental Counsellor. In 1947
married Freya Stark, marriage dissolved
1952; Colonial Secretary, Barbados,
1947–50; Principal Advisor, Cyrenaica,
1950–51. After retirement in 1952 embarked
on career as writer, historian, travel lecturer,
publishing over twenty books on Near East
history, geography and religion, and also
designing postage stamps, medals and
currency notes for many territories.

Plumer, Field Marshal Lord Herbert
(1857–1932). Created Viscount, of Messines
in 1929. After Eton, he passed as Lieutenant
directly into the Army, and saw active
service in India, Egypt, and South Africa.
He was promoted Major-General after Boer
War. Commanding the Second Army in
France in 1915, he was one of the few
successful British generals of the First World
War, winning large-scale battles at Messines
and Ypres and helping stabilize the Italian
front. Appointed Governor of Malta in
1919, and served 1925–28 as High
Commissioner of Palestine, retiring early
because of ill health. Known for his robust
common sense, he was widely popular in
Palestine, where his High
Commissionership was distinguished for
public tranquillity and firm governance.

Samuel, Sir Herbert Louis (1870–1963).
Created Viscount 1937. Born into an Anglo-
Jewish banking family, he was raised in
Orthodox tradition, educated at Balliol
College, Oxford. Elected Liberal MP,
1902–18 and 1929–35, he joined the Cabinet
in 1909, the first Jew to join a British

Cabinet, and was appointed Home
Secretary in 1916, following Asquith out of
Government. From 1914 advocated plans
for Jewish settlement in Palestine, and
helped achieve the Balfour Declaration. In
1920 appointed first High Commissioner in
Palestine and largely established
administration for the country. In 1925,
reluctantly returned to British politics, was
chairman of Royal Commission on coal
industry; Liberal leader; and Home
Secretary, 1931–32. Opposed to 1939 White
Paper, he spoke against it in the House of
Lords. Became a respected and popular
elder statesman, publishing books on
philosophy, ethics, and science as well as
memoirs.

Storrs, Sir Ronald (1881–1955).
Charterhouse and Pembroke College,
Cambridge, where took First Class in
Classical Tripos. Egyptian Government,
Ministry of Finance, 1904, and other
branches of Egyptian Government until
1909. Was Oriental Secretary to British
Agency, Egypt, then Assistant Political
Officer to Anglo-French Political Mission,
European Expeditionary Force, 1917.
Liaison Officer, Mesopotamia; Secretary of
War Cabinet, 1917; Military Governor of
Jerusalem, 1917–20, Civil Governor of
Jerusalem and Judaea, 1920–26; Governor
and Commander in Chief, Cyprus, 1926–32,
where suffered the loss of his notable
personal art and antiquities collection when
Government House burned in riots; posted
to Northern Rhodesia in 1932–34, was
invalided from tropical service in 1934. In
retirement was Trustee and active in
numerous cultural institutions, especially
musical societies. Published memoirs,
Orientations, in 1937.

Teague, Colonel John (1896–1983). Completed Portsmouth Grammar School, where studied music and was assistant organist at a local church; then served in France in First World War, where was wounded and mentioned in despatches. Then attached to the Indian Army, and the Indian Political Service as Vice Consul in Shiraz in 1919. Saw service in the Iraq insurrection in 1920, and was appointed to General Staff, Intelligence, at Baghdad. Severely wounded in Kurdistan operations in 1922. Married in 1926 Heather Fairley, who died in 1966. Also served on the Northwest Frontier, India, 1930; as an interpreter in Persia, 1933; and as Liaison Officer with the Royal Air Force in Palestine during the Arab revolt in 1936–39. Posted to General Headquarters Middle East in 1942; and from 1945 was with the Foreign Office, being Director of Passport Control from 1953 to 1958.

Wauchope, Major-General Sir Arthur (1874–1947). Of a Scottish military family, appointed Lieutenant in the Black Watch, 1893. Saw service in the Boer War, then in India; and in the First World War in France and Mesopotamia was wounded several times and decorated for gallantry. Served in occupied Germany 1929–31, and was then appointed General Officer Commanding in Northern Ireland. Appointed High Commissioner of Palestine in 1931; the only one to serve for two terms. Despite the Arab rebellion, remained enthusiastic in pursuit of his reconciliation policy, and in retirement after 1938 maintained an active interest in Palestine affairs, spending much of his personal fortune in various Palestine educational and cultural projects. Never married, he enjoyed the company of artists, musicians and those of unorthodox opinions, and was generous in support of the arts.

Photo Credits

Select Bibliography

Antonius, George *The Arab Awakening* (London, 1938)
Ashbee, C.R. *A Palestine Notebook, 1918–1923* (London, 1923)
Bauer, Yehuda *Flight and Rescue: Brichah* (New York, 1970)
Bentwich, Norman and Helen *Mandate Memories 1918–1948* (London, 1965)
Bethell, Nicholas *The Palestine Triangle: the Struggle for the Holy Land, 1935–48* (London, 1979)
Bowden, Tom *The Breakdown of Public Security: the Case of Ireland 1916–1921 and Palestine 1936–1939* (London, 1977)
Bowman, Humphrey *Middle East Window* (London, 1944)
Charters, David A. *The British Army and Jewish Insurgency in Palestine, 1945–47* (London, 1989)
Cohen, Michael J. *Palestine: Retreat from the Mandate* (New York, 1978)
Courtney, Roger *Palestine Policeman: an account of eighteen dramatic months in the Palestine Police Force during the great Jew-Arab Troubles* (London, 1939)
Crossman, R.H.S. *Palestine Mission* (New York, 1947)
Duff, Douglas *Palestine Picture* (London, 1936)
Elon, Amos *The Israelis,Founders and Sons* (New York, 1983)
Friedman, Isaiah *The Question of Palestine 1914–1918* (London, 1973)
Friesel, Evyatar, "Through a Peculiar Lens: Zionism and Palestine in British Diaries, 1927–31", *Middle Eastern Studies*, vol. 29, no.3 (July 1993), pp.419–44.
Hamilton, R.W. *Letters from the Middle East by an Occasional Archaeologist* (Edinburgh, 1992)
Hodgkin, Thomas *Letters from Palestine, 1932–36*, ed. E.C. Hodgkin (London, 1986)

Hopwood, Derek *Studies in Arab History; the Antonius Lectures, 1978–87* (Oxford, 1990)
Hopwood, Derek *Tales of Empire: the British in the Middle East, 1880–1952* (London, 1989)
Horne, Edward *A Job Well Done: A History of the Palestine Police Force 1920–48*, (London, 1982)
Hourani, Albert, "The Arab Awakening Forty Years After", in Hopwood, *Studies in Arab History* (Oxford, 1990)
Hyam, Ronald *Empire and Sexuality: the British Experience* (Manchester, 1990)
Hurewitz, J.C. *The Struggle for Palestine* (New York, 1950)
Jones, Philip, ed. *Britain and Palestine 1914–1948; archival sources for the history of the British Mandate* (London, 1979)
Kedourie, Elie *England and the Middle East: the destruction of the Ottoman Empire, 1914–1921* [rev. ed.] ,(London, 1956)
Kedourie, Elie, "Herbert Samuel and the Government of Palestine", *Middle Eastern Studies*, vol. 5, no. 1 (January 1969), pp.44–68
Kedourie, Elie & Sylvia G. Haim, eds. *Zionism and Arabism in Palestine and Israel* (London, 1982)
Kisch, F. H. *Palestine Diary* (London, 1938)
Kolinsky, Martin *Law, Order and Riots in Mandatory Palestine, 1928–35* (New York, 1993)
Lazar, Hadara *Hamandatorim: Erets Yisrael, 1940–1948* (Jerusalem, 1990)
Louis, Wm. Roger *The British Empire in the Middle East, 1945–1951* (Oxford, 1984)
Louis, Wm. Roger and Robert W. Stookey, eds. *The End of the Palestine Mandate*, (Austin, 1986)
Luke, Harry Charles & Keith-Roach, Edward, eds. *The Handbook of Palestine and Trans-Jordan* (London, 1930)

Marlow, John *The Seat of Pilate* (London, 1959)

Meinertzhagen, Richard *Middle East Diary, 1917–1956* (London, 1959)

Monroe, Elizabeth *Britain's Moment in the Middle East* (London, 1963)

Morris, Benny *1948 and After: Israel and the Palestinians* (Oxford, 1990)

Ovendale, Ritchie, "1947: the Decision to Withdraw", *International Affairs*, vol. 56, no.1 (January 1980)

Samuel, Edwin *A Lifetime in Jerusalem* (London, 1970)

Samuel, Herbert *Memories* (London, 1945)

Samuel, Horace *Unholy Memories of the Holy Land* (London, 1930)

Sykes, Christopher *Crossroads to Israel* (London, 1956)

Sykes, Christopher *Orde Wingate* (London, 1959)

Tidrick, Kathryn *Heart Beguiling Araby: the English romance with Arabia,* (London, 1989)

Tidrick, Kathryn *Empire and the English Character* (London, 1992)

Ullendorff, Edward *The Two Zions: Reminiscences of Jerusalem and Ethiopia* (Oxford, 1988)

Vatikiotis, P.J. *Among Arabs and Jews: a personal experience, 1936–1990* (London, 1991)

Wasserstein, Bernard *The British in Palestine: the Mandatory Government and the Arab-Jewish Conflict 1917–1929* (2nd ed., Oxford, 1991)

Wasserstein, Bernard *Herbert Samuel: A Political Life* (Oxford, 1992)

Wasserstein, Bernard, "Clipping the Claws of the Colonizers: Arab Officials in the Government of Palestine, 1917–1948", *Middle Eastern Studies*, vol. 13, no. 2 (May 1977), pp.171–94

Index